B.J. Summers' Guide to Coca-Cola

FIFTH EDITION

Identifications
Current Values

Sign of Good Taste

1958 February

cb

COLLECTOR BOOKS

A Division of Schroeder Publishing Co., Inc.

34041

Front Cover:
P. 114 Hanging, paper, "Sign of Good Taste," couple with snowman, 1958, M, $200.00 C. *Mitchell Collection.*
p. 153 Hobbleskirt, glass, gold-dipped 100th anniversary bottle, 1986, EX, $65.00 D.
p. 192 Wall, metal and glass, "Drink Coca-Cola," 1930 – 1940s, 18" dia., VG, $775.00 B. *Metz Superlatives Auction.*
p. 211 Buddy L, metal, "Drink Coca-Coca the Pause That Refreshes!" 1960s, EX, $325.00 – 450.00 C.
p. 140 Solid back, cardboard, "Drink Coca-Cola...Quality Carries On," 1950s, EX, $85.00 C. *Mitchell Collection.*

Not listed in book: Poster, cardboard, "I'm Heading For Coca-Cola," $675.00 C.
Bottle, blue glass, "The Coca-Cola Bottling Company," $75.00 C.
Coke Selzer Bottle, green glass, $195.00 C.

Back Cover:
P. 50 Flat mount, paper, "Drink Coca-Cola...Coca-Cola Brings You Edgar Bergen with Charlie McCarthy...,"
1949, 22" x 11", EX, $250.00 C. *Mitchell Collection.*
P. 76 Poster, cardboard, "Play Refreshed," 1950s, 36" x 20", VG, $395.00 C.
p. 83 Poster, cardboard, "Thirst Knows No Season," 1940, 56" x 27", EX, $500.00 B. *Metz Superlatives Auction.*

Cover design by Beth Summers
Book layout by Holly C. Long

Collector Books
P.O. Box 3009
Paducah, Kentucky 42002-3009
www.collectorbooks.com

Copyright © 2005 B. J. Summers

Searching for a publisher?

We are always looking for people knowledgeable within their fields. If you
feel that there is a real need for a book on your collectible subject and have
a large comprehensive collection, contact Collector Books.

❧ Contents ❧

Dedication & Acknowledgments

This book is dedicated to Hayley,
a young lady any parent would be proud and pleased to call his daughter.
Best wishes for luck, love, and happiness in the future.

I would like to extend my sincere thanks to the following people and businesses, without whose help this book would have been impossible.

Earlene Mitchell
c/o Collector Books
P.O. Box 3009
Paducah, KY 42002-3009
   One of the nicest ladies you'll ever meet. She has been collecting since the 1960s, and is a constant source of information. She remains a very active collector.

Gary Metz's Muddy River Trading Co.
P.O. Box 1430
Salem, VA 24153
Ph. 540-387-5070
Fax 540-387-3233\e-mail: mudauction@aol.com
   Gary Metz remains a mainstay in the advertising auction world. Gary's primary emphasis is Coca-Cola, but his auctions always have a broad spectrum of collectible advertising.

Antiques, Cards, and Collectibles
203 Broadway
Paducah, KY 42001
Ph. 270-443-9797\e-mail: ray@haylan.net
   Located in historic downtown Paducah, Kentucky, the old Michael Hardware Store is a great place for an afternoon of browsing. Ray Pelley and his friendly staff offer a full line of antiques and collectibles.

Charlie's Antique Mall
303 Main St., P.O. Box 196
Hazel, KY 42049
Ph. 270-492-8175/e-mail: charlies10@aol.com
   Located in the historic community of Hazel, Kentucky, on Main Street, this place has it all. The manager, Ray Gough, has some great dealers with a wide variety of antiques and collectibles and some of the friendliest help you'll find. This border-town mall can keep even the pickiest collector busy for the better part of a day.

Farmer's Daughter Antiques
6330 Cairo Rd.
Paducah, KY 42001
Ph. 270-444-7619
   This is a neat shop full of primitives and advertising. Easily located one mile west off I-24 at exit 3.

Collectors Auction Services
Rt. 2 Box 431, Oakwood Dr.
Oil City, PA 16301
Ph. 814-677-6070
   CAS offers a great phone and mail auction. Call and get one of its full-color catalogs. You'll be hooked on its services after just one auction.

Eric Reinfeld
87 Seventh Avenue
Brooklyn, NY 11217
Ph. 718-783-2313
   Eric is an avid collector of Whistle and Coca-Cola. He's always interested in selling and buying, so give him a call.

Riverbend Auction Company
103 South Monroe St.
P.O. Box 800
Alderson, WV 24910

Patrick's Collectibles
612 Roxanne Dr.
Antioch, TN 37013
Ph. 615-833-4621
   If you happen to be around Nashville, Tennessee, during the monthly flea market at the state fairgrounds, be certain to look for Mike and Julie Patrick. They have some of the sharpest advertising pieces you'll ever hope to find. And if Coca-Cola is your field, you won't be able to walk away from the great restored drink machines. Make sure to look them up — you certainly won't be sorry.

Pleasant Hill Antique Mall & Tea Room
315 South Pleasant Hill Rd.
East Peoria, IL 61611
Ph. 309-694-4040
   Bob Johnson and the friendly staff at this mall welcome you for a day of shopping. And it'll take that long to work your way through all the quality antiques and collectibles here. When you get tired, stop and enjoy a rest at the tea room, where you can get some of the best home-cooked food found anywhere. All in all, a great place to shop for your favorite antiques.

Creatures of Habit
406 Broadway
Paducah, KY 42001
Ph. 270-442-2923

This business will take you back in time with its wonderful array of vintage clothing and advertising. If you are ever in western Kentucky, stop and see Natalya and Jack.

The Illinois Antique Center
308 S.W. Commercial
Peoria, IL 61602
Ph. 309-673-3354

This is a day-long stop. Dan and Kim have restored an old, very large warehouse overlooking the river in downtown Peoria. It's full of great advertising and collectibles. Stop by and see Dan and Kim and their very friendly staff, and plan on being amazed.

Rare Bird Antique Mall
212 South Main St.
Goodlettsville, TN 37072
Ph. 615-851-2635

If you find yourself in the greater Nashville area, stop by this collectors' paradise. Jon and Joan Wright have assembled a great cast of dealers whose offerings run the gamut of collectible merchandise. So step back into a time when the general store was the place to be, and be prepared to spend some time.

Riverside Antique Mall
P.O. Box 4425
Sevierville, TN 37864
Ph. 423-429-0100

Located in a new building overlooking the river, this is a collectors' heaven, full of advertising, with lighted showcases and plenty of friendly help. You need to allow at least half a day for a quick look through this place that sits in the shadows of the Smoky Mountains.

Bill and Helen Mitchell
226 Arendall St.
Henderson, TN 38340
Ph. 901-989-9302

Bill and Helen have assembled a great variety of advertising with special emphasis on Coca-Cola, and they are always searching for new finds. So if you have anything that fits the bill, give them a call or drop them a letter.

Richard Opfer Auctioneering, Inc.
1919 Greenspring Drive
Timonium, MD 21093
Ph. 410-252-5035

Richard Opfer Auctioneering, Inc., provides a great variey of antiques and collectibles auctions. Give his friendly staff a call for his next auction catalog.

Wm. Morford
RD #2
Cazenovia, NY 13035
Ph. 315-662-7625

Wm. Morford has been operating one of the country's better cataloged phone auction businesses for several years. He doesn't list reproductions or repairs that are deceptive in nature. Each catalog usually has a section with items that are for immediate sale. Try out this site and tell him where you got his name and address.

If I have omitted anyone who should be here, please be assured it is an oversight on my part and is not intentional.

COCA-COLA!!! Just the magic name will bring a smile to the lips and memories of good times. These memories are different for each of us. One might be the family dinner on Christmas Eve — nothing better than Kentucky Bar-B-Que, chips, fresh moist coconut cake, and of course, ice-cold Coca-Cola. Maybe one is of the ballpark on a clear summer day, with a light breeze and a stadium vendor with cold Coke. One of my favorite memories involves a large shade tree in the country at the grandparents, surrounded by family, with ice-cold Coke and peanuts in the small hobbleskirt bottle. And when finished there was always a bet on the city.

Probably no one, including Coke inventor Dr. John Pemberton or Atlanta businessman and visionary Asa Griggs Chandler, could have imagined the far-reaching effects of this magic elixir. Coke is now loved and recognized all over the world. In all of America's good times, Coke has been a steady product, like a big brother. During time of turmoil, Coke has been a pillar of strength. During World War II, Coke established bottling plants overseas to supply American GIs with the familiar hometown drink. And in an effort to help bolster the folks at home, advertising was geared toward a feeling of peaceful better times. Kids the world over regularly leave a cold bottle of Coke for Santa. With the image of Coke Santa in mind, of course, as provided by artist Haddom Sundblom. Coke needs no introduction. It's as American as both Mom's apple pie and baseball.

The Coca-Cola company has always believed in advertising, and that belief has lead it to the top of the mountain. To become an American icon and hold the lion's share of the market for so many

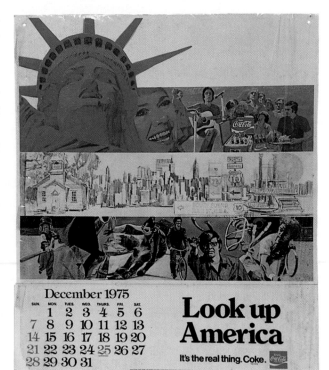

"Look up America — It's the Real Thing. Coke." See page 113.

years is no small feat. So much of Coke's fame is due to advertising. *Fantastic, colorful, wholesome, memory provoking,* and of course *plentiful* are just a few of the words and phrases that describe Coca-Cola advertising. For us collectors, to be at a Coke swap meet is to be like a kid in a toy store at Christmas.

This book is meant only as a *guide*, and not as the last word on values. It is another tool in the collector's arsenal of information; remember, an informed collector is the one who is smiling at the end of the day.

I've attempted to help both the advanced and beginning collector with this book. I don't attempt to set prices on any Coke memorabilia, only to report values. *These values are meant to be only a guide, not absolute.* If you're buying, you will no doubt like that sentence. But if you're selling, it won't be as appealing. When you look at the caption, you will see that I have keyed the prices so that you'll know the origin of the value. You'll see the following key symbols throughout this book:

> C — a value given to me by a collector(s)
>
> B — a value determined by an auction price (Remember on auction values that two determined bidders can run a price far past fair market value. Likewise, lack of interest will sometimes let a collectible sell for less than it should.)
>
> D — a value determined by a dealer

Condition will be graded by the following key:

> NOS — refers to new old stock, usually found in a warehouse or store closed for some time
>
> NRFB — never removed from box

MIB — absolutely mint, still in the original container

M — mint condition; however, has been out of the container

NM — near mint, nothing to detract from display

EX — excellent; very minor distractions, such as shelf wear, don't detract from the focal point

VG — very good, may have light scratches on the edges or back, but nothing to detract from the face

G — good, the usual used condition, with scratches and nicks on the item front, but still desirable

F — fair, some bad detractions

P — poor; pick it up only because of its rarity or because it is a piece you don't have in your collection.

Cardboard stand-up Santa Claus. See page 235.

Of course other factors, such as location, will affect price. Generally speaking, an item with a $100.00 price in my area (the Midwest and the South) may sell in the $150.00 – 175.00 range on the East Coast and in the Northeast, and in the $200.00 – 225.00 range on the West Coast.

How tough is the demand in my area? I'm a long-time collector of items from my hometown of Paducah, Kentucky. Fortunately for me, the city has a very colorful and rich history, with some great memorabilia. Unfortunately for me, there are several die-hard collectors like myself, and among us, we keep the prices artificially high due to the demand for those few items that are always surfacing.

Probably the last consideration of pricing is condition. This is where I find the most problems. If an item in the price guide is labeled as mint at $200.00, and you see one in a store in fair condition at $200.00, it's overpriced. Don't buy it! I've attempted to make sure all of the listings in this book have the condition listed. This should help when it's time to buy or haggle. It's extremely difficult to find a seller and a buyer that agree on an item's value. A buyer shouldn't be hesitant about making an offer, and a seller shouldn't be offended by an offer. Good luck buying, selling, and collecting.

Many collectors have contacted me in the past. Some have gotten to me and some — unfortunately — haven't. Please mail correspondence to:

Collector Books
ATTN: B. J. Summers
P.O. Box 3009
Paducah, KY 42002-3009

Please realize it might take some time to receive and answer the mail. I'm sometimes guilty of allowing it to pile up on my desk. Also, some questions require some research on my part. Phone calls aren't very good because I'm rarely in a situation where I can take them. If messages are left on the answering machine, they will probably not be returned due to the volume of calls and the associated long-distance charges. Probably the best method for reaching me is via e-mail at bjsummers@mchsi.com.

SCHMIDT MUSEUM

of Coca-Cola®

MEMORABILIA

This Museum is a non-profit entity which is neither owned by nor affiliated with the Coca-Cola Company.

Scheduled to open in Spring 2005, the 32,000 square foot facility will house rotating exhibits of the Schmidt Museum Collection which contains over 80,000 items. The new facility will feature a larger museum store and visitor comforts along with expanded displays and exhibits, historic vehicles, a turn-of-the-century bottling plant exhibit, neon sign displays, vending machines, and of course the only complete serving tray collection known to exist. Anything and everything with a Coca-Cola trademark will be on display!

Our interim location in the Tourism Visitors' Center will remain open until the new facility is complete!

The Museum has the only complete classic Coca-Cola serving tray collection known to exist.

Schmidt Museum of Coca-Cola Memorabilia
1030 North Mulberry
Elizabethtown, KY 42701
Phone – (270) 234-1100
E-mail – schmidtmuseum@yahoo.com

THE WORLD'S LARGEST PRIVATE COLLECTION

of COCA-COLA

Antiques, Artifacts, and Collectibles

The displays, selected from the world's largest privately owned collection of Coca-Cola memorabilia, at the Schmidt Museum are bound to have you saying; "Oh! I remember that!" In addition to the famous Coca-Cola serving trays and calendars, visitors to the museum will find everyday items such as bottles, beverage glasses, toys, neon and metal signs, sheet music, and more all bearing the famous trademark. You will also see rare vending machines and antique bottling equipment used over 100 years ago. This "window" to our past will educate and delight the viewer and make you want to see more of the larger collection planned for display in the future. The Schmidt Museum continues to add rare, authentic Coca-Cola artifacts to the collection with special exhibits added and rotated throughout the year. The current location is at 1030 North Mulberry, Elizabethtown, Kentucky, in the Tourism Visitors' Center building.

Start refreshed

DRINK **Coca-Cola**

DIRECTIONS:
⅓ mile west of I-65 at exit 94
on US 62 in Elizabethtown, Kentucky.
Open May through September:
Monday–Friday 9am–6pm, Sat 10am–2pm
Rest of the Year: Monday–Friday 9am–5pm
Closed Thankgiving, Christmas, and New Years Day.
Admission:
Adults $2.00, Seniors and Tour Groups $1.50,
Students $.50, Preschoolers Free,
handicapped accessible.

Frankfort
Louisville   Lexington

★ Elizabethtown

Paducah

www.schmidtmuseum.com

Aluminum, die-cut script, "Drink Coca-Cola in Bottles," designed for truck radiator, 1920s, 17½" x 7½", EX, $375.00 B. *Metz Superlatives Auction.*

Banner, canvas, "Drink Coca-Cola from the Bottle through a Straw," with straight-sided bottle at left, 1910, 70" x 16", EX, $4,000.00 B. *Metz Superlatives Auction.*

Banner, vinyl and canvas, "Drink Coca-Cola Ice Cold," with fishtail logo in center, 1960s, 8' x 14", EX, $200.00 B. *Metz Superlatives Auction.*

Base, crossing guard or cast iron, "Drink Coca-Cola." There are a lot of reproductions of this — most have a different measurement and the lettering is different, so be careful. 21" dia., VG, $225.00 C.

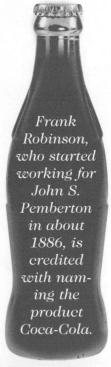

Frank Robinson, who started working for John S. Pemberton in about 1886, is credited with naming the product Coca-Cola.

Banner, canvas, "Coca-Cola brings you Edgar Bergen with Charlie McCarthy..." truck mounted, 1950s, 60" x 42", EX, $1,100.00 B. *Metz Superlatives Auction.*

Bottle, cardboard, hobbleskirt bottle with no message, Canadian, 13" x 33", EX, $475.00 B. *Metz Superlatives Auction.*

Bottle, cardboard, "Take Home Enough," flat mount, die-cut bottle in hand, 1952, VG, $195.00 C.

Bottle, celluloid, "Eis-kalt," flat mount, bottle in hand, foreign, 6½" x 16", VG, $225.00 B. *Metz Superlatives Auction.*

Bottle, celluloid, "Drink ...Delicious and Refreshing," straight-sided bottle with paper label, 1900s, 6" x 13", VG, $2,600.00 B.

Bottle, cardboard, with courtesy panel for pricing, NOS, new, 14" x 45", NM, $10.00 C.

Bottle, metal, "Buvez Coca-Cola," large embossed hobbleskirt bottle, 17¼" x 53", G, $145.00 C. *Metz Superlatives Auction.*

Bottle, metal, "Coca-Cola," die cut with white lettering, 1951, 6' tall, G, $550.00 B. *Metz Superlatives Auction.*

Bottle, metal, "Coca-Cola...Sign of Good Taste," self framing with fishtail logo and hobbleskirt bottle, 1960s, 31¼" x 11¼", G, $295.00 C.

Bottle, metal, "Drink Coca-Cola" flat mount, embossed hobbleskirt bottle, 1931, 4½" x 12½", VG, $375.00 B. *Metz Superlatives Auction.*

Bottle, metal, "Drink Coca-Cola...Sold Here Ice Cold," flat mount, vertical, self framing with Christmas bottle in center, 1932, EX, $695.00 D. *Rivervside Antique Mall.*

Bottle, metal, "Drink Coca-Cola," flat mount, horizontal, featuring tilted hobbleskirt bottle in yellow spotlight, 1948, 54" x 18", VG, $395.00 C.

Bottle, metal, flat mount, die cut of Christmas bottle, 1933, 36" tall, EX, $1,100.00 C.

Bottle, metal, "Drink Coca-Cola," self framing with hobbleskirt bottle to right of message, 1950s, 54" x 18", EX, $450.00 C. *Eric Reinfield.*

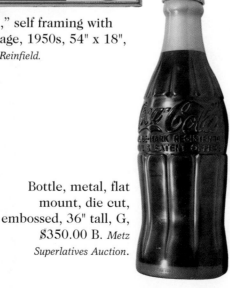

Bottle, metal, flat mount, die cut, embossed, 36" tall, G, $350.00 B. *Metz Superlatives Auction.*

Bottle, metal, "Have a Coke...Coca-Cola," flat mount, vertical, bottle in center yellow spotlight, 1940s, 18" x 54", EX, $395.00 C.

Bottle, metal over cardboard, "Drink Coca-Cola" with 1915 bottle, 1920s, 6" x 13", VG, $1,200.00 B. *Metz Superlatives Auction.*

Bottles, cardboard, "Coca-Cola...Delicious and Refreshing," flat mount, die cut of six-pack carton, 1954, EX, $750.00 B. *Metz Superlatives Auction.*

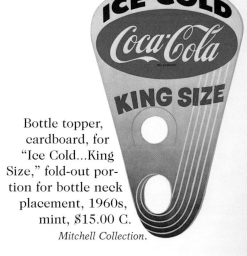

Bottle topper, cardboard, couple on bench ready to enjoy a bottle of the product, Canadian, "Refresh Yourself," hard to locate this one, it fits over two bottle necks, 1926, 13" x 13", EX, $3,600.00 B. *Metz Superlatives Auction.*

Bottle topper, cardboard, die-cut pretty redheaded girl with tray, when placed over the neck of a bottle gives a 3-D effect, 1920s, 11½" x 14", NM, $2,600.00 B. *Metz Superlatives Auction.*

Bottle topper, cardboard, for "King Size Ice Cold," also has string for use as a hanger or pull, 1960s, $100.00 – 175.00 C. *Joe Wilson.*

Bottle topper, cardboard, for "Ice Cold...King Size," fold-out portion for bottle neck placement, 1960s, mint, $15.00 C. *Mitchell Collection.*

Bottle topper, cardboard, six-pack and food in basket, top hole fits over bottle neck, 1950s, 8" x 7", NM, $550.00 B.

Bottle topper, cardboard, with bathing girl holding a bottle, "Drink Coca-Cola Delicious and Refreshing," a very rare item, 1929, EX, $1,800.00 B. *Metz Superlatives Auction.*

Bottle topper, paper, "Regular Size Coca-Cola" with Santa's elves looking around the carton, 9" x 11¾", EX, $45.00 – 55.00 C.

Bottle topper, plastic, designed to sit on top of a hobbleskirt bottle, "We Let You See the Bottle," 1950s, EX, $495.00 – 550.00 C. *Mitchell Collection..*

Bottlers advance calendar print, paper, "Autumn Girl" holding a glass of Coca-Cola. By getting this advance, the bottlers knew roughly a year in advance what the calendar would look like. Again, an extremely rare item, framed under glass, 1921, NM, $8,500.00. *Mitchell Collection.*

Bottlers advance calendar print, paper. "Garden Girl" is the name most often used on this image; however, closer examination will show her on a golf course, holding a hobbleskirt bottle. Extremely rare piece, framed under glass, 1919, NM, $8,500.00 C. *Mitchell Collection.*

Bottlers advance calendar print, paper, "Two Ladies at the Beach," extremely rare piece, framed under glass, 1917, NM, $8,500.00 C. *Mitchell Collection.*

Baseball scoreboard, cardboard, very heavy stock, advertising panel at top , "Drink...in Bottles 5¢," unusual item and still with good colors, 1930s, 30" x 20", EX, $1,000.00 B. *Metz Superlatives Auction.*

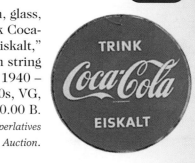

Bumper sticker, vinyl, with Max Headroom "Don't Say
The 'P' Word," 1980s, EX, $15.00 C.

Button, glass,
"Trink Coca-
Cola Eiskalt,"
German string
hung, 1940 –
1950s, VG,
$190.00 B.
*Metz Superlatives
Auction.*

Calendar top, paper,
pretty girl sitting on
a slant-back bench
drinking Coke from a
straight-sided bottle
with a straw, wearing
a large brimmed hat,
1913, 16" x 24", G,
$4,500.00 C. *Collectors
Auction Services.*

Button, metal,
"Coca-Cola"
with bottle,
1950s, 48" dia,
EX, $600.00 B.
*Metz Superlatives
Auction.*

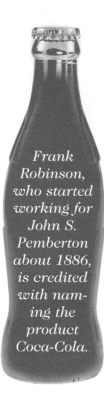

*Frank
Robinson,
who started
working for
John S.
Pemberton
about 1886,
is credited
with nam-
ing the
product
Coca-Cola.*

Cardboard, set of 20 "America's Fighting Planes." If sold
individually, 1940s, VG. Prices will range between $75.00 and
100.00 each; a complete set with the original envelope will range
from $2,100.00 to $2,400.00.
Mitchell Collection.

During WWII, Coca-Cola pro-duced a few items used to promote air-craft identifi-cation…

…There were two decks of "Spotter" playing cards, a booklet titled Know Your War Planes, and four series of large framed pictures showing war planes. Artist and aircraft professional William Heaslip painted all the aircraft.

Cardboard, set of 20 war planes, not all shown, during WWII Coke produced four different series of "Know Your War Planes," each had different names, 1943, EX. Prices generally run in the $75.00 – 100.00 range when buying individually; when complete with original envelope, prices run in the $2,100.00 – 2,400.00 range. *Mitchell Collection.*

Cash register topper, metal and plastic, "Drink Coca-Cola," 1950s, EX, $950.00 B.
Metz Superlatives Auction.

Cooler panel insert, metal, "Serve yourself...Drink Coca-Cola...Please Pay the Clerk," 1931, 31" x 11", G, $140.00 B.
Metz Superlatives Auction.

Counter, celluloid over cardboard, "Coca-Cola...Delicious...Refreshing" with easel back, never unfolded and original label on back, 1940s, 9" dia., NM, $300.00 B. *Wm. Morford Investment Grade Collectibles.*

Counter top, metal, "Lunch with Us..." light-up by Price Brothers, 1950s, 19" x 8½", EX, $900.00 B. *Metz Superlatives Auction.*

Probably the earliest script logo was used around June 1887.

Decal, paper, "Drink Coca-Cola Ice Cold," shield shaped with hobbleskirt bottle, 1934, 18" x 15", EX, $130.00 B. *Metz Superlatives Auction.*

Crossing guard, metal and cast iron, "Slow School Zone." *Note: these have been reproduced. Usually the details and thickness of the metal give away the fakes; also watch for fake bases — they aren't the same diameter of the originals and the lettering isn't the same. Pricing is still volatile, ranging between $1,000.00 and $3,500.00 depending upon condition and how it is sold, whether auction, dealer, etc.,* 1950s.

Decal, vinyl, "Drink Coca-Cola...Air Conditioned Inside," 1950 – 1960s, EX, $15.00 C.

Decal, vinyl, "Drink Coca-Cola...Please Pay Cashier," 1960s, 13" x 6", EX, $10.00 C. *Collectors Auction Services.*

Decal, vinyl, "Drink...in Bottles," 1950s, 15" x 9", EX, $50.00 B. *Metz Superlatives Auction.*

Decal, vinyl, "Drink Coca-Cola...Please Pay Cashier," 1960s, EX, $30.00 C.

Delivery truck, porcelain, "Drink Coca-Cola Ice Cold," designed for a truck cab, 1950s, 50" x 10", EX, $350.00 B. *Metz Superlatives Auction.*

Display, cardboard, "Bartender on Duty...," unusual find, 1950 – 1960s, 14" x 12", NM, $350.00 B. *Metz Superlatives Auction.*

Dispenser, stainless steel, "Drink Coca-Cola," horizontal lettering with border trim, 6½" x 3¼", G, $95.00 B. *Metz Superlatives Auction.*

The Coca-Cola trademark was registered January 31, 1893, but had been in the market since 1886.

Display, cardboard, bottle in hand die cut, framed and matted, 1950s, NM, $650.00 B. *Metz Superlatives Auction.*

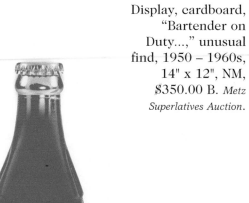

Display, cardboard, "Boy-oh Boy!" 3-D set-up of boy in front of store cooler with a bottle of Coke, 1937, 36" x 34", VG, $925.00 C. *Mitchell Collection.*

Display, cardboard, "Buy the Case Coke...10 oz. Size," "$1.25 Plus Deposit," EX, $65.00 – 95.00 C.

Display, cardboard, cherub holding a tray with a glass of the product, die cut, matted and framed, super rare item, 1908, VG, $4,000.00 B. *Metz Superlatives Auction.*

Display, cardboard, Christmas tree–shaped string hanger with dynamic wave sign, 1970s, 14" x 24", VG, $32.00 – 50.00 D.

Display, cardboard, clown balancing on a bottle of Coke while holding a 12-pack with one hand and juggling a button on a foot, 1950s, EX, $875.00 B – 1,200.00 C. *Metz Superlatives Auction.*

Display, cardboard, "Coca-Cola...Dale Earnhardt" die-cut life-size standup. Prices shot up to around $100.00 – 125.00 immediately after his death; before that, they had been in the $10.00 – 15.00 range. They have started a very slow decline. NM, $85.00 C.

Display, cardboard, "Coca-Cola...Ice Cold," die cut with diamond can in hand, 1960s, NM, $230.00 B. *Metz Superlatives Auction.*

Display, cardboard, "Coca-Cola...Ice Cold," featuring a king-size bottle die cut, 1960s, NM, $160.00 B. *Metz Superlatives Auction.*

Display, cardboard, cut-out of woman with glass of Coke, very similar to the 1930s serving tray, 1930s, 21" x 38", G to EX, $600.00 A – 1,050.00 C. *Metz Superlatives Auction.*

Display, cardboard, die-cut arrow and disc, layered to make 3-D effect, 1944, 20" x 12", VG, $195.00 D. *Metz Superlatives Auction.*

Display, cardboard, die-cut bathing girl in horseshoe, could be used for a window display or wall hanging, matted and framed, 1910s, F, $1,450.00 B. *Metz Superlatives Auction.*

Display, cardboard, die-cut bottle in hand beside sign, on post that reads "Drink...Delicious and Refreshing," 1900s, 9" x 19", F, $525.00 C.

Display, cardboard, die-cut bell glass of Coke, easel back, snow at base, 1930s, 17" x 27", EX, $500.00 B. *Metz Superlatives Auction.*

The first Coca-Cola bottling plant was opened in Chattanooga, TN, in 1899.

Display, cardboard, die-cut boy and girl drinking Coke from a glass through a straw, button in front and "So Refreshing," 1950s, 20" x 13", VG, $195.00 C. *Metz Superlatives Auction.*

Display, cardboard, die-cut boy with dog, sitting on stump and fishing, bottle of Coke in one hand, "Friends for Life," unusual piece, not seen very often, 1935, 36" tall, VG, $2,650.00 B. *Metz Superlatives Auction.*

Display, cardboard, die cut, easel back, three guys with glasses of Coke, "So Refreshing," 1953, 3" x 1½" VG, $225.00 C. *Metz Superlatives Auction.*

Display, cardboard, die-cut French Canadian bottle in hand, 1939, 12" x 16", NM, $600.00 B. *Metz Superlatives Auction.*

Display, cardboard, die-cut hobbleskirt bottles, "Every Bottle Sterilized," matted and framed, 1930s, 14" x 12", EX, $1,300.00 C.

Display, cardboard, die cut of snowman holding a bell glass with "Drink...," easel back, 1953, 19" x 32", EX, $800.00 B. *Metz Superlatives Auction.*

Display, cardboard, die cut of lady with parasol and a straight-sided paper-label bottle, 1900s, 24" x 27", VG, $5,200.00 B. *Metz Superlatives Auction.*

Display, cardboard, die cut of woman holding a six-pack carton, 1940s, 5' tall, EX, $275.00 C. *Metz Superlatives Auction.*

Display, cardboard, die cut of two pretty girls on a bicycle built for two, matted and framed. This was part of a larger bottle display that, when in place, gave a 3-D effect to the bicycle riders. 1960s, EX, $325.00 C.

Display, cardboard, die cut of young boy on bicycle, "Have a Coke," 1950s, 29" x 20", G, $275.00 C.

Display, cardboard, die-cut "Old Man North" with a carton of Cokes, "Serve Ice Cold," 1953, 16" x 21", NM, $275.00 B. *Metz Superlatives Auction.*

Display, cardboard, die cut Sailor girl with signal flags "Take...Home," matted and framed, 1952, 11" x 7", NM, $375.00 B. *Metz Superlatives Auction.*

Display, cardboard, die cut, three ladies at table with Coke, "Be Refreshed," 24" x 18", VG, $450.00 B. *Metz Superlatives Auction.*

Display, cardboard, die-cut unit for "Beverage Dept." with a "Drink" button at top, 1954, 26" x 36", EX, $700.00 B. *Metz Superlatives Auction.*

Display, cardboard, die-cut servicewoman in uniform holding a bottle of Coke, 1944, 25" x 64", EX, $600.00 B. *Auctions Center.*

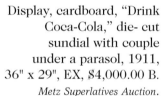

Display, cardboard, die cut WWII battleship, matted and under glass, 1940s, 26" x 14", NM, $1,300.00.
Metz Superlatives Auction.

Display, cardboard, die-cut winter girl with glasses of Coke in snow, 1930 – 1940s, 32" x 19", EX, $695.00 C.

Display, cardboard, die cut with Lionel Hampton, 1953, 12" x 15", EX, $975.00 B. *Metz Superlatives Auction.*

Display, cardboard, double-sided string-hung mobile, movies are more fun with a Coke and popcorn, 1957, 32" tall, NM, $425.00 C. *Metz Superlatives Auction.*

Display, cardboard, "Drink Coca-Cola...Coke Brightens Every Bite," die-cut easel-back standup, 1959, 2' x 3', EX, $275.00 B. *Metz Superlatives Auction.*

Display, cardboard, "Drink Coca-Cola," die-cut sundial with couple under a parasol, 1911, 36" x 29", EX, $4,000.00 B. *Metz Superlatives Auction.*

Display, cardboard, "Drink Coca-Cola," die-cut easel-back boy at soda fountain with glass of Coke and a sandwich, 1936, 28" x 36", EX, $2,800.00 B. *Metz Superlatives Auction.*

Display, cardboard, "Drink Coca-Cola," trifold with cameo center with pretty girl drinking from a flare glass, for window use, 1913, VG, $5,200.00 B. *Metz Superlatives Auction.*

Display, cardboard, "Drink...," die cut of smart teacher rabbit with pointer instructing children sitting on a bench at a school desk, extremely difficult to locate, 1900s, 6½" x 7", NM, $16,000.00 B. *Metz Superlatives Auction.*

Display, cardboard, "Drive with Real Refreshment," bottle cap coming off with product emerging, 1999, 8" x 8", NM, $15.00 D.

Display, cardboard, cut-out Eddie Fisher holding a bottle of Coke, with easel back for store use. *Note to all the youngsters out there, this was a famous singer in the 1950s.* 1954, 5' tall, VG, $375.00 B – 425.00 C. *Metz Superlatives Auction.*

Display, cardboard, "Enjoy a Float with COKE," with a courtesy panel for "Today's Feature," 22" x 7", NM, $65.00 C. *Mitchell Collection.*

Display, cardboard, "Float with Coke," string hung, resembles a life ring, 1960s, 10" dia., EX, $95.00 C.

Display, cardboard, "For Extra Fun...Take More Than One," life-size cut-out of Jennifer O'Neill with a six-pack carton in each hand, 1960s, 60" x 30", EX, $130.00 B. *Metz Superlatives Auction.*

Display, cardboard, "King Size...Ice Cold," commonly known as a fan pull, or string hanger, this die cut is double sided and advertises King Size Coke, 1950 – 1960s, EX, $55.00 D.

Display, cardboard and glass, "Coca-Cola Chewing Gum," die-cut girl in woods scene in a beveled glass mirror, advertising at bottom, embossed, Kaufmann and Strauss Company, New York, 1903, 4½" x 10½", EX, $15,500.00 B. *Metz Superlatives Auction.*

Display, cardboard, "Get Your Coca-Cola Holiday Bell Soda Glass when You Buy a Large Coca-Cola," with Christmas motif and picture of bell glasses, NM, $55.00 C.

Display, cardboard, "Off to a Fresh Start," diecut woman wearing a smile and 1920 to 1930s vintage clothing, 1931, 12" x 27", EX, $875.00 B. *Metz Superlatives Auction.*

Display, cardboard, pretty young lady cut out enjoying Coke from a bottle, framed and matted, this is a hard item to find, 1936, 15" x 21", G, $475.00 B. *Metz Superlatives Auction.*

Display, cardboard and plastic, "Work Safely," light-up with C-clamp and "Safety Is a Job," 1950s, 15½" sq., EX, $775.00 B. *Metz Superlatives Auction.*

Display, cardboard, pretty lady in director's chair with a parasol and a large bottle of Coke, 1930s, 10" x 18½", EX, $1,475.00 C – 1,775.00 C. *Mitchell Collection.*

Display, cardboard, rack sign, die-cut Eddie Fisher, 1954, 12" x 20", EX, $175.00 C.

Display, cardboard and plastic, "Work Safely," light-up with three work figures carrying a banner that reads, "Work Safety-wise," 1950s, 15½" sq, EX, $725.00 B. *Metz Superlatives Auction.*

25

Display, cardboard, Red Hot Summer game cup promotion, 1994, 20" x 12", NM, $40.00 D.

Display, cardboard, Red Hot Summer promotion for a new Mustang, 1994, 12" x 20", NM, $40.00 C.

Display, cardboard, die-cut woman wearing a hat and sitting on wooden bench drinking Coke from a bottle, "Coca-Cola in Bottles," 1900s, 18" x 28½", VG, $8,500.00 C. *Metz Superlatives Auction.*

Display, cardboard, ringmaster and assistant die-cut pieces, matted and framed under glass, 1920 – 1930s, 32" tall, EX, $550.00 C. *Metz Superlatives Auction.*

Display, cardboard, "This Pizza Calls for a Coke," bottom folds for countertop display, 11½" x 14½", NM, $25.00 C.

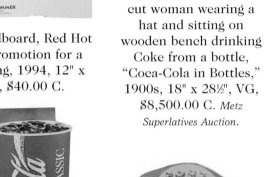

Display, cardboard, "Take Enough Home...2 Convenient Sizes," 1956, 29" x 32", EX, $525.00 B. *Metz Superlatives Auction.*

Display, cardboard, "The Refreshing Custom," die cut of three pretty women having a glass of Coke, easel back designed for window display, 1939, 41" x 32", EX, $775.00 B. *Metz Superlatives Auction.*

Display, cardboard, "The Pause That Refreshes" cutout, hard to locate this piece, 1937, 34" x 14", VG, $200.00 B – 325.00 C. *Metz Superlatives Auction.*

Display, cardboard, Toonerville cut-out standups, 14 pieces form a village, G, $1,900.00 B. *Metz Superlatives Auction.*

Display, cardboard, waitress cutout holding a tray full of refreshing Coca-Cola, 17" x 20", VG, $475.00 B. *Metz Superlatives Auction.*

Display, cardboard, two-piece with two couples having a picnic, "Buy Coca-Cola Now...for Picnic Fun," 1950s, EX, $135.00 – 185.00 C. *Mitchell Collection.*

Display, cardboard, "Win a Trip to the NFL Pro Bowl in Hawaii," with panel to the right for dealer or retailer information, 12" x 18", NM, $15.00 D. *Collectors Auction Services.*

Display, cardboard, window cutout from Niagara Litho Co., NY, with woman in front of cooler holding a bottle of Coke, 1940s, 32½" x 42½", EX, $975.00 – 1,400.00 C. *Mitchell Collection.*

Original cost of this item was a whopping 17¢.

Display, cardboard with boys playing around a real bottle of Coke, Canadian item and very hard to locate, 1930s, 11½" x 11½", EX, $4,700.00 B. *Metz Superlatives Auction.*

Display, cardboard, woman shopping and carrying a carton of Coke in her basket, cutout with easel bracket for countertop use, 1944, 17½" tall, NM, $1,900.00 B. *Metz Superlatives Auction.*

Display, cardboard, "Zing for your Supper with Ice Cold Coke," young man in early version of space suit, 1960s, EX, $145.00 C. *Mitchell Collection.*

Display, celluloid, "Coca-Cola...Delicious and Refreshing 5¢," metal frame with chain hanger, 1900s, EX, $9,000.00 B.

Display, glass, "Drink Coca-Cola 5¢," 1900s, 8" dia., F, $2,300.00 D. *Collectors Auction Services.*

Display, celluloid, "Drink Coca-Cola Highballs," 1921, 11¼" x 6", EX, $6,500.00 D. *Metz Superlatives Auction.*

Display, glass, "Drink Coca-Cola 5¢," oval shaped, 1906, 9" x 6½", VG, $2,500.00 C. *Collectors Auction Services.*

Display, glass and metal, "Coca-Cola...Sign of Good Taste," hanging light up with fishtail logo, 1960s, 38" x 20" x 9", EX, $350.00 B. *Metz Superlatives Auction.*

Display, glass, "Drink Coca-Cola...Please Pay When Served...Thank You," back bar mirror, 1930s, 11" dia., VG, $650.00 C. *Mitchell Collection.*

Display, glass and metal, "Drink Coca-Cola," reverse painting with original chain hanger, chrome frame, 1932, 20" x 12", EX, $1,500.00 B. *Metz Superlatives Auction.*

Display, glass and plastic, "Always Feels Right, Always Coca-Cola," light-up counter display with newer plastic bottle, 1990s, 12" x 13", NM, $250.00 B. *Metz Superlatives Auction*.

Display, glass mirror, "Drink Carbonated Coca-Cola 5¢ in bottles," round, good, $600.00 C. *Mitchell Collection*.

Display, glass and plastic, "Drink Coca-Cola...Please Pay Cashier," light-up counter sign with Coke glass at each end, 1950s, 18½" x 8", EX, $2,600.00 B. *Metz Superlatives Auction*.

Display, glass and plastic, "Drink Coca-Cola...Pause and Refresh" on left side and fan image of bottle in hand on right side, 1940s, 19" x 15½", EX, $675.00 B. *Metz Superlatives Auction*.

Display, metal and glass, "Open...," four-sided revolving sign on raised base, light-up, 1960s, 20" tall, NM, $1,600.00 B. *Metz Superlatives Auction*.

Display, metal and glass, "Please Pay when Served," light-up counter sign, 1948, 20" x 12", VG, $2,000.00 C. *Metz Superlatives Auction*.

Display, metal, "Coca-Cola," hobbleskirt bottle on flat background giving a 3-D effect with raised border trim, NOS, 24" x 48", NM, $325.00 B. *Metz Superlatives Auction*.

Display, metal, "Coca-Cola Sold Here," 1920s, VG, $850.00 B. *Metz Superlatives Auction.*

Display, metal, "Curb Service...Coca-Cola...Sold Here Ice Cold," embossed lettering, driveway sign, 1931, 20" x 28", EX, $125.00 B. *Metz Superlatives Auction.*

Display, metal, "Drink Coca-Cola, Delicious and Refreshing" by "The Icy-O Company, Inc., Charlotte, N.C.," hobbleskirt bottle at left of message, EX, $850.00 B. *Metz Superlatives Auction.*

Display, metal, "Drink Coca-Cola," and seven other advertisements on spinning paddles, NOS, 1950s, NM, $750.00 B. *Metz Superlatives Auction.*

Display, metal, "Drink Coca-Cola...Enjoy That Refreshing New Taste," horizontal fishtail design with bottle at right, 1960s, 32" x 12", EX, $400.00 B. *Metz Superlatives Auction.*

Display, metal, "Drink Coca-Cola...Fountain Service," double-sided shield, 1934, 23" x 26", NM, $1,600.00 C.

Display, metal, "Drink Coca-Cola," horizontal embossed Dasco Coke, 1930s, 17¾" x 5¾", EX, $375.00 B. *Metz Superlatives Auction.*

Display, metal, "Drink Coca-Cola...Ice Cold," horizontal, tag design with bottle, 1950s, EX, $700.00 B. *Metz Superlatives Auction.*

Display, metal, "In Any Weather...Drink Coca-Cola in Bottles...Sold Here" on front side with thermometer on left of message, reverse side reads, "Thanks...Call Again," 1930s, EX, $2,100.00 B. *Metz Superlatives Auction.*

Display, metal, "Enjoy Coca-Cola...While We Check Your Tires," 1960s, EX, 225.00 C.

Display, metal, "Drink Coca-Cola in Bottles," on metal surrounded by bent wire frame, 1950s, EX, $300.00 B. *Metz Superlatives Auction.*

Display, metal and glass, "Drink Coca-Cola," reverse-painted glass designed to be lit from the back, 1930s, 13" x 9", G, $835.00 C. *Mitchell Collection.*

Display, metal, "Gas Today...Drink Coca-Cola While You Wait," with courtesy panel for gas prices, 1929 – 1930, 28" x 20", EX, $4,500.00 B. *Metz Superlatives Auction.*

In 1950, Edgar Bergen and Charlie McCarthy appeared in the first live TV program sponsored by Coca-Cola.

Display, metal and glass, "Drink Coca-Cola," reverse-painted glass with original metal frame and chain, 1932, 20" x 12", EX, $3,500.00 B. *Metz Superlatives Auction.*

Display, metal and glass, "Drink Coca-Cola," light-up topper for cash register, 1940 – 1950s, EX, $950.00 B. *Metz Superlatives Auction.*

Display, metal and glass, "Drink...Sign of Good Taste," disc inside wire circle, 1965, 14" dia., EX, $400.00 B. *Metz Superlatives Auction.*

Display, metal and glass, "Drink ...in Bottles," disc-shaped motion light, 1950, 11½" dia., NM, $675.00 B. *Metz Superlatives Auction.*

Display, metal and glass, "Pause and Refresh...Drink Coca-Cola in Bottles" light-up counter sign with waterfall illusion at left, 1950s, EX, $1,150.00 B.

Display, metal and glass, "Have a Coke...Refresh Yourself," light-up arrow pointing at cup, difficult to locate, 1950s, 17" x 10" x 3", NM, $1,400.00 B. *Metz Superlatives Auction.*

Display, metal and glass, "Pause...Drink Coca-Cola...Have a Coke," illusion light behind the word *pause*, 1950s, EX, $925.00 C. *Metz Superlatives Auction.*

Display, metal and glass, "Work Safely...Work Refreshed," light-up workplace piece in its original box, 1950s, 16" x 16", EX, $675.00 B. *Metz Superlatives Auction*

Display, metal, "Ice Cold...Coca-Cola...Enjoy That Refreshing New Feeling," horizontal, fishtail logo with bottle, 1960s, EX, $525.00 B. *Metz Superlatives Auction.*

Display, metal and plastic, "Drink Coca-Cola," light-up with starburst effect in back of cup, 1960s, 14" x 16", EX, $575.00 C. *Collectors Auction Services.*

Display, metal and plastic, "Drink Coca-Cola...Baby Needs...Toys — Gifts," double-sided light-up, "Cosmetics and Prescriptions" on reverse sign with directional arrow, 1950s, 28" x 23", EX, $1,900.00 B. *Metz Superlatives Auction.*

Display, metal and plastic, "Drink Coca-Cola in Bottles...Shop Refreshed...Take Enough Home," light-up with rotating top, 1950s, 21" tall, EX, $525.00 B. *Metz Superlatives Auction.*

Display, metal and plastic, "Drink Coca-Cola," light-up with unusual halloween scene of jack-o-lantern on table with woman in witch costume, 1940s, 10" x 8", EX, $2,000.00 B. *Metz Superlatives Auction.*

Display, metal and plastic, "Have a Coke Here" on one side and "In Bottles" on the other side, light-up halo-type sign, 1950s, 16" dia., EX, $1,400.00 B. *Metz Superlatives Auction.*

Display, metal and plastic, "Drink Coca-Cola," round illusion light, 1960s, 11" dia., NM, $775.00 B. *Metz Superlatives Auction.*

Display, metal and plastic, "Drink Coca-Cola...Thank You...Call Again," double-sided light-up with "Fountain and Prescriptions" on the reverse side, 1950s, 28" x 23", EX, $1,900.00 B. *Metz Superlatives Auction.*

Display, metal and plastic, "Same Quality as Bottled...Coca-Cola Now in Cups," light-up double-sided halo-type sign with 1950s cup on both sides, 1950s, 16" dia., EX, $2,400.00 B. *Metz Superlatives Auction.*

Display, metal and plastic, "Have a Coke" with bottle in hand, light-up with beveled edge, 1940s, 18" x 12", EX, $775.00 B. *Metz Superlatives Auction.*

Display, neon and metal, "Drink Coca-Cola in Bottles," with the original crinkle paint, super early piece, influenced by the Art Deco era and difficult to find. *Caution: this item has been reproduced; however, the reproduction is very easy to detect.* 1939, 17" x 13½", G, $1,700.00 B. *Metz Superlatives Auction.*

Display, paper, "Drink Coca-Cola," die-cut glass for window use, unusual item, 12" x 20", EX, $1,800.00 B. *Metz Superlatives Auction.*

Display, neon and metal, "Coca-Cola in Bottles," Art Deco–influenced base, rubber feet for counter use, 1950s, EX, $3,000.00 B. *Metz Superlatives Auction.*

Display, paper, "Drink Coca-Cola...See Kit Carson TV Show..." featuring Kit Carson, 1953, 24" x 16", EX, $145.00 C. *Mitchell Collection.*

Display, paper, "Home Refreshment" with die-cut six-pack carton, 1941, 22" x 16", NM, $45.00 B. *Metz Superlatives Auction.*

Display, neon and metal, "Coke with Ice," nice showy three-color piece, 1980s, EX, $450.00 C. *Metz Superlatives Auction.*

Display, plastic and metal, "Pause...Drink Coca-Cola...Refresh," light-up plastic center in metal frame, designed for outdoor use, 1960s, 3' x 3', EX, $225.00 B. *Metz Superlatives Auction.*

Display, neon and metal, "The Official Drink of Summer," a modern multicolored sign, 1989, EX, $1,100.00 B. *Metz Superlatives Auction.*

Display, plastic, "Wherever You Go... Whatever You Do," three-piece unit, 1950s, 12" x 14" disc, 46" x 15" ends, EX, $1,250.00 B. *Metz Superlatives Auction.*

Display, wood and glass, "Coca-Cola...Have a Coke," plastic crest with bottle on top, rare item, 1948, 18" x 12", VG, $650.00 B.

Display, wood, "Drink Coca-Cola," diamond shaped with bottle in yellow spotlight at bottom, 1946, 42" x 42", NM, $950.00 B. *Metz Superlatives Auction.*

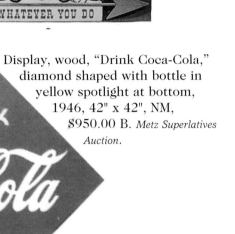

Display, wood, "Coca-Cola" glass being held by pretty blond die-cut woman, 1940s, 42" x 40", VG, $550.00 B. *Metz Superlatives Auction.*

Display, wood and plastic, "Drink Coca-Cola..." fishtail design over courtesy panel, 1960s, 15½" x 12", VG, $145.00 C.

Display, wood, "Drink Coca-Cola...Ice Cold," triangle shaped with arrow pointing down, 1933, EX, $575.00 B. *Metz Superlatives Auction.*

Display, wood, "Drink Coca-Cola...Ice Cold," cooler shaped, 1950s, EX, $275.00 B. *Metz Superlatives Auction.*

Display, wood, "Drink Coca-Cola...Fountain Service" die-cut fountain heads on sides of sign, 1930s – 1940s, 27" x 14", EX, $1,200.00 B. *Metz Superlatives Auction.*

Display; wood, glass, and chrome; "Coca-Cola," plain version of the cash register topper, 1940s, 11½" x 5", good, $475.00 B. *Metz Superlatives Auction.*

Display; wood, glass, and chrome; "Coca-Cola...Please Pay when Served," cash register topper, 1940s, 11½" x 6", EX, $900.00 B. *Metz Superlatives Auction.*

Display, wood and metal, "Drink Coca-Cola," die-cut wood cooler in center of wire circle with arrow through the cooler, 1940s, 32" x 16", NM, $550.00 B. *Metz Superlatives Auction.*

Display, wood and metal, "Drink Coca-Cola...Ice Cold" on disc with bottle and arrow, 1939, 17" dia., good, $450.00 C.

Driveway, metal, "Drink Coca-Cola Refresh," lollipop sign with correct base, 1940 – 1950s, F, $595.00 D.

Displays, plastic, "Things Go Better with Coke," scenes of race cars, 1960s, 13" x 16" each, EX, $575.00 B. *Metz Superlatives Auction.*

Driveway, metal, "Drink Coca-Cola Refresh!" lollipop, not on correct base, 1950s, VG, $495.00 D. *Riverside Antique Mall.*

Flange, metal, "Drink Coca-Cola...Enjoy That Refreshing New Feeling," center fishtail logo, 1960s, 18" x 15", VG, $350.00 C.

Flange, metal, "Drink Coca-Cola...Enjoy That Refreshing New Feeling," horizontal, fishtail design on white background with green stripes, 1963, 18" x 15", EX, $450.00 B. *Metz Superlatives Auction.*

Flange, metal, "Coca-Cola...Sign of Good Taste," horizontal fishtail design, 1960s, VG, $225.00 B. *Metz Superlatives Auction.*

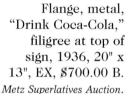

Flange, metal, "Drink Coca-Cola," filigree at top of sign, 1936, 20" x 13", EX, $700.00 B. *Metz Superlatives Auction.*

Flange, metal, "Drink Coca-Cola...Hart Cafe" with die-cut arrow, 1950s, EX, $1,800.00 B. *Metz Superlatives Auction.*

Flange, metal, "Drink Coca-Cola...Ice Cold," die cut with button top and arrow flange arm, hobbleskirt bottle, EX, $575.00 D.

Flange, metal, "Drink Coca-Cola...Lunch," button at top and arrow mounting "Lunch" message, 1950s, 18" x 22", NM, $4,000.00 B. *Metz Superlatives Auction.*

Flange, metal, "Drink Coca-Cola in Bottles...Ice Cold" with glass in arrow, 1954, EX, $2,500.00 B. *Metz Superlatives Auction.*

Flange, metal, "Drink Coca-Cola...Soda," button on top, 1950s, EX, $3,300.00 B. *Metz Superlatives Auction.*

Flange, metal, "Drink Coca-Cola," with bottle in yellow spotlight in lower corner of flange, 1947, 24" x 20", VG, $625.00 C.

Flange, metal, "Enjoy Coca-Cola in Bottles," round with bottle in circle, 1954, EX, $4,500.00 B. *Metz Superlatives Auction.*

Flange, metal, "Sign of Good Taste," double sided with fishtail logo in center, green stripes, NOS, 1960s, 17¾" x 15", NM, $300.00 B. *Wm. Morford Investment Grade Collectibles.*

Flange, metal, "Vendemos Coca-Cola Bien Fria," Italian, 1920s, 16" x 12", NM, $1,500.00 B. *Metz Superlatives Auction.*

Flange, porcelain, "Buvez Coca-Cola Glace," French Canadian, 1950s, 18" x 19", NM, $225.00 B. *Metz Superlatives Auction.*

Flange, porcelain, "Coca-Cola Iced Here," 18" x 20", EX, $775.00 C.

Flat mount, glass, "Drink Coca-Cola," reverse-painted glass, 1920s, 10" x 6", EX, $1,350.00 C.

Flange, porcelain, "Coca-Cola...Rafraichissez Vous...Vendu Ici Glace," foreign, double sided, 17" x 20", VG, $495.00 C.

Flange, porcelain, "Coca-Cola...Refresh yourself...Sold Here, Ice Cold," double-sided shield design, 1930s, 17" x 20", G, $525.00 B. *Metz Superlatives Auction.*

Flange, porcelain, "Drink Coca-Cola Here," 1940s, NM, $850.00 B. *Metz Superlatives Auction.*

The Coca-Cola secret formula is known as "7X" and is probably one of the most closely guarded secrets in the business world.

Flat mount, metal and wire, "Drink Coca-Cola...Wherever You Go" with snow ski scene, 1960s, 14" x 18", EX, $225.00 C.

Flat mount, metal and wire, "Drink Coca-Cola...Wherever You Go," beautiful tropical island scene, 1960s, 14" x 18", EX, $225.00 C.

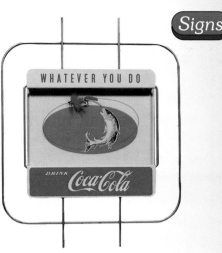

Flat mount, metal and wire, "Drink Coca-Cola...Wherever You Go," fishing scene, 1960s, 14" x 18", EX, $225.00 C.

Flat mount, metal and wire, "Drink Coca-Cola...Wherever You Go" with saddle on fence, 1960s, 14" x 18", EX, $225.00 C.

Flat mount, metal, "Coca-Cola...at Home...Handy Home Carton Sold Here...Now Enjoy," cardboard six-pack, Canadian, hard to find, 1930s, 18" x 54", F, $1,050.00 B. *Metz Superlatives Auction.*

Flat mount, metal, "Coca-Cola...Candy-Cigarettes" with fishtail design logo and white-letter bottle, 1960s, EX, $300.00 B. *Metz Superlatives Auction.*

Flat mount, metal, "Coca-Cola...Delicious and Refreshing 5¢," Lillian Nordica with fan and standing in front of large mirror, 1905, 8¼" x 10¼", VG, $7,500.00 C.

Flat mount, metal, "Coca-Cola...Delicious and Refreshing," oval self framing, Lillian Nordica beside table, rare item, 1904, 8½" x 10¼", EX, $8,500.00 D.

Flat mount, metal, "Coca-Cola," fishtail die cut, 1962, 26" x 12", NM, $200.00 B. *Metz Superlatives Auction.*

Flat mount, metal, "Coca-Cola...Drink...Delicious and Refreshing," Hilda Clark in the round metal variation, difficult to find, 1903, 6" dia., EX, $5,700.00 B.

Flat mount, metal, "Coca-Cola...Delicious and Refreshing...Take a Case Home Today," painted, 19½" x 27¾", VG, $250.00 D.

Flat mount, metal, "Coca-Cola...Enjoy Big King Size...Ice Cold Here," horizontal, with fishtail design and bottle, 1960s, 28" x 20", G, $295.00 D. *Metz Superlatives Auction.*

Flat mount, metal, "Coca-Cola... Ice Cold...Sold Here," embossed, painted round, with trademark in tail of O, 1932, 20" dia., NM, $1,250.00 B. *Metz Superlatives Auction.*

Flat mount, metal, "Coca-Cola," Hilda Clark oval, rarely found in the metal version shown here, 1903, 16¼" x 19½", EX, $3,700.00 B. *Metz Superlatives Auction.*

Flat mount, metal, "Coca-Cola...Ice Cold...Sold Here," round with green painted border, 1933, 20" dia., G, $225.00 B. *Metz Superlatives Auction.*

Flat mount, metal, "Coca-Cola" self framing, hobbleskirt bottle decal, vertical design, 1940 – 1950s, 16" x 50", EX, $425.00 B. *Metz Superlatives Auction.*

Flat mount, metal, "Coca-cola," self framing oval with pretty girl with a Coke bottle, 1926, 11" x 8", VG, $1,000.00 D.

Signs

Flat mount, metal, "Coca-Cola," self framing with fishtail logo, diamond can on right and bottle on left, 1960s, 54" x 18", NM, $850.00 B. *Metz Superlatives Auction.*

Flat mount, metal, "Coca-Cola...Sign of Good Taste," fishtail design on striped frame, 1960s, 46" x 16", EX, $325.00 C.

Flat mount, metal, "Coca-Cola with Soda 5¢," manufactured by Tuchfarber Co. of Cincinnati, 1902, 17" x 12", G, $7,200.00 B. *Metz Superlatives Auction.*

Flat mount, metal, "Delicatessen," fishtail design with diamond can and bottle, self framing, 1960s, 60" x 24", EX, $650.00 B. *Metz Superlatives Auction.*

Flat mount, metal, die-cut "6 for 25" carton, 1950, 11" x 13", EX, $775.00 B. *Metz Superlatives Auction.*

Flat mount, metal, die-cut 12-bottle carton, 1954, NM, $3,000.00 B. *Metz Superlatives Auction.*

Flat mount, metal, die-cut six-pack of bottles with "Regular Size" in yellow spotlight, 1958, 11" x 12", NM, $1,500.00 B. *Metz Superlatives Auction.*

Flat mount, metal, die-cut embossed six-bottle pack, "King Size" at top of carton, 1963, 36" x 30", EX, $725.00 B. *Metz Superlatives Auction.*

41

Flat mount, metal, "Drink Coca-Cola 5¢," Lillian Nordica promoting both fountain and bottle sales, embossed, self framing, 1904 – 1905, EX, $8,700.00 D.

Flat mount, metal, die-cut embossed six-pack with "King Size" panel at bottom, 1963, 36" x 30", EX, $700.00 B. *Metz Superlatives Auction.*

Flat mount, metal, "Drink Coca-Cola," couple with bottle of Coke, self framing, 1940s, 35" x 11", EX, $595.00 D.

Flat mount, metal, "Drink Coca-Cola...Delicious-Refreshing," embossed and painted with 1923 bottle, 1934, 54" x 30", EX, $525.00 B. *Metz Superlatives Auction.*

Flat mount, metal, "Drink Coca-Cola...Delicious and Refreshing...," embossed with bottle in hand, 14" x 10", F, $225.00 B. *Metz Superlatives Auction.*

Flat mount, metal, "Drink Coca-Cola," embossed and painted kick plate with 1923 bottle, 1933, 35" x 11", EX, $935.00 C.

Flat mount, metal, "Drink Coca-Cola...Delicious and Refreshing," with hobbleskirt bottle to left side of courtesy panel, 1930s, 36" x 12", EX, $595.00 C. *Mitchell Collection.*

Flat mount, metal, "Drink Coca-Cola...Enjoy That Refreshing New Feeling," with fishtail logo and a bottle on striped background, self framing, 1960s, 32" x 12", VG, $275.00 C.

Flat mount, metal, "Drink Coca-Cola...Home Cooking Served with a Coke," self framing in horizontal design, 1950s, 50" x 16", EX, $300.00 B. *Metz Superlatives Auction.*

Flat mount, metal, "Drink Coca-Cola ...Enjoy That Refreshing New Feeling," vertical fishtail logo over bottle, self framing, 1960s, 18" x 54", VG, $300.00 B. *Metz Superlatives Auction.*

Flat mount, metal, "Drink Coca-Cola...Ice Cold 5¢," vertical design with hobbleshirt bottle, 1936, EX, $2,700.00 B. *Metz Superlatives Auction.*

Flat mount, metal, "Drink Coca-Cola... Delicious and Refreshing," *Notice anything different about this sign, which was rejected by Coca-Cola? I included this sign because of the auction interest by collectors, but the "Drink..." message is not in the button but on a somewhat bizarre background, probably a production malfunction.* 1954, 18" x 54", EX, $750.00 B. *Metz Superlatives Auction.*

Flat mount, metal, "Drink Coca-Cola...Ice Cold," embossed with shadowed 1923 bottle to left of message panel, 1936, 28" x 20", EX, $850.00 B. *Metz Superlatives Auction.*

Flat mount, metal, "Drink Coca-Cola...Ice Cold...Gas...Today... Drink...Sold Here," vertical version, 1936, 18" x 54", G, $750.00 B. *Metz Superlatives Auction.*

Flat mount, metal, "Drink Coca-Cola...Ice Cold," self framing shadow bottle in vertical design, 1936, 18" x 54", G, $600.00 B. *Metz Superlatives Auction.*

Flat mount, metal, "Drink Coca-Cola...Ice Cold...," self framing, fishtail design with bottle, 1960s, 56" x 32", EX, $300.00 B. *Collectors Auction Services.*

43

Flat mount, metal, "Drink Coca-Cola...Ice Cold" with hob-bleskirt shadowed bottle, 1937, 28" x 20", good, $525.00 B. *Metz Superlatives Auction.*

Flat mount, metal, "Drink Coca-Cola...in Bottles... 5¢," horizontal tacker, 1922, 23½" x 6", NM, $1,350.00 B. *Metz Superlatives Auction.*

Flat mount, metal, "Drink Coca-Cola...in Bottles...," embossed painted kick plate with bottle in left of message panel, 1931, 27" x 10", EX, $750.00 B. *Metz Superlatives Auction.*

Flat mount, metal, "Drink Coca-Cola...Lunches and Home Made Chili...," green striped background with rolled edges, 1960 – 1970s, 65" x 35", EX, $235.00 C.

Flat mount, metal, "Drink Coca-Cola...Refresh Yourself...Sold Here Ice Cold," with bottle to right of message, Canadian, 1930s, 28" x 20", G, $350.00 B. *Metz Superlatives Auction.*

Flat mount, metal, "Drink Coca-Cola...," oval from McRae Distributors with pretty redheaded lady, 1910, EX, $3,650.00 D.

Flat mount, metal, "Drink Coca-Cola...Refresh Yourself...Sold Here Ice Cold," 1927, 28" x 29", VG, $450.00 B. *Metz Superlatives Auction.*

Flat mount, metal, "Drink Coca-Cola," screen print bottle in hand; most of the bottle in hand scenes are decals, making this one unusual; 1954, 18" x 54", EX, $2,100.00 B. *Metz Superlatives Auction.*

Flat mount, metal, "Drink Coca-Cola," self framing horizontal variation with "Trade Mark" in tail, 1927, 32" x 10½", VG, $750.00 B. *Metz Superlatives Auction.*

Flat mount, metal, "Drink Coca-Cola," self framing, horizontal lettering with bottle in yellow spotlight in lower right-hand corner, 1946, 28" x 20", EX, $350.00 B. *Metz Superlatives Auction.*

Flat mount, metal, "Drink Coca-Cola," self framing, designed for outdoor use, with courtesy panel at top, 1950 – 1960s, 72" x 36", F, $95.00 B. *Metz Superlatives Auction.*

Flat mount, metal, "Drink Coca-Cola," self framing new Betty with a hobbleskirt bottle, 1940s, 28" x 20", VG, $325.00 C.

Flat mount, metal, "Drink Coca-Cola," self framing with girl drinking from a bottle of Coke, 1940s, 34" x 12", EX, $475.00 B. *Metz Superlatives Auction.*

Flat mount, metal, "Drink Coca-Cola...Sign of Good Taste," vertical fishtail over bottle, 1960s, 18" x 54", EX, $350.00 B. *Metz Superlatives Auction.*

Flat mount, metal, "Drink Coca-Cola...Take Home a Carton," six-pack in yellow center spotlight, Canadian, 1940, 36" x 60", G, $275.00 C.

Flat mount, metal, "Drink Coca-Cola...Take Home a Carton," yellow background seen so often on these Canadian pieces, 1950, 35" x 53", EX, $625.00 B. *Metz Superlatives Auction.*

Flat mount, metal, "Drink Coca-Cola...Take Home a Carton" vertical design with six for 25¢ carton in yellow spotlight in sign center, Canadian made, 1942, 17" x 53½", EX, $825.00 C.

Flat mount, metal, "Drink Coca-Cola...the Delicious Beverage," known as a turtle sign due to its design, 1920s, 20" x 15", G, $1,800.00 B. *Metz Superlatives Auction.*

Flat mount, metal, "Drink Coca-Cola...Things Go Better With Coke," self framing, courtesy panel at top, 1960s, 60" x 36", good, $275.00 B. *Metz Superlatives Auction.*

Flat mount, metal, Elaine holding a glass, embossed self framing, sign was meant to promote fountain sales, 1916, 20" x 30", VG, $6,000.00 C.

Flat mount, metal, "Drink Coca-Cola," unusual "marching" bottles, 1937, 54" x 18", NM, $800.00 B. *Metz Superlatives Auction.*

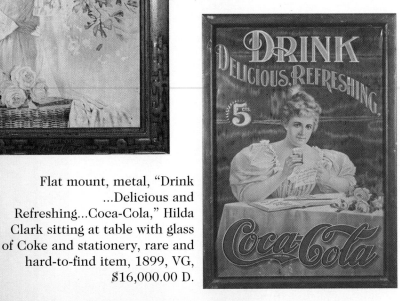

Flat mount, metal, "Drink ...Delicious and Refreshing...Coca-Cola," Hilda Clark sitting at table with glass of Coke and stationery, rare and hard-to-find item, 1899, VG, $16,000.00 D.

Flat mount, metal, "Drink Delicious Refreshing Coca-Cola," Hilda Clark at table with stationary, super rare and desirable, 1900s, 20" x 28", EX, $15,500.00 C.

Flat mount, metal, "Drink Coca-Cola...While You Wait...Gas...Today," 1926, 23½" x 15", G, $775.00 B. *Metz Superlatives Auction.*

Flat mount, metal, "Enjoy Big King Size...Coca-Cola...Ice Cold," self framing, fish-tail logo with bottle, 1960s, 56" x 32", EX, $375.00 B. *Metz Superlatives Auction.*

Flat mount, metal, "Enjoy Coca-Cola...Coke Adds Life to Everything Nice," rolled self-framing edges, 1960s, EX, $295.00 C.

Flat mount, metal, "Enjoy Coca-Cola," with dynamic wave logo and unusual stripped background, 1970s, 35" x 13", EX, $125.00 B. *Metz Superlatives Auction.*

Flat mount, metal, "Ice Cold...Prepared by the Bottler of Coca-Cola" with ice cold beverage in a cup, self framing, 1960s, 20" x 28", NM, 300.00 B. *Metz Superlatives Auction.*

Flat mount, metal, "Enjoy Coke...Have a Coke and a Smile...Coke Adds Life," painted, with self-framing rolled edges, 1960 – 1970s, EX, $165.00 C.

Flat mount, metal, "Enjoy Coca-Cola Ice Cold," painted, with bottle under message panel, 1960s, 18" x 54", VG, $250.00 C.

Flat mount, metal, "Ice Cold...Prepared by the Bottler of Coca-Cola," with 1960s cup on unusual blue background, 1960s, 28" x 20", NM, $675.00 B. *Metz Superlatives Auction.*

Flat mount, metal, "Ice Cold...Prepared by the Bottler of Coca-Cola," 1960s cup on striped background, 1960s, 28" x 20", G, $325.00 B. *Metz Superlatives Auction.*

Flat mount, metal, "Ice Cold...Prepared by the Bottler of Coca-Cola," vertical version of 1960s cup, 1960s, 20" x 28", EX, $550.00 B. *Metz Superlatives Auction.*

Flat mount, metal, "Luncheonette... Coca-Cola," with fishtail logo and bottle and diamond can, 59¼" x 23¼", EX, $425.00 C.

Flat mount, metal, "Pause...Drink Coca-Cola," self framing with horizontal detail. This one is considered rare due to the 1939 – 1940 cooler in yellow spotlight, 1940, 42" x 18", EX, $2,400.00 B. *Metz Superlatives Auction.*

Flat mount, metal over cardboard, "Coca-Cola," Chinese, beveled edge, 11" x 8", EX, $695.00 C.

Flat mount, metal, "Pause...Drink Coca-Cola," vertical with yellow spotlight and tilted bottle, 1940, 18" x 54", VG, $775.00 B. *Metz Superlatives Auction.*

Flat mount, metal, "Pause...Refresh Yourself," with various sports scenes and a tilted hobbleskirt bottle, 1950s, 28" x 10", VG, $255.00 C. *Mitchell Collection.*

Flat mount, metal, "Take Home a Carton," six-pack carton with "6 Bottles" in circle, 1957, 20" x 28", EX, $850.00 B. *Metz Superlatives Auction.*

"Pause and refresh yourself" introduced in 1924.

Flat mount, metal, "Pickup 6...for Home Refreshment," with six-pack carton pictured, self framing with rolled edges, 1956, 50" x 16", NM, $1,450.00 B. *Metz Superlatives Auction.*

Flat mount, metal, "Pickup 12...Refreshment for All," 12-pack of bottles in center, self-framing rolled edges, 1960s, 50" x 16", EX, $595.00 C.

Flat mount, metal, "Take Home a Carton...Drink Coca-Cola," self framing, vertical design with yellow spotlight and six-pack carton, 1930s, 18" x 54", G, $250.00 B. *Metz Superlatives Auction.*

Flat mount, metal, "Things Go Better with Coke," horizontal design with paper cup, difficult to locate this sign, 1960s, 28" x 20", NM, $600.00 B. *Metz Superlatives Auction.*

Flat mount, metal, "Taste TAB...Flavor In — Calories Out...a Product of the Coca-Cola Company," self framing with rolled edges, 1960s, 31½" x 12", VG, $275.00 C.

"Things go better with Coke" slogan debuted in 1963.

Flat mount, metal, "Things Go Better with Coke, vertical design with king-size bottle, 1960s, 18" x 54", NM, $475.00 B. *Metz Superlatives Auction.*

Flat mount, metal, "Things Go Better with Coke," horizontal design with paper cup, 1960s, 20" x 28", EX, $950.00 B. *Metz Superlatives Auction.*

Flat mount, metal, "Things Go Better with Coke," picture of bottle, rolled edges, self framing, 1960s, 35¼" x 35¼", G, $295.00 C.

Flat mount, metal, "Things Go Better with Coke," self framing with king-size hobbleskirt bottle, 1960s, 36" sq., EX, $300.00 B. *Metz Superlatives Auction.*

Flat mount, neon and porcelain, "Coca-Cola...Drug Store...Fountain Service," large single-sided sign, 86" x 58" x 8", G, $3,500.00 B. *Metz Superlatives Auction.*

Flat mount, metal, "Tomese Coca-Cola," embossed painted Spanish kick plate with straight-sided bottle on each side of message, 1908, 36" x 12", EX, $2,300.00 B. *Metz Superlatives Auction.*

Flat mount, oil on canvas, Coca-Cola in glasses being served by soda jerk, dry mounted on board and marked on the back "Forbes Litho," 1940s, 22" x 17", F, $2,300.00 B. *Metz Superlatives Auction.*

Flat mount, original art work on board, "Drink Coca-Cola" on large tent-like building, 1970s, 30" x 20", EX, $150.00 B. *Metz Superlatives Auction.*

In 1950, Edgar Bergen and Charlie McCarthy appeared in the first live TV program sponsored by Coca-Cola.

Flat mount, oil cloth, "Coca-Cola at Soda Fountains 5¢ Delicious Refreshing," scene with Lillian Nordica holding a large fan beside a table with a glass of Coke, extremely rare. As you can imagine, this item is worth whatever someone with deep pockets, is willing to pay. The price I'll give here is the last price I saw this one sell for at auction. 1904, 25" x 47", EX, $13,000.00 B.

Flat mount, paper, "Drink Coca-Cola 5¢," Hilda Clark with flowers, 1901, EX, $7,800.00 C.

Flat mount, original oil artwork on board, "Coca-Cola" being enjoyed on a break by western actors on location, 1950 – 1960s, 22" x 14", NM, $1,000.00 B.

Flat mount, paper, "Drink Coca-Cola Delicious and Refreshing," hot dog and hobbleskirt bottle, 1950s, EX, $195.00 C. *Mitchell Collection.*

Flat mount, paper, "Drink Coca-Cola...Coca-Cola Brings You Edgar Bergen with Charlie McCarthy...CBS Sunday Evenings," Edgar and Charlie in front of an old CBD microphone, 1949, 22" x 11", EX, $250.00 C. *Mitchell Collection.*

Flat mount, paper, "Drink Coca-Cola, Quick Refreshment," with hobbleskirt bottle and hot dog, framed, EX, $195.00 C. *Mitchell Collection.*

Flat mount, paper, Gibson Girl drinking from a straight-sided bottle with a straw, matted, framed and under glass, some slight water stains, 1910s, 20" x 30", VG, $4,600.00 C. *Mitchell Collection.*

Flat mount, paper, pretty girl with large red bow on white dress drinking from a straight-sided bottle with a straw, matted, framed and under glass, 1910s, F, $3,950.00 C. *Mitchell Collection.*

Flat mount, paper, "Tome Coca-Cola" with swimming star Lupe Velez holding up a bottle of Coke, 1932, 11" x 21½", NM, $1,250.00 C. *Mitchell Collection.*

Flat mount, porcelain, "Bevete Coca-Cola," Italian button inside square frame, 22" sq., EX, $225.00 B. *Metz Superlatives Auction.*

Flat mount, porcelain, "Buvez Coca-Cola Vendu Ici Glace," French, single sided, 30½" x 12", EX, $225.00 C.

Flat mount, porcelain, "Delicious Refreshing" with hobbleskirt in center, 1950s, 24" sq., EX, $325.00 C. *Metz Superlatives Auction.*

Flat mount, porcelain, "Coca-Cola...Sold Here Ice Cold," 1940s, 29" x 12", EX, $325.00 C.

Flat mount, porcelain, "Coca-Cola...verfrist U het best...Drink Coca-Cola," foreign, 1950 – 1960s, 18" x 24", EX, $225.00 B. *Metz Superlatives Auction.*

Flat mount, porcelain, "Drink Coca-Cola...Fountain Service," 28" x 12", EX, $800.00 B. *Metz Superlatives Auction.*

Flat mount, porcelain, "Drink Coca-Cola...Fountain Service," 1950s, 30" x 12", G, $325.00 B. *Metz Superlatives Auction.*

Flat mount, porcelain, "Drink Coca-Cola...Delicious and Refreshing...Fountain Service," self framing with design detail on top, 60" x 45½", EX, $2,400.00 C.

Flat mount, porcelain, "Drink Coca-Cola...Fountain Service," Canadian, 1935, 27" x 14", NM, $1,425.00 D. *Metz Superlatives Auction.*

Flat mount, porcelain, "Drink Coca-Cola...Fountain Service," horizontal design, 1950s, 28" x 12", EX, $700.00 B. *Metz Superlatives Auction.*

Flat mount, porcelain, "Drink Coca-Cola," with rolled ends, 1950s, 44" x 16", M, $325.00 B.

Flat mount, porcelain, "Drink Coca-Cola...Ice Cold," vertical version with hobbleskirt bottle and button, 1950 – 1960s, 16" x 4", NM, $475.00 B. *Metz Superlatives Auction.*

Flat mount, porcelain, "Drink Coca-Cola" shield design, 1942, 36" x 24", EX, $325.00 B.

Flat mount, "Serve...Coca-Cola...at Home," vertical design with six-pack in yellow spotlight in center, 1951, 18" x 54", EX, $350.00 B.

Flat mount, tin, "Drink a Bottle of Carbonated Coca-Cola" with straight-sided paper-label bottle, 1900s, 8½" x 10½", G, $6,000.00 C.

Flat mount, wood and cardboard, "Take Home the New HomeCase...," cardboard case in center spotlight on wooden back, 1940s, 18" x 48", EX, $1,600.00 B. *Metz Superlatives Auction.*

Frame, wood, "Drink Coca-Cola" crest at top rail of fancy Kay Displays frame for horizontal cardboard signs, 1930s, 40" x 24", F, $175.00 B – 300.00 C. *Metz Superlatives Auction.*

Frame, wood, Coke bottle crest in center of lower leg, made for upright posters, 1940s, EX, $400.00 – 450.00 C.

Frame, wood, original factory for 36" x 20" cardboard signs, 1940s, EX, $275.00 B – 300.00 C. *Metz Superlatives Auction.*

Hanging, glass, "Please Pay when Served...Coca-Cola," reverse glass, 1950s, 19" x 9½", EX, $550.00 B. *Metz Superlatives Auction.*

Hanging, metal, "Drink Coca-Cola," Kay Displays, 1940s, F, $80.00 B. *Metz Superlatives Auction.*

Hanging, metal, "Drink Coca-Cola...Ice Cold," wrought iron hanging arm, sign has filigree on top, 1937, EX, $4,000.00 B. *Metz Superlatives Auction.*

Hanging, metal, "Coca-Cola...Sold Here...Ice Cold," die cut, double sided, arrow shaped. *Caution: This sign has been heavily reproduced.* 1927, 30" x 8", VG, $495.00 D.

Hanging, metal over cardboard, "Drink Coca-Cola," string handle, 1922, 8" x 4", EX, $900.00 B. *Metz Superlatives Auction.*

Hanging, metal, "Rx Drug Rx...Coca-Cola...Store," designed to hang on arm over sidewalk, EX, $1,300.00 C.

Hanging, metal, "Savourez Coca-Cola A La Maison," French Canadian, 1930-40s, 11" x 16", EX, $200.00 B. *Metz Superlatives Auction.*

Hanging, porcelain, "Drink Coca-Cola," designed to hang on arm over sidewalk, 5' x 3', VG, $400.00 B. *Metz Superlatives Auction.*

Hanging, porcelain, "Drink Coca-Cola...Delicious and Refreshing...Prescriptions," double sided, "Made in U.S.A. 1933, Tenn Enamel Mfg Co., Nash.," designed to be a sidewalk hanger, 1933, 60½" x 46½", EX, $1,450.00 C.

Hanging, porcelain, "Drink Coca-Cola," double-sided die cut with courtesy panel at top and yellow bottle spotlight at bottom, 60" x 60", VG, $850.00 B. *Metz Superlatives Auction.*

Hanging, porcelain, "Drink Coca-Cola," double-sided, add-on bottle disc on bottom adds a 3-D effect, 1923, 48" x 60", G, $675.00 C.

Hanging, porcelain, "Drink Coca-Cola," double sided, 52½" x 35½", F, $150.00 C. *Collectors Auction Services.*

Hanging, porcelain, "Drink Coca-Cola Ice Cold," single-head fountain dispenser, with metal frame, 28" x 27", G, $975.00 C.

Hanging, porcelain, "Drink Coca-Cola...Pause Refresh...Lunch," double sided, 1950s, 28" x 25", NM, $1,500.00 B. *Metz Superlatives Auction.*

Hanging, porcelain, "Drink Coca-Cola...Tourist Stop...Gas...Food," double sided, die cut, with bottom sign attached to main sign for a 3-D effect, 40" x 58", VG, $1,495.00 C.

Hanging, porcelain, "Drink Coca-Cola," very early counter dispenser, 1941, 25" x 26", EX, $2,200.00 B. *Metz Superlatives Auction.*

Hanging, porcelain, "Fountain Service...Drink Coca-Cola...Delicious and Refreshing," 1930s, 5' x 3½', F, $450.00 B. *Metz Superlatives Auction.*

Hanging, porcelain, "Have a Coca-Cola," double sided, 17½" x 19", EX, $475.00 C. *Metz Superlatives Auction.*

Kay display, wood, "Please Pay Cashier" medallion with glass at top, 1940s, 13" dia., EX, $950.00 B. *Metz Superlatives Auction.*

Kay Displays flange, wood and metal, "Drink Coca-Cola...Please Pay when Served," bent metal, double sided, 1940 – 1950s, 15" x 12", EX, $1,250.00 B. *Metz Superlatives Auction.*

Kay Displays, plywood, "Drink Coca-Cola" with applied wood war ships, complete set of five, 1940s, 25" x 8½", EX, $1,900.00 B. *Metz Superlatives Auction.*

Kay Displays, wood and brass, "Drink Coca-Cola," filigree at top of shield shaped sign and marching bottles in center, 1940s, 9" x 11", EX, $525.00 B. *Metz Superlatives Auction.*

Kay Displays, wood and chrome, "Drink Coca-Cola...Thirst Asks Nothing More," very scarce item, 38" x 10", G, $775.00 B. *Metz Superlatives Auction.*

Kay Displays, wood and metal, with bowling scene in center on wood, outlined by wire frame, 1940s, 16" dia., EX, $425.00 B. *Metz Superlatives Auction.*

Kay Displays, wood and brass, "Drink Coca-Cola," shield shaped with die-cut filigree at top, 1940s, 19" x 20", G, $800.00 B. *Metz Superlatives Auction.*

"Thirst asks nothing more" introduced in 1938.

Kay Displays, wood and masonite, "Coca-Cola...Ice Cold," yellow spotlighted bottle at bottom, metal arrow running along back of disc, 1940s, 17" dia., EX, $2,000.00 B. *Metz Superlatives Auction.*

Kay Displays, wood, "Drink Coca-Cola...Ice Cold," with painted disc, bottle and arrow, 17" dia., F, $500.00 B. *Metz Superlatives Auction.*

Kay Displays, wood, "Drink Coca-Cola," die cut of '40s-era airplane and both sides of the globe, 1940s, 27" x 7", EX, $650.00 B. *Metz Superlatives Auction.*

Kay Displays, wood and Masonite, "Drink Coca-Cola Delicious Refreshing," silhouette girl, metal hangers, 1940s, 36" x 14", EX, $625.00 C. *Metz Superlatives Auction.*

Kay Displays, wood, "Drink Coca-Cola...Ice Cold," arrow pointing down through triangle with bottle in point of arrow, 1940s, 24" x 28", G, $750.00 B. *Metz Superlatives Auction.*

Kay Displays, wood, "Drink Coca-Cola...Please Pay When Served," 13" dia., G, $600.00 B. *Metz Superlatives Auction.*

Kay Displays, wood, "Drink Coca-Cola," medallion shaped with die-cut leaves and bottle at top, 1930s, EX, $1,365.00 D. *Metz Superlatives Auction.*

Kay Displays, wood, "Drink Coca-Cola," "Work Refreshed," occupational theme with center medallion supporting "Education," 1940s, 23" x 11½", EX, $375.00 B. *Metz Superlatives Auction.*

Kay Displays, wood, "Have a Coke," teenager on disc in different poses, shown here are two of four made, all are extremely difficult to locate, 1950s, 12" dia., EX, $2,200.00 B. *Metz Superlatives Auction.*

Kay Displays, wood, "Here's Refreshment" with bottle and horseshoe on plank, 1940s, 16½" x 12", $395.00 C.

Kay Displays, wood, "Lunch with Us...a Tasty Sandwich with Coca-Cola," scarce item, 1940s, 9" x 13", EX, $2,900.00 B. *Metz Superlatives Auction.*

Kay Displays, wood, "Lunch with Us" medallion with glass at top, 1940s, 13" dia., EX, $800.00 B. *Metz Superlatives Auction.*

Kay Displays, wood and metal, "Drink Coca-Cola," badminton scene, wooden center with wire outside frame, part of a set, 1930 – 1940s, EX, $425.00 C.

Kay Displays, wood and metal, "Drink Coca-Cola," center displays golfing scene, 1930 – 1940s, EX, $425.00 C.

57

Kay displays, wood and metal, "Drink Coca-Cola," die-cut center of United States, disc with glass at bottom, surrounding double metal rings display directions of the compass, unusual item, 1930s, 16" dia., EX, $1,200.00 B. *Metz Superlatives Auction.*

Kay Displays, wood and metal, "Drink Coca-Cola," soda glass shield sign, 1930s, 9" x 11½", NM, $825.00 B. *Metz Superlatives Auction.*

Kay Displays, wood, "Pause...Drink Coca-Cola...Refresh," Art Deco influence is very apparent, 1940s, 14" x 10½", EX, $2,900.00 B. *Metz Superlatives Auction.*

Kay Displays, wood and metal, "Drink Coca-Cola," recreational scene with girl in water with beach ball, 1930 – 1940s, EX, $425.00 C.

Magazine ad, paper, "Sun-worship with Us This Week at the Beach of Your Choice," pretty girl laying on beach with a bottle of Coke, 1960s, EX, $75.00 C. *Mitchell Collection.*

Light-up, plexglass, "Drink Coca-Cola," part of a dispensing unit featuring the Dee-lish kids, 1950 – 1960s, 13" x 21", EX, $375.00 B. *Metz Superlatives Auction.*

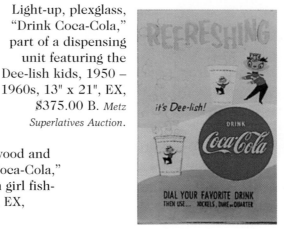

Kay Displays, wood and metal, "Drink Coca-Cola," sports scene with girl fishing, 1930 – 1940s, EX, $425.00 C.

Pilaster, metal, "Drink Coca-Cola in Bottles...Pickup 12...Refreshment for All," with 16" button at top and 12-pack carton, 1954, 16" x 55", NM, $3,300.00 B. *Metz Superlatives Auction.*

Kay Displays, wood and metal, "Drink Coca-Cola...Pause here," 1930s, 37" x 10", G, $1,625.00 D.

Pilaster, metal, "Drink Coca-Cola...Refresh Yourself," unusual version with the "Refresh" top tag, 1950s, 16" x 52", EX, $1,400.00 B. *Metz Superlatives Auction.*

Pilaster, metal, "Drink Coca-Cola...Serve Coke at Home," 16" button at top with 6 pack carton, 1948, 16" x 54", NM, $700.00 D.

Pilaster, metal, "Serve Coke at Home" with wooden handled six-pack, minus top button normally seen on these items, 1947, 16" x 40", VG, $300.00 B. *Metz Superlatives Auction.*

Pilaster, metal, "Take Home a Carton of Quality Refreshment," with a cardboard six-pack carton at the bottom, 1950s, 16" x 55", NM, $875.00 B. *Wm. Morford Investment Grade Collectibles.*

Poster, cardboard, "58 Million a Day," with large bottle, 1957, 17½" x 28½", F, $150.00 C. *Metz Superlatives Auction.*

Poster, cardboard, "12 Bottle Carton...More for Everybody," framed and under glass, 1950s, 16" x 27", VG, $155.00 B. *Metz Superlatives Auction.*

Poster, cardboard, "7 Million Drinks a Day," woman seated with parasol holding a glass of Coke, 1926, 18" x 31", VG, $1,500.00 C.

Poster, cardboard, "A Great Combination," open-faced hamburger and a bottle of Coke, 1950s, EX, $135.00 D.

Poster, cardboard, "Accepted Home Refreshment," couple by the fireplace enjoying Coke and popcorn, 1942, VG, $425.00 B – 550.00 D. *Metz Superlatives Auction.*

Poster, cardboard, "All Set at Our House" with young redheaded boy holding a six-pack of Cokes, 1943, EX, $650.00 B.

Poster, cardboard, "A Red Hot Summer Picnic Pack," promotion with a chance to win the picnic pack, 18" x 25", NM, $35.00 C.

Poster, cardboard, "America's Favorite Moment," couple dining in a booth with a bottle of Coke, 1940s, 36" x 20", EX, $295.00 B – 395.00 D. *Metz Superlatives Auction.*

Poster, cardboard, "At Home," vertical scene of friends and a bowl of iced Cokes, 1953, 16" x 27", VG, $475.00 B. *Metz Superlatives Auction.*

Poster, cardboard, "Be Really Refreshed...Enjoy Coke," with scene at beach, 1959, 21½" x 37½", G, $350.00 C.

Poster, cardboard, "Bacon and Tomato" with Coke glass in right corner, 1930 – 1940s, 21" x 14", EX, $200.00 B. *Metz Superlatives Auction.*

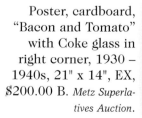

Poster, cardboard, "Be Really Refreshed," die-cut double-sided pretty woman with a glass of Coke, 1960s, 13" x 17", EX, $425.00 B. *Metz Superlatives Auction.*

Poster, cardboard, Betty in original wood frame, 1914, 30" x 38", VG, $2,895.00 C.

Poster, cardboard, "Big Refreshment Value...King Size Coke," pretty lady in wide-brimmed straw hat with bottle of Coke, in metal frame, 1960s, 36" x 20", VG, $295.00 C.

Poster, cardboard, "Buvez Coca-Cola," vertical Middle Eastern man with a bottle of Coke, 1940s, EX, $800.00 B. *Metz Superlatives Auction*.

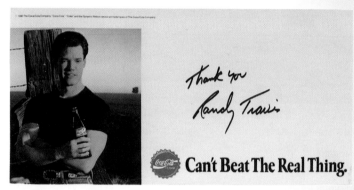

Poster, cardboard, "Can't Beat the Real Thing," picture and autograph by Randy Travis endorsing Coke, 1990, 12" x 16", EX, $30.00 C.

Poster, cardboard, "Coca-Cola Belongs," couple with a picnic basket and a metal bucket of iced Cokes, 1942, EX, $750.00 B. *Metz Superlatives Auction*.

Poster, cardboard, "Coca-Cola 5¢," woman with broad-brimmed hat seated with bamboo fan, 1912, EX, $4,900.00 D.

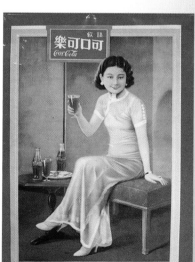

Poster, cardboard, "Coca-Cola Belongs," military couple at booth, 1930s, 36" x 20", EX, $1,100.00 B. *Metz Superlatives Auction*.

Poster, cardboard, "Coca-Cola," Chinese girl seated with a glass of Coke, 1936, 14½" x 22", NM, $1,450.00 C.

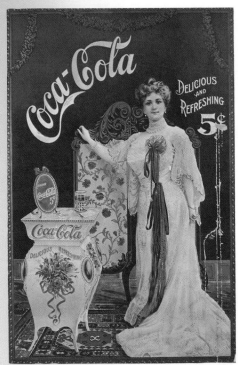

Poster, cardboard, "Coca-Cola," good and unusual picture of marching glasses, framed, 1948, 34" x 11", EX, $725.00 B. *Metz Superlatives Auction.*

Poster, cardboard, "Coca-Cola," litho of sandwich and bottle of Coke for 35¢, used in lunchrooms and fountains, 1952, 11" x 16", VG, $225.00 C.

Poster, cardboard, "Coca-Cola," party scene with Coke iced in metal tub, rare piece, 1952, G, $300.00 B. *Metz Superlatives Auction.*

Poster, cardboard, "Coca-Cola Delicious and Refreshing 5¢" with Lillian Nordica standing beside a high table, 1904, 26" x 40", EX, $9,700.00 C. *Collectors Auction Services.*

Poster, cardboard, "Coca-Cola ...Rafraichissement Chez Soi," horizontal French Canadian, pretty girl with Coke and tulips, 1949, EX, $125.00 B. *Metz Superlatives Auction.*

Poster, cardboard, "Coca-Cola Refreshing" young lady enjoying a bottle of Coke, in original wooden frame, 1949, G, $375.00 B. *Metz Superlatives Auction.*

Poster, cardboard, "Coke Belongs," picnickers pulling cold Coke bottles from cooler, back sides shows girl at refrigerator, 1950s, 16" x 27", EX, $900.00 B. *Metz Superlatives Auction.*

"Coke Belongs" introduced in 1941.

Poster, cardboard, "Coca-Cola" vertical, woman with small kitten and ball of twine being offered a Coke, foreign, 1950s, 16" x 27", EX, $250.00 B. *Metz Superlatives Auction.*

Poster, cardboard, "Coke Belongs" with young couple sharing a bottle of Coke, 1944, EX, $700.00 B. *Metz Superlatives Auction.*

Poster, cardboard, "Coke for Me, Too" couple with Coke and hot dogs, 1946, 36" x 20", EX, $450.00 D.

Poster, cardboard, "Coke," double-sided vertical display with Old Man North on one side and bottles of Coke being passed around on the other side, French Canadian, 16" x 27", VG, $225.00 C. *Metz Superlatives Auction.*

Poster, cardboard, "Coke Convient" with six pack and family at table, 1948, 18" x 24", NM, $200.00 B – 250.00 C.

Poster, cardboard, "Coke...for Hospitality" with couples enjoying Coke and sandwiches, 1948, 36" x 24", EX, $425.00 B. *Metz Superlatives Auction.*

Poster, cardboard, "Coke Time...Join the Friendly Circle," people in pool with float holding a cooler with ice cold Coke, 1955, 36" x 20", EX, $375.00 B. *Metz Superlatives Auction.*

Poster, cardboard, "Coke Head-quarters" with a young couple at the refrigerator with Coke, 1947, EX, $455.00 D.

Poster, cardboard, "Coke is Coca-Cola...Coca-Cola is Coke," in original wooden frame, 1949, EX, $600.00 B. *Metz Superlatives Auction.*

Poster, cardboard, "Coke Knows No Season," couple in back-ground waving, Coke bottle in snow bank, with original wooden frame, 1946, 62" x 33", G, $450.00 C.

63

Poster, cardboard, "Coke Time," pretty woman in cowboy hat, bottle of Coke, border is surrounded by various cattle brands, 1955, VG, $375.00 C.

Poster, cardboard, "Coke Time" pretty girl being offered a bottle of Coke, 1950s, F, $250.00 C.

Poster, cardboard, "Coke Time" two couples enjoying themselves with Coke, in original restored frame, 1954, NM, $600.00 B. *Metz Superlatives Auction.*

Poster, cardboard, "Come Over for Coke" with pretty hostess at table, 1947, 36" x 20", G, $275.00 C.

Poster, cardboard, "Coke Time" with group having fun, 1954, 36" x 20", EX, $1,200.00 B. *Metz Superlatives Auction.*

Poster, cardboard, "Cooling," Florine McKinney, MGM actress, at patio table, 1935, 13½" x 30", F, $425.00 B. *Metz Superlatives Auction.*

Poster, cardboard, "Dancing Lady," lobby card featuring Clark Gable and Joan Crawford, 1930s, EX, $1,900.00 B. *Metz Superlatives Auction.*

Poster, cardboard, "Cooling Lift," redheaded beauty in pool with a bottle of Coke, 1958, EX, $500.00 B. *Metz Superlatives Auction.*

Poster, cardboard, "Coke Time," young couple on bleachers enjoying Coke in bottles, in original wooden frame, EX, $950.00 B. *Metz Superlatives Auction.*

Poster, cardboard, "Demand the Genuine by Full Name, Nicknames Encourage Substitution" with straight-sided paper-label bottle, 1914, 30" x 18", F, $500.00 B. *Metz Superlatives Auction*.

Poster, cardboard, "Delicious...Refreshing" with Lillian Nordica holding a fan, 1905, F, $9,300.00 C.

Poster, cardboard, "Drink Coca-Cola...Be Alert," soda jerk with extended glass of Coke, easel back for counter use, unusual piece, 1930s, 21" x 37", EX, $4,300.00 B. *Metz Superlatives Auction*.

Poster, cardboard, "Drink Coca-Cola 50th Anniversary" with two women sitting on a Coke disc, 1936, 27" x 47", VG, $1,500.00 B. *Metz Superlatives Auction*.

Poster, cardboard, "Drink Coca-Cola," circus scene with performers enjoying a bottle of Coke, 1936, 32" x 50", EX, $4,500.00 B. *Metz Superlatives Auction*.

Poster, cardboard, "Drink Coca-Cola...Delicious and Refreshing...Refreshment You Go For," horizontal with girl on bicycle with front basket full of Cokes, 36" x 20", NM, $675.00 B. *Metz Superlatives Auction*.

Poster, cardboard, "Drink Coca-Cola Delicious and Refreshing," matted, framed and under glass, 1914, 21" x 11", F to EX, $800.00 C $3,400.00 C. *Mitchell Collection*.

Poster, cardboard, "Drink Coca-Cola...Come up Smiling" with Johnny Weissmuller and Maureen O'Sullivan sitting on a springboard, 1934, 13½" x 29½", EX, $3,100.00 C. *Mitchell Collection*.

Poster, cardboard, "Drink Coca-Cola," Hostess Girl sitting on the arm of chair and enjoying a bottle of Coke, 1935, 16" x 27", F, $250.00 D.

Poster, cardboard, "Drink Coca-Cola," Hostess Girl with a glass of refreshment, 1935, 30" x 50", G, $375.00 B. *Metz Superlatives Auction.*

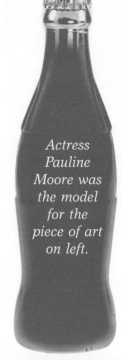

Actress Pauline Moore was the model for the piece of art on left.

Poster, cardboard, "Drink Coca-Cola...Delicious and Refreshing," vertical, Coke being iced down in metal bucket, 1926, EX, $850.00 C.

Poster, cardboard, "Drink Coca-Cola...Delicious and Refreshing," vertical with bottle over button, 1954, 27" x 56", VG, $500.00 B. *Metz Superlatives Auction.*

Poster, cardboard, "Drink Coca-Cola...Delicious with Good Food," woman with serving tray full of food and Cokes, Canadian, 1931 – 1932, 18" x 32", EX, $4,100.00 B. *Metz Superlatives Auction.*

Poster, cardboard, "Drink Coca-Cola Ice Cold," youngster holding a bottle, 1950s, 16" x 27", EX, $625.00 B. *Metz Superlatives Auction.*

Poster, cardboard, "Drink Coca-Cola," lady in red outfit at stadium with a bottle of Coke, 1940, 30" x 50", EX, $1,400.00 B. *Metz Superlatives Auction.*

Poster, cardboard, "Drink Coca-Cola," pretty dark-haired lady with a horse and a bottle, 1938, 30" x 50", G, $1,050.00 D.

Poster, cardboard, "Drink Coca-Cola ...Refresh Yourself," horizontal, three cheerleaders with Cokes, 1953, 27" x 16", EX, $675.00 B. *Metz Superlatives Auction.*

Poster, cardboard, "Drink Coca-Cola...Refreshing," vertical running girl as used on the 1937 tray, 1937, 14" x 30", EX, $400.00 C.

Poster, cardboard, "Drink Coca-Cola," pretty girl by the ocean in swimsuit, vertical version, 1938, 30" x 50", EX, $4,000.00 B. *Metz Superlatives Auction.*

Poster, cardboard, "Drink Coca-Cola" woman at beach with red towel, wearing a yellow swimsuit and holding a bottle of Coke, 1930s, 30" x 50", EX, $1,700.00 B. *Metz Superlatives Auction.*

Poster, cardboard, "Drink Coca-Cola," vertical scene with bathing beauty, 1940, EX, $1,200.00 B. *Metz Superlatives Auction.*

Poster, cardboard, "Drink...," pretty girl lifeguard on stand with a glass of Coke, 1929, 17" x 29½", VG, $1,000.00 B. *Metz Superlatives Auction.*

Poster, cardboard, "Drink Royal Palm," Royal Palm Beverages by the Coca-Cola Company, 1930s, 17" x 11¼", G, $155.00 D.

Poster, cardboard, "Drink Coke in Bottles," three boxers, including Floyd Patterson, 1954, F, $375.00 B. *Metz Superlatives Auction.*

Poster, cardboard, "Easy to Take Home," woman with a carton of Coke fresh from a store rack, 1941, EX, $800.00 B. *Metz Superlatives Auction.*

Poster, cardboard, "Enjoy Coke" with dynamic wave and courtesy panel on right side of sign, 1970 – 1980s, EX, $12.00 D.

Poster, cardboard, "Enjoy Frosty, Refreshing, Sugar Free Fresca," snowy background with bottle of Fresca, 1960s, VG, $200.00 D.

Poster, cardboard, "Entertain Your Thirst," singer at microphone with a bottle of Coke, 1940s, 36" x 20", EX, $750.00 C.

Poster, cardboard, "Enjoy That Refreshing New Feeling," couple at waters edge with refreshing Coke in bottles, 1960s, 19" x 27", EX, $175.00 C.

Poster, cardboard, "-et Coke, Aussi," French Canadian with mother and daughter at table with bottles of Coke, 1946, 16" x 27", VG, $275.00 C. *Metz Superlatives Auction.*

Poster, cardboard, "Entertain Your Thirst," two ballerinas resting with a bottle of Coke, 1942, 16" x 27", VG, $600.00 B. *Metz Superlatives Auction.*

Poster, cardboard, "Entertain Your Thirst...the One Drink Most Guests Prefer," 1956, 16" x 15", EX, $130.00 B. *Metz Superlatives Auction.*

Poster, cardboard, "Face Your Job Refreshed," pretty woman in work environment at drill press, 1940s, 59" x 30", VG, $900.00 D.

Poster, cardboard, "Extra Bright Refreshment," couple at party holding bottles of Coke, 33" x 53", EX, $325.00 C.

Poster, cardboard, "For Good Eating," staggered bottles of Coke and food, 1950s, 36" x 20", G, $295.00 C.

Poster, cardboard, "Familiar Refreshment" with bottle of Coke and sandwich, 1940, 14" x 31", F, $250.00 B.
Metz Superlatives Auction.

Poster, cardboard, "Face the Sun Refreshed," young woman using one hand to shield eyes from the sun and holding a bottle of Coke with the other hand, vertical display, 1941, 30" x 53½", VG, $675.00 C.
Collectors Auction Services.

Poster, cardboard, famous bather from Snyder and Black with round blue background, framed and under glass, considered to be a rare piece, 1938, 22" x 23", EX, $2,850.00 C.
Mitchell Collection.

Poster, cardboard, "For People on the Go," vertical, service man and pretty lady walking with a bottle of Coke, 1944, 28" x 36", EX, $1,300.00 B. *Metz Superlatives Auction.*

Poster, cardboard, "For the Party," soldier and pretty girl on bicycle for two with a basket full of Coke bottles, 1940s, 29" x 50½", EX, $525.00 C.

Poster, cardboard, "Friendly Pause," three women with bottle Cokes, 1948, 16" x 27", NM, $1,500.00 B. *Metz Superlatives Auction.*

Poster, cardboard, "Get Both sizes in cartons," with woman and both sizes on the table, 1956, NM, $500.00 B. *Metz Superlatives Auction.*

Poster, cardboard, "Good Taste," 50s girl and furniture, 1955, 16" x 27", EX, $625.00 B. *Metz Superlatives Auction.*

Poster cardboard, "Good Pause Drink Coca-Cola in Bottles," pretty circus performer on trapese, 1954, 36" x 20", G, $525.00 C.

Poster, cardboard, "Good Taste for All," bottle in hand, , 1955, 16" x 27", EX, $295.00 C.

Poster, cardboard, "Good," woman about to take a drink from a Coke bottle, 1957, NM, $400.00 B. *Metz Superlatives Auction.*

Poster, cardboard, "Got Enough Coke on Ice?" three teenage girls on sofa with telephone, Canadian, 1945, 36" x 20", G, $400.00 C.

Poster, cardboard, "Have a Coke," bottle of Coke in snowbank, in original wooden frame, 1946, NM, $550.00 B. *Metz Superlatives Auction.*

Poster, cardboard, "Have a Coke...Coca-Cola," couple at a masquerade ball, F, $275.00 C.

Poster, cardboard, "Have a Coke," pretty cheerleader with megaphone in one hand and a bottle of Coke in the other, 1946, EX, $750.00 B. *Metz Superlatives Auction.*

Poster, cardboard, "Have a Coke" pretty girl pulling on skates, 1955, F, $500.00 B. *Metz Superlatives Auction.*

Poster, cardboard, "Have a Coke" with pretty girl handing forth a Coke, 1940s, EX, $650.00 B. *Metz Superlatives Auction.*

Poster, cardboard, "Here's a Glass for You...Drink Coca-Cola," woman with flare glass at table, 1909, F, $6,800.00 D.

Poster, cardboard, "Have a Coke," redheaded young lady with a Coke bottle in each hand, in front of a drink machine, 1940s, 16" x 27", EX, $395.00 C.

Poster, cardboard, "Hello Refreshment," vertical version, pretty girl coming out of swimming pool, 1942, EX, $600.00 B. *Metz Superlatives Auction.*

Poster, cardboard, "Have a Coke," vertical pretty young lady with a bottle of Coke, 1948, EX, $1,800.00 B. *Metz Superlatives Auction.*

Poster, cardboard, "Hello Refreshment," horizontal version, pretty girl coming out of swimming pool to a refreshing bottle of Coke, 1942, 36" x 20", EX, $1,700.00 B. *Metz Superlatives Auction.*

71

Poster, cardboard, "Here's Something good!" party scene with people enjoying a Coke, 1951, EX, $375.00 C. *Metz Superlatives Auction.*

Poster, cardboard, "Here's to Our G.I. Joes," two young ladies sitting beside a globe, 1944, G, $600.00 B. *Collectors Auction Services.*

Poster, cardboard, "Home Refreshment," double sided with picnic scene on one side and girl by refrigerator on other side, 1950s, NM, $675.00 B. *Metz Superlatives Auction.*

Poster, cardboard, "Home Refreshment," horizontal picture with woman holding flowers and a bottle of Coke, 1950s, 50" x 29", EX, $350.00 C.

Poster cardboard, "Hospitality Coca-Cola," a bottle of Coke and a pretty girl with flower in hair lighting a candle, 1950, 59" x 30", EX, $950.00 D. *Collectors Auction Services.*

Poster, cardboard, "Home Refreshment on the Way," extremely attractive young woman wearing a wide-brimmed hat and carrying a basket of Coke, 1940s, 24½" x 50", VG, $650.00 B. *Metz Superlatives Auction.*

Poster, cardboard, "Home Refreshment" with a pretty girl sitting talking to a man in military uniform, 1944, EX, $1,300.00 B. *Metz Superlatives Auction.*

Poster, cardboard, "Hospitality in Your Hands," smiling pretty woman hostess with a tray of Cokes, 1948, EX, 425.00 B. *Metz Superlatives Auction.*

Poster, cardboard, "Home Refreshment," young woman in front of an open refrigerator, holding a bottle of Coke, 1950s, 16" x 27", NM, $550.00 B. *Metz Superlatives Auction.*

Poster, cardboard, "Inviting You to Refreshment," pretty girl at table with bottles of Coke, 1940s, EX, $650.00 B. *Metz Superlatives Auction.*

Poster, cardboard, "It's a Family Affair," family enjoying a Coke, Canadian, 1941, EX, $400.00 B. *Metz Superlatives Auction.*

Poster, cardboard, "Ice Cold," snowman with arm around bottle, Canadian item that's difficult to locate, 1941, 16" x 27", NM, $225.00 B. *Metz Superlatives Auction.*

Poster, cardboard, "It's Twice Time," horizontal view with a couple dressed in white on a white scooter, large truck size, 1960s, 67" x 32", EX, $225.00 B. *Metz Superlatives Auction.*

Poster, cardboard, "James Brown," with psychedelic artwork, hard to locate this one, 1960s, 16" x 27", EX, $200.00 B. *Metz Superlatives Auction.*

Poster, cardboard, Kit Carson, promotional item for the TV cowboy, with a six-pack the buyer could get an official kerchief, 1950s, 16" x 24", EX, $225.00 B. *Metz Superlatives Auction.*

Poster, cardboard, "Join the Friendly Circle," double sided featuring young people gathered around a cooler of Cokes, 1954, G, $500.00 B. *Metz Superlatives Auction.*

Poster, cardboard, "La pause...," vertical French Canadian scene of pretty girl with tennis racket, 1946, EX, $450.00 B. *Metz Superlatives Auction.*

Poster, cardboard, "Join Me," young lady fencing contestant resting on a store cooler with a cold bottle of Coke, 16" X 27", 16, EX, $775.00 B. *Metz Superlatives Auction.*

Poster, cardboard, "Let's Watch for'em" with school girl crossing intersection, 1950s, 66" x 32", NM, $850.00 B. *Metz Superlatives Auction.*

Poster, cardboard, "Let's Have a Coke," young lady majorette sitting on top of a store cooler, 16" x 27", EX, $395.00 C.

Poster, cardboard, "Lunch Refreshed," working men and woman taking their lunch break, 1943, EX, $1,000.00 B. *Metz Superlatives Auction.*

Poster, cardboard, lettered "Fountain Service" with Coke disc to right of message, 1950s, 30" x 12", EX, $450.00 B. *Metz Superlatives Auction.*

Poster, cardboard, "Match your Thirst...Drink Coca-Cola...ice cold...Regular...King size," horizontal with couple drink from each size bottle through a straw, 1956, 27" x 16", EX, $160.00 B. *Metz Superlatives Auction.*

Poster, cardboard, "Lunchez rafraichi," vertical, pretty girl with hat and a bottle of Coke, French Canadian, 1948, 16" x 27", EX, $850.00 B. *Metz Superlatives Auction.*

Poster, cardboard, "Me, Too!" young bright eyed boy eager for a bottle of Coke, 62" x 33", G, $525.00 C.

Poster, cardboard, "Lunch refreshed," vertical scene with waitress holding a tray of Cokes and sandwiches, 1948, 16" x 27", NM, $1,600.00 B. *Metz Superlatives Auction.*

Poster, cardboard, "Mind Reader," pretty girl sunning and being handed a bottle of Coke, 1960s, EX, $650.00 C. *Metz Superlatives Auction.*

Poster, cardboard, "Nothing Refreshes Lke a Coke," couple with bicycles, man in uniform, both enjoying Coke from bottles, 1943, EX, $1,700.00 B. *Metz Superlatives Auction.*

Poster, cardboard, "Now for a Coke!" woman in swimsuit, 1951, 36" x 20", NM, $1,250.00 B., *Metz Superlatives Auction.*

Poster, cardboard, "Mom Knows Her Groceries" with girl at refrigerator holding a couple of bottles of Coke, 1946, VG, $450.00 B. *Metz Superlatives Auction.*

Poster, cardboard, "Pause and Refresh" with pretty girl sitting a soda fountain with dispenser, 1948, 41" x 23½", NM, $2,300.00 B. *Metz Superlatives Auction.*

Poster, cardboard, "On the Refreshing Side," couple with bottles of Coke at sporting event, 1941, 30" x 50", VG, $600.00 B. *Metz Superlatives Auction.*

Poster, cardboard, "Party Pause," woman in clown suit being offered a bottle of Coke, 1940s, 36" x 20", G, $395.00 C. *Mitchell Collection.*

Poster, cardboard, "Pause for Coke," girl at railing at ballpark, 1948, 16" x 27", EX, $850.00 B. *Metz Superlatives Auction.*

Poster, cardboard, "Pause...Refresh... Drink Coca-Cola," vertical, bottle in festive background, Canadian, framed and under glass, 1949, 16" x 27", EX, $425.00 B. *Metz Superlatives Auction.*

Poster, cardboard, "Pause...Refresh," vertical, couple at soda fountain enjoying a glass of Coke, Canadian, 1948, 28" x 36", EX, $1,400.00 B. *Metz Superlatives Auction.*

Poster, cardboard, "Pause," with skating scene and clown, still in an original factory frame, 1930s, EX, $850.00 B – 925.00 D. *Metz Superlatives Auction.*

Poster, cardboard, "Play Refreshed," pretty young woman tennis player relaxing on a Coke cooler enjoying a bottle of Coke, 1949, NM, $2,700.00 B. *Metz Superlatives Auction.*

Poster cardboard, "Play Host to Thirst," vertical, friends around a large tub of iced Cokes, 1950s, 16" x 27", EX, $375.00 B. *Metz Superlatives Auction.*

Poster, cardboard, "Planning Hospitality," carton of Cokes beside flowers, 27" x 16", EX, $425.00 D.

Poster, cardboard, "Play Refreshed," woman with ocean-fishing rod and reel and with a bottle of Coke, 1950s, 36" x 20", VG, $395.00 C.

Poster, cardboard, "Play Refreshed," cowgirl with bottle of Coke, still in original wooden frame, 1951, EX, $700.00 B. *Metz Superlatives Auction.*

Poster, cardboard, "Play Refreshed," woman on carousel horse, still in original factory frame, 1940s, EX, $1,200.00 B. *Metz Superlatives Auction.*

Poster, cardboard, printer's proof that was left in the estate of Mrs. Diana Allen, one of the models for this scene, 1922, 15¼" x 25", EX, $8,000.00 B. *Metz Superlatives Auction.*

Poster, cardboard, "Quality You Can Trust," sports stars Jesse Owens and Alice Coachman with bottles of Coke, 1952, EX, $925.00 B. *Metz Superlatives Auction.*

Poster, cardboard, "Refresh your taste," sailing scene with pretty girl holding a bottle of Coke, in original wooden frame, 1950s, 16" x 27", EX, $775.00 C. *Mitchell Collection.*

Poster, cardboard, "Refresh" with pretty majorette about to enjoy a bottle of Coke, 1952, G, $325.00 D.

Poster, cardboard, "Refreshment Right Out of the Bottle," redheaded girl with skates drinking from a bottle of Coke, in front of a store cooler, 1941, EX, $750.00 B. *Metz Superlatives Auction.*

Poster, cardboard, "Refreshing New Feeling," couple laying on the beach with bottled Coke, truck sized, 1960s, 67" x 32", NM, $125.00 B. *Metz Superlatives Auction.*

Poster, cardboard, "Refreshing New Feeling" woman in pool with King Size Coke, wearing large-brimmed hat, truck side advertising, 1960s, 67" x 32", EX, $135.00 B. *Metz Superlatives Auction.*

Poster, cardboard, "Refresh Yourself" with horses and riders, 1957, 16" x 27", VG, $425.00 D.

-et Coke, aussi

Poster, cardboard, "Refreshment," young party girl by pool with cart full of Cokes, 1949, 33½" x 54", EX, $695.00 C.

RIDE ALONG
WITH THE COCA-COLA RACING FAMILY!

Poster, cardboard, "Ride Along," Dale Earnhardt and a Coke store advertising, 36" x 46", EX, $35.00 – 55.00 C.

Right off the ice

Poster, cardboard, "Right Off the Ice," girl at skating rink with a bottle of Coke, 1946, 16" x 27", EX, $400.00 B. *Metz Superlatives Auction.*

SERVE YOURSELF
ICE COLD
Coca-Cola
...Delicious, Refreshing!

Poster, cardboard, "Serve Yourself" with glass in hand, 1949, 13" x 11", NM, $170.00 B. *Metz Superlatives Auction.*

Poster, cardboard, "Round the World 1944", die cut lady in heavy coat with a glass of Coke, framed, 1944, EX, $325.00 D. *Riverside Antique Mall.*

Shop refreshed

Poster, cardboard, "Shop Refreshed," pretty red-head at counter with fountain dispenser, 1948, 41" x 23½", NM, $2,000.00 B. *Metz Superlatives Auction.*

SERVES 3 OVER ICE-NICE!
Coca-Cola
BIG 16 OZ. SIZE

Poster, cardboard, "Serves 3 Over Ice – Nice...Drink Coca-Cola...Big 16 oz. Size," horizontal with a lady at kitchen table, 1950s, 27" x 16", EX, $350.00 B. *Metz Superlatives Auction.*

Shop *refreshed*

Poster, cardboard, "Shop Refreshed," young woman at vending machine with a bottle of Coke, 1948, EX, $600.00 B. *Metz Superlatives Auction.*

BE REALLY REFRESHED!

Poster, cardboard, skiers in winter snow scene, "Be Really Refreshed," in metal frame, 1955, 36" x 20", EX, $335.00 C.

Poster, cardboard, "So Delicious," woman in heavy winter coat with hood, 1950s, VG, $475.00 B. *Metz Superlatives Auction.*

Poster, cardboard, "So Easy to Carry Home," woman walking home in rain with umbrella and a carton of Cokes, vertical-style positioning, 1942, EX, $495.00 C. *Metz Superlatives Auction.*

Poster, cardboard, "So Easy," hostess preparing for the party by candlelight, 1950s, VG, $495.00 C.

Poster, cardboard, "So Good with Food," vertical, girl at Coke picnic cooler with friends, 1952, 16" x 27", EX, $575.00 B. *Metz Superlatives Auction.*

Poster, cardboard, swimsuit girl with bottle, the companion piece to the 1938 version, this one has a diamond shaped background and other small changes, very desirable item, framed and under glass, 1940, 23" x 22", EX, $2,000.00 C. *Mitchell Collection.*

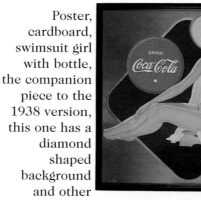

Poster, cardboard, "Start Refreshed," couple at roller skating rink, man in Naval uniform, two bottles of Coke, 1943, 16" x 27", EX, $425.00 C.

Poster, cardboard, "So Easy...So Welcome...Serve Coca-Cola," horizontal, small girl serving Coke in bottles in outdoor scene, 1952, 56" x 27", EX, $850.00 B. *Metz Superlatives Auction.*

Poster, cardboard, "Stop...Go Refreshed," glass of Coke and 1950s-style steering wheel, 1950s, 16" x 27", VG, $295.00 C.

Poster, cardboard, "So Refreshing...Drink Coca-Cola" girl with Coke bottle, vertical, 1941, EX, $750.00 B. *Metz Superlatives Auction.*

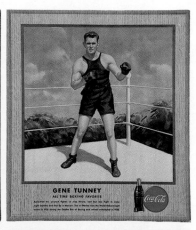

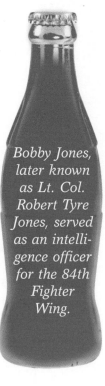

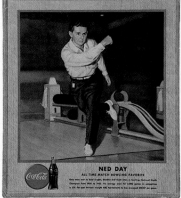

Bobby Jones, later known as Lt. Col. Robert Tyre Jones, served as an intelligence officer for the 84th Fighter Wing.

Poster, cardboard, sports favorites, pictured are nine of set of ten, individually these sell in the $110.00 – 200.00 range, 1947, EX, $2,100.00 – 2,500.00 C full set. *Mitchell Collection.*

Poster, cardboard, TAB advertising with a courtesy panel on the right side of the sign, 1960s, EX, $75.00 D.

Poster, cardboard, "Take Coke Along," young couple picnicking with basket and cooler of ice cold Cokes, 1951, 16" x 27", EX, $700.00 B. *Metz Superlatives Auction.*

Poster, cardboard, "Take Some Home Today," young girl in party scene, in original frame, 1950s, 16" x 27", VG, $675.00 C. *Collectors Auction Services.*

Poster, cardboard, "Take Home a Carton...Easy to Carry" with woman carrying a carton of Cokes, 1937, 14" x 32", EX, $1,600.00 B. *Metz Superlatives Auction.*

Poster, cardboard, "Talk about Good," cowboy with bottle of Coke, 1954, 16" x 27", EX, $800.00 B. *Metz Superlatives Auction.*

Poster, cardboard, "The Best of Taste," young lady being offered a Coke, 1956, EX, $750.00 B. *Metz Superlatives Auction.*

Poster, cardboard, "Talk about Refreshing," young ladies on beach with bottles of Coke, 1943, VG, $800.00 B. *Metz Superlatives Auction.*

Poster, cardboard, "The Best is Always the Better Buy," girl carrying a bag of groceries and a six-pack carton of Coke, 1943, EX, $975.00 B. *Metz Superlatives Auction.*

Poster, cardboard, "The Calendar Girls through the Years," horizontal scene of 12 well-known models, difficult to find this one, 1939, 56" x 27", EX, $850.00 B. *Metz Superlatives Auction.*

Poster, cardboard, "Talk about Refreshing," young lady with umbrella and a bottle of Coke in front of a store cooler, 1942, EX, $600.00 C.

Poster, cardboard, "The Best of Taste," young lady being offered a bottle of Coke, 1956, VG, $350.00 B. *Metz Superlatives Auction.*

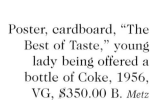

Poster, cardboard, "The Pause That Refreshes at Home," woman sitting with bottle and six-pack in background, VG, $675.00 C. *Mitchell Collection.*

Poster, cardboard, "The Drink They All Expect," couple getting ready for guests with bottles of Coca-Cola, 1942, EX, $700.00 B. *Metz Superlatives Auction.*

Poster, cardboard, "The Pause That Refreshes," three workers around a cooler, vertical version, 1940s, EX, $375.00 D.

Poster, cardboard, "The Rest-Pause That Refreshes" with military women seated and enjoying bottles of Coke, 1943, 36" x 20", EX, $425.00 B. *Metz Superlatives Auction.*

Poster, cardboard, "The Pause That Refreshes," young lady tennis player being handed a bottle of Coke, vertical version, 1943, EX, $500.00 B. *Metz Superlatives Auction.*

Poster, cardboard, "The Pause That Refreshes," pretty red headed lady resting in a chaise with a bottle of Coke, reproduction frame, 1940s, 36" x 20", EX, $925.00 B. *Metz Superlatives Auction.*

Poster, cardboard, "The Pause That Refreshes," young woman in the moonlight, 1939, G, $550.00 B. *Metz Superlatives Auction.*

Poster, cardboard, "The Pause That Refreshes," woman on beach in swimsuit, 1950s, 36" x 20", G, $375.00 C. *Metz Superlatives Auction.*

Poster, cardboard, "Things Go Better with Coke," couple roller skating, 1960s, EX, $140.00 B. *Metz Superlatives Auction.*

Poster, cardboard, "They All Want Coca-Cola" waitress with a tray of burgers ordering Cokes, 36" x 20", EX, $425.00 B. *Metz Superlatives Auction.*

Poster, cardboard, "Thirst Asks Nothing More," vertical with two girls at a floor cooler taking a break from basketball, in original frame, 1940s, 16" x 27", EX, $1,300.00 B. *Metz Superlatives Auction.*

Poster, cardboard, "Things Go Better with Coke," pretty girl in swimsuit with a bottle of Coke, 1960s, 24" x 20", VG, $195.00 D. *Metz Superlatives Auction.*

Poster, cardboard, "Things Go Better with Coke," scene of food platter and bottle of Coke, 1960s, F, $145.00 D.

Poster, cardboard, "Time Out for Food and Drink," with pretty girl in shorts enjoying a bottle of Coke and some food, 1938, G, $625.00 B. *Metz Superlatives Auction.*

"Thirst knows no season" introduced in 1922.

Poster, cardboard, "Thirst Knows No Season" couple building large snowman, 1942, 30" x 50", NM, $775.00 C.

Poster, cardboard, "Thirst Knows No Season" woman drinking from a bottle with her arm propped on a case of Cokes, 1940, 56" x 27", EX, $500.00 B. *Metz Superlatives Auction.*

Poster, cardboard, "We Sell Coca-Cola Part of Every Day," two-piece window ad, by Snyder & Black, 1942, EX, $595.00 C. *Mitchell Collection.*

Poster, cardboard, "To Be Refreshed," with woman with a Coke bottle in each hand. EX, $495.00 C.

Poster, cardboard, vertical, "Drink Coca-Cola...the Pause That Refreshes," military couple with Cokes, 1943, 27" x 56", EX, $350.00 B. *Metz Superlatives Auction.*

Poster, cardboard, "Wherever Thirst Goes," pretty girl in row boat with bucket of iced Cokes, 1942, EX, $750.00 C.
Metz Superlatives Auction.

Poster cardboard, "Welcome Home," woman reaching for a couple of bottles of Coke and talking to a man in uniform, 1944, 36" x 20", EX, $450.00 C.

Poster, cardboard, "Welcome Friend," lettering on background designed to resemble simulated oak, 1957, 14" x 12", EX, $375.00 C. *Mitchell Collection.*

Poster, cardboard, "Welcome Pause," young lady tennis player enjoying a bottle of Coke, 1942, 30" x 50", NM, $795.00 C.

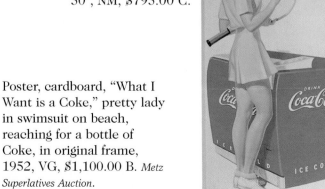

Poster, cardboard, "What I Want is a Coke," pretty lady in swimsuit on beach, reaching for a bottle of Coke, in original frame, 1952, VG, $1,100.00 B. *Metz Superlatives Auction.*

Poster cardboard, "Yes," woman in swimsuit with a bottle of Coke, 1947, 15" x 25", F, $375.00 B. *Metz Superlatives Auction.*

Poster, cardboard, "You Taste Its Quality," with pretty girl wearing flowers in her hair and drinking Coke from a bottle, 1942, 36" x 20", EX, $1,150.00 B. *Metz Superlatives Auction.*

Poster, cardboard, "Wherever You Go," travel scenes and a cold bottle of Coke, 1950s, EX, $325.00 C. *Mitchell Collection.*

Poster, cardboard, "Yes," girl on beach being offered a bottle of Coke, horizontal version, 1946, 56" x 27", EX, $625.00 C. *Mitchell Collection.*

Poster, paper, "All Over the World It's Coca-Cola...Delicious and Refreshing...at Soda Fountains," couple with a glass of Coke, 1912, 38" x 49", F, $16,500.00 B. *Metz Superlatives Auction.*

Poster, cardboard, "Yield to the Children," kids in street crossing, truck size ad, 1960s, 67" x 32", EX, $115.00 C.

Poster, paper, "Drink Coca-Cola Delicious and Refreshing," woman in flapper hat with a bottle of Coke and a straw, 1927 – 1928, 12" x 20", VG, $675.00 B. *Metz Superlatives Auction.*

Poster instructions, paper, "The Hand and Bottle for Outdoor Signs," instruction sheet for use, EX, $135.00 B. *Metz Superlatives Auction.*

Poster, paper, "Coca-Cola...Refreshing" with bottle in snow bank, 1957, 57" x 19", NM, $400.00 B. *Metz Superlatives Auction.*

Poster, paper, "Drink Coca-Cola...Cold" with bottle laying on iceberg, 1942, 57" x 18", EX, $165.00 C.

Poster, paper, "Drink Coca-Cola...Refresh," hobbleskirt bottle in snow, 1940s, 57" x 18", EX, $300.00 B. *Metz Superlatives Auction.*

Poster, paper, "Drink...Delicious and Refreshing..." framed, under glass, 1890 – 1900s, VG, $1,500.00 B.

Poster, paper, "Let's Have a Coke," couple in uniform, 1930s, 57" x 20", G, $850.00 B. *Mitchell Collection.*

Poster, paper, "Such a Friendly Custom," with two women in uniform at a soda fountain, 1930s, EX, $375.00 B. *Metz Superlatives Auction.*

Poster, paper, Ritz Boy used for the first time, "60,000,000 Drinks a Day," 1920s, F, $735.00 C. *Mitchell Collection.*

Poster, paper, "Pause a Minute...Refresh Yourself" with pretty girl and a bottle, 1927 – 1928, 12" x 20", EX, $1,800.00 B. *Metz Superlatives Auction.*

Poster, paper, "That 'Taste-Good' Feeling," young boy with a bottle of Coke and a hot dog, 1920s, EX, $650.00 B. *Metz Superlatives Auction.*

Poster, paper, "Treat Yourself Right," man with a sandwich opening a bottle of Coke, 1920s, 12" x 20", F, $550.00 B. *Metz Superlatives Auction.*

Poster, paper, "Sold Everywhere 5¢," pretty woman drinking from a glass with a straight-sided bottle on the table, extremely rare piece, in mint condition it would command 10 – 15 times the price shown, 1908, 14" x 22" has been trimmed, F, $1,050.00 B. *Metz Superlatives Auction.*

Print, cardboard, "Drink Coca-Cola," couple at beach with large towel, 1932, 29" x 50", F, $650.00 C. *Mitchell Collection.*

Poster, paper, "Which." This item has been trimmed; that has eliminated the wording. Pretty girl with a straight-sided bottle in one hand and Gold-elle Ginger Ale in the other. If this were in mint condition the value would be doubled, 1905, G, $4,900.00 C. *Mitchell Collection.*

Poster, paper; two pretty ladies, each with straight-sided Coke bottle, with ocean scene in the background; 1912, 16" x 22", VG, $4,900.00 C. *Metz Superlatives Auction.*

Rack mount, metal, "Serve Coca-Cola...Sign of Good Taste," double-sided bottle rack top attachment, 1960s, 17" x 10", EX, $175.00 C.

Rack mount, metal, "Drink Coca-Cola...Big King Size," designed to fit a bottle rack, 1960s, 9" x 17", EX, $145.00 C. *Metz Superlatives Auction.*

Rack mount, metal, "Coca-Cola...Take Home a Carton...6 bottles 25¢ plus Deposit," double sided, 1930s, 13" dia., G, $275.00 C. *Collectors Auction Services.*

Rack mount, metal, "Take Home a Car-ton...Coca-Cola...6 Bottles 25¢ Plus Deposit," round rack mounted, 1930 – 1940s, EX, $200.00 B. *Metz Superlatives Auction.*

Rack mount, metal, "Take Home a Carton...Drink Coca-Cola...6 Bottles 25¢," 1930s, 18" x 9", EX, $225.00 B. *Metz Superlatives Auction.*

Rack mount, metal, "Things Go Better with Coke...Drink Coca-Cola...Please Place Empties Here," rolled edges for bottle rack, 1960s, 14½" x 5", VG, $135.00 C.

Rack mount, card-board, with diamond cans, 1960s, NM, $85.00 D.

School crossing, plywood, "Enjoy Coca-Cola...Slow School Zone...Drive Safely" with silhouette of school girl running, 1950 – 1960s, EX, $995.00 C.

Sidewalk, metal, "Take a Case Home Today...Quality Refreshment," with a 24-bottle case, 1957, EX, $300.00 D.

Side walk, metal, "Drink Coca-Cola...Ice Cold," fishtail sidewalk sign, 1960s, 22½" x 33", EX, $500.00 C.

Sidewalk insert, metal, "Coca-Cola...Sign of Good Taste," fishtail logo and king size bottle, 1960s, 20" x 28", EX, $450.00 B. *Metz Superlatives Auction.*

Sidewalk insert, metal, "Take Home a Carton...Big King Size," fishtail logo and six-pack King Size, 1958, 20" x 28", EX, $800.00 B. *Metz Superlatives Auction.*

Sidewalk insert, metal, "Coca-Cola...Take Home a Carton," fishtail logo and six-bottle package, 1959, 20" x 28", NM, $950.00 B. *Metz Superlatives Auction.*

Sidewalk insert, metal, "Drink Coca-Cola...Things Go Better with Coke," 1960s, 20" x 28", VG, $500.00 B. *Metz Superlatives Auction.*

Sidewalk, metal, "Coca-Cola...Take Home 8 Bottle Carton...Regular Size," fishtail sidewalk insert with eight-bottle carton, 1960s, 20" x 28", EX, $4,000.00 B. *Metz Superlatives Auction.*

Sidewalk, metal, "Coca-Cola...Sign of Good Taste...Take Home a Carton," fishtail sidewalk insert with six-bottle carton of regular size bottles, 1959, 20" x 28", EX, $1,300.00 B. *Metz Superlatives Auction.*

Sidewalk, metal, "Drink Coca-Cola," double-sided curb insert, Canadian, 1949, 58" x 28", EX, $1,350.00 D. *Collectors Auction Services.*

Early Coca-Cola contained as much as ¹/₁₀ grain of cocaine per drink, and three to four times the caffeine used today.

Sidewalk, metal, "For Headache and Exhaustion Drink Coca-Cola...5¢ a glass... Delicious and Refreshing," an early one and not too many of these around, manufactured by Ronemers & Co., Baltimore, MD, 1895 – 1900, G, $7,500.00 B. *Metz Superlatives Auction.*

String holder, metal, "Take Home Coca-Cola in Cartons," double sided with same image of six-pack carton, 1930s, EX, $1,100.00 B. *Metz Superlatives Auction.*

Sidewalk, porcelain, "Drink Coca-Cola...Stop Here" metal frame and legs, 1941, 27" x 46", VG, $850.00 B. *Metz Superlatives Auction.*

Sidewalk, metal, "Drink Coca-Cola...Enjoy That Refreshing New Feeling....Take Home a Carton...Big King Size," fishtail curb insert with six-pack carton of king-size bottles, 1961, 20" x 28", NM, $1,500.00 B. *Metz Superlatives Auction.*

Sidewalk, metal, "French Wine Cola," embossed with 9" legs, 1885 – 1888, 27¼" x 19¼", VG, $7,500.00 B. *Metz Superlatives Auction.*

Sidewalk, metal, "Take Home a Carton," embossed with a six-pack in center yellow spotlight, 1942, 20" x 28", EX, $450.00 D. *Metz Superlatives Auction.*

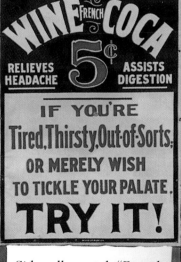

Sidewalk, metal, "French Wine Coca...Relieves Headache... 5¢...Assists Digestion," forerunner to Coca-Cola, extremely rare item, 1880s, 20" x 28", NM, $10,000.00 B. *Metz Superlatives Auction.*

Trolley car, cardboard, "Around the Corner from Anywhere," woman in 1920s vintage hat, matted and framed and under glass, 1927, 21" x 11", EX, $2,600.00 B. *Metz Superlatives Auction.*

"Around the corner from anywhere" debuted in 1927.

Trolley car, cardboard, "Coca-Cola...From a Bottle...Through a Straw...Absolutely Sanitary...," pretty girl with a bottle and straw, 1912, 21" x 11", F, $2,300.00 B. *Metz Superlatives Auction.*

Trolley car, cardboard, "Four Seasons," with the four models in seasonal attire, matted and framed and under glass, 1923, 21" x 11", EX, $4,000.00 B. *Metz Superlatives Auction.*

Trolley car, cardboard, "Drink Coca-Cola...Delicious and Refreshing All the Year Round," with the "Four Seasons Girls," matted and framed, 1923, 21" x 11", EX, $3,200.00 B. *Metz Superlatives Auction.*

Trolley car cardboard, "Delicious and Refreshing...Drink Coca-Cola...at Fountains...in Bottles," matted and framed and under glass, 1905, 21" x 11", G, $1,850.00 B. *Metz Superlatives Auction.*

Trolley car, cardboard, "Drink Coca-Cola Delicious and Refreshing," matted and framed and under glass, 1910s, 21" x 11", EX, $675.00 B. *Metz Superlatives Auction.*

Trolley car, cardboard, "Get It With Your Groceries," scene of a six-pack carton in a woven hand-carried basket, 1930s, 21" x 11", EX, $1,300.00 B. *Metz Superlatives Auction.*

Trolley car, cardboard, "Good Company" with a toast being presented with Coke glasses, 1927, 21" x 11", EX, $3,000.00 B. *Metz Superlatives Auction.*

Trolley car, cardboard, "The Drink Every-one Knows" with winged button saying "Pause...Go Refreshed," 1941, 21" x 11", EX, $1,150.00 B. *Metz Superlatives Auction.*

Trolley car, cardboard, "Relieves Fatigue, Sold Everywhere," man enjoying the product; mat-ted, framed, and under glass; 1907, 21" x 11", EX, $3,400.00 C. *Metz Superlatives Auction.*

Trolley car, cardboard, "Work Refreshed," with bottle in hand view, 1941, 21" x 11", EX, $875.00 B. *Metz Superlatives Auction.*

By the mid 1920s, the Coca-Cola Company was spending over one mil-lion a year on advertis-ing, and Coke was the most advertised item in the country.

Trolley car, cardboard, "Tired? Coca-Cola Relieves Fatigue," matted and framed and under glass, 1907, 21" x 11", EX, $2,300.00 B. *Metz Superlatives Auction.*

Wall hung, porcelain, "Drug Store...Drink Coca-Cola...Delicious and Refreshing," horizontal and very heavy, 8' x 5', EX, $1,200.00 D.

Window display, card-board, "The Pause That Refreshes," die-cut pretty woman at fountain with a glass of Coke, display unfolds to obtain a 3-D effect, 1929, EX, $11,000.00 B. *Metz Superlatives Auction.*

Window display, cardboard, "Drink Coca-Cola," with endorsements by Jackie Coogan and Wallace Berry with tall Coke bottle in center, 1934, 43" x 32", EX, $7,700.00 B. *Metz Superlatives Auction*

Discs

Button, metal, bottle decal, hard to find, 1940s, 24" dia., NM, $40.00 B. *Metz Superlatives Auction.*

Button, metal, "bottle in hand" decal, 1950s, 16" dia., NM, $25.00 B. *Metz Superlatives Auction.*

Button, metal, "Buvez Coca-Cola," French Canadian, 12" dia., EX, $35.00 B. *Metz Superlatives Auction.*

Button, metal, "...Coca-Cola," Chinese, made in U.S.A. 12" dia., EX, $525.00 B. *Metz Superlatives Auction.*

Advertising button signs were available in 12", 16", 18", 24", 36", and 48" sizes, and were used into the 1960s.

Button, metal, "Drink Coca-Cola," 1950s, 12" dia., VG, $15.00 B. *Metz Superlatives Auction.*

Button, metal, "Drink Coca-Cola...Comeonin Coke," mistake on wording-Come on in shown as one word and very light weight material, dynamic wave logo, 1970 – 1980s, 12" dia., EX, $10.00 B. *Metz Superlatives Auction.*

Button, metal. "Drink Coca-Cola in bottles", 1954, 12" dia., EX, $25.00 B. *Metz Superlatives Auction.*

Button, metal, "Drink Coca-Cola in bottles," 1955, 16" dia., NM, $55.00 B. *Metz Superlatives Auction.*

Button, metal, "Drink Coca-Cola...Sign of Good Taste," 1958, 16" dia., EX, $30.00 B. *Metz Superlatives Auction.*

Button, metal, "Drink Coca-Cola...Sign of Good Taste," two-color lettering, 1953, 24" dia., EX, $475.00 B. *Metz Superlatives Auction.*

Button, metal, "Drink Coca-Cola," made in and for use in U.S.A., 1957, 16" dia., EX, $475.00 B.

Button, metal, "Drink Coca-Cola" with metal arrow, 1960s, 18" dia., VG, $775.00 C.

Button, metal, "Drink...in Bottles," with arrow from a different sign, not the original flat metal arrow, 1950s, 16" dia., EX, $85.00 B. *Metz Superlatives Auction.*

Button, metal, "Match Your Thirst...Ice Cold," decal showing regular and large bottle, 1950s, 16" dia., NM, $45.00 B. *Metz Superlatives Auction.*

Button, metal, "Tome Coca-Cola," Mexican, 12" dia., EX, $20.00 B. *Metz Superlatives Auction.*

Button, metal, "Standard 6 Bottle Package," with cardboard six pack, 1950s, 16" dia., NM, $425.00 B. *Metz Superlatives Auction.*

Button, porcelain, "Coca-Cola" with bottle in center, 36" dia., EX, $625.00 C. *Metz Superlatives Auction.*

Button, porcelain, "Drink Coca-Cola," 24" dia., NM, $475.00 C. *Metz Superlatives Auction.*

Button, porcelain, "Drink Coca-Cola...'Coke'...Ask for It Either Way," 1940s, 9" dia., EX, $395.00 C. *Mitchell Collection.*

Button, porcelain, "Drink Coca-Cola in Bottles," 24" dia., NM, $575.00 C. *Metz Superlatives Auction.*

Button, porcelain, "Drink Coca-Cola Sign of Good Taste," 24" dia., EX, $525.00 C. *Metz Superlatives Auction.*

Display, celluloid, "Coca-Cola," round disc with bottle, 1950s, 9" dia., EX, $295.00 C.

Button sign, metal, "Yes! Coke is still 5¢," 1950s, 16" dia., EX, $775.00 B. *Metz Superlatives Auction.*

Button sign, metal, "Have a Coke" with decal of Sprite Boy and bottle, 1950s, 16" dia., NM, $775.00 B. *Metz Superlatives Auction.*

Display, composition, "Pause...Go Refreshed," heavily embossed wings, with bottle in hand, at bottom of disc, 1941, 9½" dia., NM, $2,100.00 B. *Metz Superlatives Auction.*

Display, celluloid, "Pause Go Refreshed," round disc with bell glass in center, unusual white background with red trim, 1942, 9" dia., EX, $4,700.00 B. *Metz Superlatives Auction.*

Display, metal and plastic, "Drink Coca-Cola...Sign of good taste," light up disc type sign, 1950s, 16" dia., EX, $495.00 C. *Mitchell Collection.*

Display, metal, "Drink Coca-Cola," round iron frame with button on each side in center, 24" dia., VG, $1,100.00 C.

Flange, metal, "Drink Coca-Cola...Soda," button on top, 1950s, EX, $3,300.00 B. *Metz Superlatives Auction.*

Display, metal, "Please Pay Cashier," built to back light the center disc, 1930s, 12" x 14", EX, $2,600.00 B. *Metz Superlatives Auction.*

Flat, metal over card-board, "Drink Coca-Cola...Coke," contrasting color edge, 12" dia., EX, $50.00 B. *Metz Superlatives Auction.*

 BEVERAGES

Flat mount, metal, "Drink Coca-Cola...Beverages" with a 12" button at each end, 1950s, 70" x 12", EX, $95.00 B. *Metz Superlatives Auction.*

Rack mount, metal, "Take Home a Carton...Coca-Cola," double sided, 1940s, 13" dia., EX, $325.00 B. *Metz Superlatives Auction.*

Pilaster, metal, "Coca-Cola" bottle in hand decal, no top button, 1940s, 16" x 40", EX, $175.00 D.

Pilaster, metal, "Drink Coca-Cola," button at top and bottle decal, 1948, 16" x 55", EX, $625.00 B. *Metz Superlatives Auction.*

Pilaster, metal, "Drink Coca-Cola...Serve Coke at Home," 16" button at top with six-pack carton, 1948, 16" x 54", NM, $700.00 D.

Pilaster, metal, "Drink Coca-Cola in Bottles...Pickup 12...Refreshment for All" with 16" button at top and 12-pack carton, 1954, 16" x 55", NM, $330.00 B. *Metz Superlatives Auction.*

Sign, masonite and metal, "Sundaes...Malts," beautiful Kay Displays wings with center 12" button and Sprite Boy and bottle at each end, 1950s, 78" x 12", EX, $1,050.00 B. *Metz Superlatives Auction.*

Sign, masonite, "Beverage Department," featuring a "Drink..." button in center of wings that have Sprite Boy on each end, Kay Displays, 1940s, 78" x 12", EX, $85.00 B – 1,000.00 C. *Metz Superlatives Auction.*

Wall, metal, "Drink Coca-Cola in Bottles...Quality Refreshment," button at top and scale-type reading, 1950s, EX, $225.00 C. *Mitchell Collection.*

Sign, wood, "Drink Coca-Cola in Bottles," wing sign with Sprite Boy and bottle on each end and 12" button in center, 1940s, 36" x 12", NM, $130.00 B. *Metz Superlatives Auction.*

Wall hung, wood and metal, "Drink Coca-Cola" button at bottom, slide menu strips, 1940s, EX, $65.00 B. *Metz Superlatives Auction.*

Wall hung, wood and metal, "Drink Coca-Cola in bottles," slide-type menu slots with 16" dia. button at top, Kay Displays, 17" x 29", EX, $525.00 B. *Metz Superlatives Auction.*

Wooden Kay Displays signs were made during WWII to conserve metal.

⚜ **Festoons** ⚜

Back bar, cardboard, "Be Really Refreshed," nine pieces with original envelope and instruction sheet, 1958, 12' long, NM, $1,600.00 B. *Metz Superlatives Auction.*

Back bar, cardboard, "Drink Coca-Cola," framed, under glass, 1918, 96" long, EX, $4,500.00 B. *Metz Superlatives Auction.*

Back bar, cardboard, "Refreshment through the Years," pictured with only centerpiece, 1951, NM, $1,200.00 B. *Metz Superlatives Auction.*

Back bar, cardboard, "Know Your State Tree," in original envelope, 1950s, EX, $750.00 – 850.00 C. *Mitchell Collection.*

Back bar, cardboard, "The Pause That Refreshes," five pieces, 1930s, VG, $775.00 B – 925.00 C. *Metz Superlatives Auction.*

Back bar, cardboard, "Verbena," only center pictured, total of five pieces, 1932, EX, $1,500.00 B. *Metz Superlatives Auction.*

Back bar, cardboard, Autumn Leaves, five pieces, woman with glass of Coke and colorful fall leaves, 1927, good $1,000.00 B. *Metz Superlatives Auction.*

Back bar, cardboard, "Drink Coca-Cola," woman with glass of Coke, with original envelope, 1937, EX, $4,000.00 B. *Metz Superlatives Auction.*

Back bar, cardboard, "Poppies," with original envelope, Canadian item, five pieces, 1938, EX, $1,050.00 B. *Metz Superlatives Auction.*

Back bar, cardboard, "Lily Pads," five-piece with great girl in center with a glass of Coke, 1935, EX, $2,600.00 B. *Metz Superlatives Auction.*

Back bar, cardboard, "Snowman," Canadian piece featuring a snowman with a fountain attendant's hat, five pieces, 1936, 14', EX, $7,500.00 B. *Metz Superlatives Auction.*

Back bar, cardboard, "Parasols," five pieces with centerpiece featuring a pretty girl with an extended glass of Coke, 1927, G, $4,700.00 B. *Metz Superlatives Auction.*

Back bar, cardboard, "Swans," 1930s, excellent $1,500.00 B.
Metz Superlatives Auction.

Back bar, cardboard, "Times Around the World," with clock times and different cities, this set is missing two cities, 1953, 22" x 18" center, 22" x 13" ends, EX, $300.00 B. *Metz Superlatives Auction.*

Back bar, cardboard, Square Dance, five pieces with original envelope, couples dancing and enjoying a glass of Coke, 1957, G, $1,400.00 B. *Metz Superlatives Auction.*

Back bar, masonite, "Howdy Partner," three pieces with the message "...Pause...Refresh," EX, $850.00 B.
Metz Superlatives Auction.

Back bar, metal and wood, "Drink Coca-Cola," life preserver centerpiece only, but a very hard item to find; completed, the festoon has a metal fish on each side; 1937, NM, $1,800.00 B. *Metz Superlatives Auction.*

Back bar, wood, "Drink Coca-Cola," Kay Displays three-piece with marching Coke glasses, 1930s, 37" x 10" center, 9" x 11½" ends, NM, $2,800.00 B. *Metz Superlatives Auction.*

Back bar, plywood and metal, "Weidelich Pharmacies," super item used until the stores closed in the 1960s, 36" x 20" center, 36" x 18" ends, G, $4,000.00 B. *Metz Superlatives Auction.*

Back bar, wood, "Drink Coca-Cola," part of a nautical theme unit, 1930 – 1940s, 24" x 13", EX, $1,400.00 B. *Metz Superlatives Auction.*

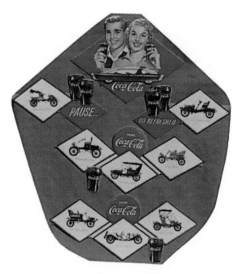

Back bar, cardboard, "Girls' Heads"; five pieces, each with a recognizable face featured; 1951, one is 21" x 22", four are 16" x 16", EX, $1,700.00 B. *Metz Superlatives Auction.*

Back bar, cardboard, "Old Cars," five pieces with original envelope, 1957, 12' long, EX, $600.00 B. *Metz Superlatives Auction.*

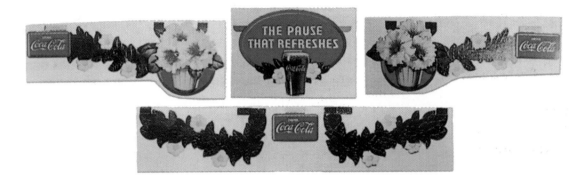

Back bar, cardboard, "Orchids," "The Pause That Refreshes," five pieces, 1941, 12' long, EX, $1,300.00 B. *Metz Superlatives Auction.*

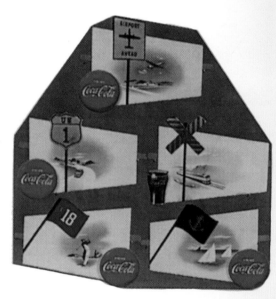

Back bar, cardboard, "Travel," with traffic signs and scenes, 1950s, 8½' long, VG, $1,300.00 B. *Metz Superlatives Auction.*

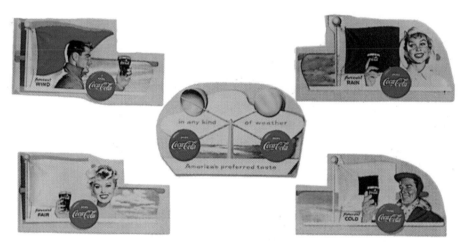

Back bar, cardboard, "Weather," five pieces with different weather scenes, approx. 10' long, EX, $1,200.00 B. *Metz Superlatives Auction.*

Display, wood, waitress and Sprite Boy centerpiece of this festoon, with waitress holding tray with four Coca-Cola glasses, 1946, 37" x 39", EX, $250.00 B. *Metz Superlatives Auction.*

Hanging, paper, "Coca-Cola At Soda Fountains 5¢," Lillian Nordica with arm on tall table that holds a glass of Coke, she's holding a large fan, partial monthly sheets, matted, framed, under glass, 1905, 7" x 15", EX, $5,400.00 D. *Metz Superlatives Auction.*

Hanging, bamboo, "Drink Coca-Cola in Bottles...Herrin Coca-Cola Bottling Co.," beautiful mountain and stream scene, strong Japanese art influence, missing bottom tear sheets, 1920s, VG, $300.00 C. *Mitchell Collection.*

Hanging, paper, 50th anniversary special with older man and young girl at a small boat enjoying a bottle of Coke, full pad, matted, framed and under glass, 1936, 12" x 24", M, $975.00 C. *Mitchell Collection.*

Hanging, bamboo, "Drink Coca-Cola in Bottles...Herrin Coca-Cola Bottling Co. ..." beautiful Japanese scene on front, bottom year sheets missing, but still a very desirable and rare piece, 1920s, VG, $300.00 C. *Mitchell Collection.*

Desk, metal, "Coca-Cola," perpetual showing month, day, and year, 1920s, EX, $450.00 C.

Hanging, paper, "America, Love It or Leave It," advertising from Brownsville, TN, with a display of a drum and fife scene, full monthly pads, 1942, EX, $155.00 C. *Mitchell Collection.*

Desk, brass, "Drink Coca-Cola" round logo, with perpetual action, VG, $225.00 C. *Mitchell Collection.*

Hanging, metal, "Drink Coca-Cola in Bottles" on button on top, 1950s, 8" x 19", EX, $415.00 B. *Metz Superlatives Auction.*

The pose in the 1932 calendar at right is from a Norman Rockwell painting titled "The Old Oaken Bucket."

Hanging, paper, boy with a bucket of Cokes and dog sitting at a well, full pad, matted, framed and under glass, 1932, 12" x 24", M, $900.00 C. *Mitchell Collection.*

Hanging, paper, baseball girl with glass, scene of early baseball game in background, matted, framed and under glass, 1922, 12" x 32", NM, $2,200.00 C. *Mitchell Collection.*

Hanging, paper, Autumn Girl, promoting fountain sales with a glass, partial monthly tear sheets, matted, framed and under glass, 1921, 12" x 32", NM, $2,300.00 C. *Mitchell Collection.*

Hanging, paper, boy with fishing pole and a couple of bottles of Coke, matted, framed and under glass, 1937, 12" x 24", M, $875.00 C. *Mitchell Collection.*

Hanging, paper, "Coca-Cola," all months displayed, 1900, 7" x 12", EX, $10,500.00 D.

Hanging, paper, "Be Really Refreshed," man and woman with snow skis and snowy mountains in background, full month pad, double month display, 1960, M, $115.00 C. *Mitchell Collection.*

Hanging, paper, "Coca-Cola at All Soda Fountains," all monthly pads displayed at once, 1897, 7" x 12", EX, $10,500.00 C.

Hanging, paper, "Coca-Cola at Soda Fountains 5¢," same Lillian Nordica as on the 1905 calendar, 1909, 3¼" x 7", EX, $1,500.00 C.

Hanging, paper, "Coca-Cola," Betty top only, rare version featured with a straight-sided bottle and a straw, 1914, VG, $2,500.00 C.

The Boy Scout calendar at right was commissioned by the Boy Scouts of America, not Coca-Cola, and was published by Brown & Bigelow, the largest calendar publisher in the country.

Hanging, paper, "Coca-Cola Bottling Works of Greenwood," scene of scouts in front of Liberty Bell, full monthly tear sheets, 1953, EX, $500.00 C. *Mitchell Collection.*

Hanging, paper, "Coca-Cola," pretty girl in big hat sitting on bench drinking from a straight-sided bottle with a straw, double value for a complete example, 1913, EX, $4,300.00 C. *Mitchell Collection.*

Hanging, paper, "Coca-Cola," girl with racquet, from Asa Chandler & Co., tear pad at bottom has been moved for better view of calendar, 1891, G, $5,500.00 C.

Hanging, paper, "Coca-Cola," Lillian Nordica standing beside a tall table with a glass of Coke, 1904, 7" x 15", EX, $4,400.00 D.

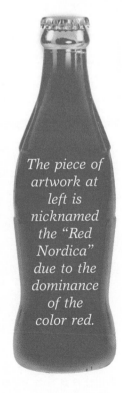

The piece of artwork at left is nicknamed the "Red Nordica" due to the dominance of the color red.

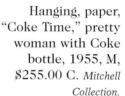

Hanging, paper, "Coke Has the Taste You Never Get Tired of," pretty girl with a bottle of Coke and a 45rpm record, double-month display, full pad, 1968, M, $90.00 C. *Mitchell Collection.*

Hanging, paper, "Coca-Cola," the Coca-Cola girl, partial monthly sheets, matted, framed and under glass, 1910, 8" x 17", EX, $5,400.00 C. *Collectors Auction Services.*

Hanging, paper, "Coke Adds Zest," party scene with girl serving Coke in bottles from a tray, double-month display, 1952, M, $225.00 C. *Mitchell Collection.*

Hanging, paper, "Coke Time," pretty woman with Coke bottle, 1955, M, $255.00 C. *Mitchell Collection.*

Hanging, paper, "Coke Refreshes You Best," lady being offered a bottle of Coke, double-month display, full pad, 1961, M, $100.00 C. *Mitchell Collection.*

Hanging, paper, "Constance" sitting at table with a glass, full pad, matted framed and under glass, 1917, EX, $2,700.00 C. *Mitchell Collection.*

Hanging, paper, "Drink Coca-Cola," bottom tear sheets below Hilda Clark with glass, framed and matted, 1903, G, $2,400.00 B. *Metz Superlatives Auction.*

Hanging, paper, "Drink Coca-Cola...Delicious and Refreshing," original metal strip on top, full monthly pad, 1914, VG, $1,750.00 C.

Hanging, paper, "Drink Coca-Cola at All Soda Fountains 5¢," monthly tear sheets at bottom, matted, under glass, framed, 1901, EX, $5,700.00 D.

Hanging, paper, "Drink Coca-Cola 5¢," matted, framed and under glass, but this example has the incorrect monthly sheet, EX, $5,800.00 D.

Hanging, paper, "Drink Coca-Cola...Delicious and Refreshing...at All Soda Fountains," top only with Hilda Clark, 1901, 7⅛" x 6", EX, $3,900.00 B. *Metz Superlatives Auction.*

Hanging, paper, "Drink Coca-Cola Delicious Refreshing," matted, framed and under glass, 1906, 7" x 15", EX, $5,300.00 C.

Hanging, paper, "Drink Coca-Cola Delicious Refreshing," lady with parasol, this example has the incorrect pad, matted, framed and under glass, 1912, EX, $2,900.00 C.

Hanging, paper, "Drink Coca-Cola Delicious Refreshing," woman drinking from a glass with syrup line, 1913, 13" x 22", VG, $2,700.00 C.

Hanging, paper, "Drink Coca-Cola," Elaine seated and drinking from a soda glass and holding a parasol, partial monthly pads, matted, framed and framed, 1915, VG, $1,750.00 D.

Hanging, paper, "Drink Coca-Cola... Relieves Fatigue...Sold Everywhere 5¢," top only, pretty woman drinking from a fountain glass, 1908, 7" x 14", EX, $3,200.00 C.

Hanging, paper, "Drink Coca-Cola...Relieves Fatigue," only one monthly sheet still in tact, 1908, 7" x 14", EX, $7,200.00 B. *Metz Superlatives Auction.*

Hanging, paper, "Drink Coca-Cola...Relieves Fatigue," full sheets, matted, framed and under glass, 1907, EX, $6,300.00 C.

Hanging, paper, "Drink Delicious Coca-Cola," Coca-Cola girl with big-brimmed hat, full monthly sheets, matted, framed and under glass, 1911, 10" x 17", M, $4,900.00 D.

Hanging, paper, "Drink Coca-Cola," with Betty drinking from a bottle with a straw, only one tear sheet, 1914, EX, $3,300.00 B. *Metz Superlatives Auction.*

Hanging, paper, "Drink Coca-Cola" top only, still has the top metal strip, pretty girl with glass in hand and one on the table, lighted building in background from World Exposition, 1909, 11" x 14", EX, $5,500.00 B. *Metz Superlatives Auction.*

Hanging, paper, Elaine drinking from a straight sided paper label bottle with a straw, partial monthly pad, matted, framed and under glass, 1916, 13" x 32", NM, $2,200.00 C.

Hanging, paper, Elaine the World War I girl holding a glass, incorrect pad, 1916, 13" x 32", NM, $2,300.00 C.

The model for the Elaine image was silent film star Faye Tincher. The image was also used on a 1916 tray.

Hanging, paper, "Entertain Your Thirst," party girl holding a bottle of Coke, double monthly display, 1951, M, $235.00 C. *Mitchell Collection.*

Hanging, paper, "Enjoy that Refreshing New Feeling," young couple enjoying a dance and Coke, 1962, M, $95.00 C. *Mitchell Collection.*

Hanging, paper, evening wear lady holding a glass of Coke, matted, framed and under glass, partial monthly tear sheets, 1928, 12" x 24", M, $1,100.00 C. *Mitchell Collection.*

Barefoot boy's name is Danny Grant. He posed for Norman Rockwell in 1930 and 1931 and is part of six images that Rockwell created for Coca-Cola.

Hanging, paper, fishing boy with sandwich and bottle of Coke, dog looking at boy, full pad, matted, framed and under glass, 1931, 12" x 24", M, $1,095.00 C. *Mitchell Collection.*

Hanging, paper; flapper girl in green dress with string of beads and holding a glass, with a bottle on the table in front of her; matted, framed and under glass, full pad, 1929, 12" x 24", M, $1,200.00 C. *Mitchell Collection.*

Hanging, paper, Garden Girl, actually misnamed since the girl is on a golf course holding a glass of Coke, matted, framed and under glass, 1920, 12" x 32", M, $2,700.00 C. *Mitchell Collection.*

Hanging, paper, "For the Taste You Never Get Tired of," five-woman team with a trophy and a cold bottle of Coke, 1967, M, $80.00 C. *Mitchell Collection.*

Hanging, paper, girl in a red dress with a bottle of Coke, full pad, matted, framed and under glass, 1940, 12" x 24", VG, $600.00 C. *Mitchell Collection.*

Hanging, paper, girl in coat with a bottle of Coke, double-month display, 1948, EX, $450.00 C. *Mitchell Collection.*

Hanging, paper, girl in tennis outfit with bright red scarf, holding a glass of Coke with a bottle on the table, matted, framed and under glass, 1926, 10" x 18", VG, $1,195.00 C. *Mitchell Collection.*

Hanging, paper, girl in sheer dress with a glass of Coke, message panel for Taylor's Billiard Parlor, matted, framed and under glass, 1927, 12" x 24", M, $1,895.00 C. *Mitchell Collection.*

Hanging, paper, girl in the afternoon, in front of blinds holding a bottle of Coke, full pad, matted, framed and under glass, 1938, 12" x 24", M, $775.00 C. *Mitchell Collection.*

Hanging, paper, girl pouring Coke from bottle to glass, matted, framed and under glass, 1939, 12" x 24", M, $675.00 C. *Mitchell Collection.*

Hanging, paper; girl smiling, in period dress and holding a glass of Coke while a bottle is sitting on the table; matted, framed and under glass, *beware of reproductions*, 1924, 12" x 24", M, $1,495.00 D. *Mitchell Collection.*

Hanging, paper, girl with ice skates and sitting on a log, displays two months at one time, 1941, EX, $450.00 C. *Mitchell Collection.*

Hanging, paper, girl with shawl and with a bottle of Coke and a straw, matted, framed and under glass, 1923, 12" x 24", VG, $1,100.00 C. *Mitchell Collection.*

Hanging, paper, "Have a Coke and a Smile," Olympic torch, full monthly pad, 1979, M, $25.00 C. *Mitchell Collection.*

Hanging, paper, "Have a Coke and a Smile," scenes of America, double-month display, full pad, 1981, M, $30.00 C. *Mitchell Collection.*

Hanging, paper, "Hospitality in Your Hands," pretty woman hostess witha tray of Coke bottles, double-month display, 1950, M, $375.00 C. *Mitchell Collection.*

Hanging, paper, June Caprice with glass, with rear of calendar in view, 1918, G, $475.00 C. *Mitchell Collection.*

Hanging, paper, Knitting Girl with bottle of Coke, partial monthly pad, framed and under glass, 1919, 13" x 32", EX, $3,200.00 D. *Mitchell Collection.*

Hanging, paper, "It's the Real Thing." This decade started a new image, and many collectors do not like it; therefore, many don't collect anything past 1970. Double-month display, full pad, 1970, M, $35.00 C. *Mitchell Collection.*

Hanging, paper, military nurse with a bottle of Coke, two months shown on each sheet, 1943, EX, $525.00 C. *Mitchell Collection.*

"Out Fishin' " was the last of six pieces produced for Coke by Norman Rockwell and was printed on nearly two million calendars.

Hanging, paper, "Out Fishin'," boy on stump and holding a bottle, full pad, matted, framed and under glass, 1935, 12" x 24", M, $875.00 C. *Mitchell Collection.*

Hanging, paper, Marian Davis holding a glass of Coke, partial monthly tear sheets, matted, framed and under glass, 1919, 6" x 10½", EX, $3,300.00 C.

Hanging, paper, "Look up America" with scenes of America, double-month display, full pad, 1976, M, $50.00 C. *Mitchell Collection.*

Hanging, paper, party girl with white fox fur around her shoulder and holding a glass of Coke, matted, framed and under glass, 1925, 12" x 24", M, $1,250.00 C.

Mitchell Collection.

Hanging, paper, pretty blond girl with snow skis, two-month display, 1947, EX, $475.00 C. *Mitchell Collection.*

Hanging, paper, pretty woman in winter scene with scarf, Sprite Boy at bottom, two months shown on one sheet, 1945, EX, $375.00 C. *Mitchell Collection.*

Hanging, paper, pretty woman with a bottle of Coke, outdoor scene in background, double months shown on each page, 1944, EX, $395.00 C. *Mitchell Collection.*

Hanging, paper, pretty girl in red hat with bottle of Coke, double-month display, 1949, M, $325.00 C. *Mitchell Collection.*

Hanging, paper, "Pause...Refresh" with sport scene behind woman with a Coke bottle, double-month display, 1954, M, $235.00 C. *Mitchell Collection.*

Hanging, paper, "Sign of Good Taste," couple with snowman that has a large bottle top for a hat, double-month display, 1958, M, $200.00 C. *Mitchell Collection.*

Hanging, paper, scenes of America the Beautiful and backpacking couple, double display, full pad, 1975, M, $30.00 C. *Mitchell Collection.*

Hanging, paper, snowman surrounded by a boy and girl, double-month display, 1942, VG, $475.00 C. *Mitchell Collection.*

Hanging, paper, southern girl on porch playing music to an elderly gentleman, full pad, matted, framed and under glass, 1934, 12" x 24", M, $875.00 C. *Mitchell Collection.*

Hanging, paper, "The Pause That Refreshes," sports event and pretty girl being offered a Coke bottle, full pad, 1959, G, $150.00 C.*Mitchell Collection.*

Hanging, paper, "The Pause That Refreshes," woman with snow skis and bottle of Coke, double-month display, 1957, EX, $125.00 C. *Mitchell Collection.*

Hanging, paper, "There's Nothing Like a Coke," pretty girl putting on ice skates, double-month display, 1956, M, $175.00 C. *Mitchell Collection.*

Hanging, paper, "The Pause That Refreshes," woman looking at clothes in a door mirror, double-month display, full pad, 1963, M, $100.00 C. *Mitchell Collection.*

Hanging, paper, "Things Go Better with Coke," couple relaxing by a log cabin, each with a bottle of Coke, double-month display, full pad, 1965, M, $100.00 C. *Mitchell Collection.*

Hanging, paper, "Things Go Better with Coke," man and woman with tray of Coke bottles, double-month display, full pad, 1966, M, $100.00 C. *Mitchell Collection.*

Hanging, paper, village blacksmith with young boy, full pad, matted, framed and under glass, 1933, 12" x 24", M, $875.00 C. *Mitchell Collection.*

Hanging, paper, "Things Go Better with Coke," young couple at cafe table, double month display, full monthly pads, 1969, M, $85.00 C. *Mitchell Collection.*

Hanging, plastic, "Drink Coca-Cola...Coke Refreshes You Best," fishtail top design, bottom daily tear sheets, all sheets present, 1960s, EX, $475.00 B. *Metz Superlatives Auction.*

Hanging, paper, "Things Go Better with Coke," pretty lady on couch being offered a Coke by a man in a suit, 1964, M, $100.00 C. *Mitchell Collection.*

Hanging, paper, canoe and a woman in a swimsuit and holding a bottle, matted, framed and under glass, partial pad, 1930, 12" x 24", M, $1,275.00 C. *Mitchell Collection.*

Hanging, paper, "Work Better Refreshed," scenes of woman working, double-month display, 1953, M, $250.00 C. *Mitchell Collection.*

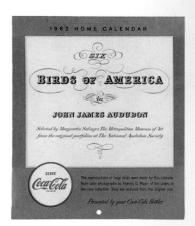

Hanging, paper, "The Drink That Makes the Whole world Kin," girl in sheer dress holding a glass of Coke and with a bottle of Coke in an insert panel, matted, framed and under glass, 1927, 12" x 24", M, $1,200.00 C.

Mitchell Collection.

Pocket, paper, "Here's to Our G.I. Joes," two girls toasting with Coke bottles, all months shown on front, 1943, EX, $70.00 C.

Mitchell Collection.

Pocket, paper, "Tastes Like Home," with sailor and all months shown on front, 1943, EX, $75.00 C.

Mitchell Collection.

Reference, paper, "Birds of America" by John James Audubon, 1962, M, $45.00 C.

Mitchell Collection.

Reference, paper, "Holiday Greetings," hobbleskirt bottles on the front, 1969, M, $25.00 C. *Mitchell Collection.*

Reference, paper, "Drink Coca-Cola," birds sitting on branch, 1959, M, $40.00 C.

Mitchell Collection.

Reference, paper, "Sign of Good Taste," scene of flowers against a brick background, 1958, M, $35.00 C.

Mitchell Collection.

Reference, paper, "Puppies," pair of dogs in Christmas stocking, 1960, EX, $35.00 C.

Mitchell Collection.

117

Change receiver, ceramic, "The Ideal Brain Tonic For Headache and Exhaustion...Coca-Cola...," rare item, 1899, EX, $6,200.00 C.

Change receiver, glass, "Drink Coca-Cola 5¢," 1907, 7" dia., EX, $1,500.00 D.

Change receiver, metal, "Change Receiver...Coca-Cola...Delicious and Refreshing," very similar to the 1901 6" tip tray with Hilda Clark, 1900, 8½" dia., EX, $4,500.00 C.

Serving, metal, "Coca-Cola...Delicious...Refraichissant," girl with umbrella and a bottle of Coke, French version, 1950s, 10½" x 13¼", G, 185.00 C. *Mitchell Collection.*

Commerative, metal, "Enjoy Coca-Cola...Bottling Company of Cape Cod...Grand Opening June 1984...45th Anniversary...June 1939 – 1984," with the "Four Seasons Girls" on front, deep lip, 1984, 15" x 12¼", EX, $45.00 C. *B. J. Summers.*

Serving, metal, "Coca-Cola," couple in early car receiving service at the curb by a soda person, 1927, 13¼" x 10½", VG, $875.00 C. *Mitchell Collection.*

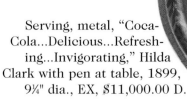

Serving, metal, "Coca-Cola...Delicious...Refreshing...Invigorating," Hilda Clark with pen at table, 1899, 9¼" dia., EX, $11,000.00 D.

Serving, metal, "Coca-Cola," featuring the "Autumn Girl," with a glass of Coke, also on the 1922 calendar, 1925, 10½" x 13¼", EX, $1,100.00 C. *Mitchell Collection.*

Serving, metal, "Coca-Cola," Flapper Girl holding a flare glass with a syrup line, 1923, 10½" x 13¼", EX, $475.00 C. *Mitchell Collection.*

Serving, metal, "Coca-Cola," Garden Girl with a flare glass featuring a flare line, 1920, 10½" x 13¼", EX, $975.00 C. *Mitchell Collection.*

Serving, metal, "Coca-Cola...Have a Coke," red hair beauty with a yellow scarf and a bottle of Coke. *Caution — these seem to have reproduced by the tons,* 1950s, 10½" x 13¼", EX, $250.00 C. *Mitchell Collection.*

Serving, metal, "Coca-Cola," Smiling Girl holding a glass of Coke, this tray can have either a brown or maroon border, 1924, 10½" x 13¼", EX, $825.00 C. *Mitchell Collection.*

Serving, metal, "Coca-Cola," Summer Girl with flare glass featuring syrup line, mfg. by H.D. Beach Company, Coshocton, Ohio, 1922, 10½" x 13¼", EX, $900.00 C. *Mitchell Collection.*

Serving, metal, "Coca-Cola," vendors cart with large basket full of goodies and cold bottles of Coca-Cola, 1958, 13¼" x 10½", EX, $30.00 D. *Metz Superlatives Auction.*

Serving, metal, "Coca-Cola is Better — Try It," topless long-haired beauty holding a bottle of Coca-Cola, designed for the bar and tavern trade, distributed by the Western Coca-Cola Company of Chicago without the permission of the home office, 1908, 12¼" dia., EX, $5,500.00 B. *Metz Superlatives Auction.*

There has been much written about this topless tray. Coke historians agree and disagree on several issues.

1) Was it approved by Asa Chandler? Most agree it was not.
2) Mr. Chandler, president of Coke, was a religous man and was opposed to drinking. So it would seem natural to think he would not have liked the use of Coca-Cola as a mixer.
3) This probably helped enforce the need for standard advertising.
4) The image is not in keeping with the wholesome Coca-Cola thinking.

Serving, metal, "Drink a Bottle of Carbonated Coca-Cola," with tilted straight sided paper label bottle, same image as on the 1903 tip tray, 1903, 9¼" dia., EX, $6,700.00 D.

Serving, metal, "Drink Coca-Cola," another American Art Works product with pretty girl in yellow swimsuit and with a bottle of Coke, 1929, 10½" x 13¼", EX, $800.00 C. *Mitchell Collection.*

Serving, metal, "Drink Coca-Cola at Soda Fountains 5¢," Lillian Nordica with a glass of coke on table, 1905, 10½" x 13", EX, $4,500.00 D.

Serving, metal, "Drink Coca-Cola" bobbed-hair girl drinking Coke through a straw from a bottle, 1928, 10½" x 13¼", EX, $825.00 C. *Mitchell Collection.*

Serving, metal, "Drink Coca-Cola," boy and dog at fishing hole eating lunch, 1931, 10½" x 13¼", EX, $1,100.00 D. *Mitchell Collection.*

Serving, metal, "Drink Coca-Cola...Delicious and Refreshing," same image that appears on the oval version of this tray, 1913, 10½" x 13¼", EX, $1,050.00 D.

Serving, metal, "Drink Coca-Cola...Delicious and Refreshing," oval shaped, with a Hamilton King Coca-Cola girl holding a glass of Coke, 1913, 12¼" x 14¼", EX, $1,050.00 D. *Collectors Auction Services.*

Serving, metal, "Drink Coca-Cola...Delicious and Refreshing" with the same image of Betty that appears on the oval and tip tray, 1914, 10½" x 13¼", EX, $875.00 C. *Mitchell Collection.*

Serving, metal, "Drink Coca-Cola...Delicious and Refreshing," with Betty as also seen on the 1914 tip tray, 1914, 12½" x 15¼", EX, $995.00 C. *Mitchell Collection.*

Serving, metal, "Drink Coca-Cola...Delicious and Refreshing," girl on springboard with a bottle of Coke, 1939, 10½" x 13¼", EX, $400.00 C. *Mitchell Collection.*

Serving, metal, "Drink Coca-Cola...Delicious and Refreshing," pretty young lady with sailor hat fishing from a dock and enjoying a bottle of Coke, 1940, 13¼" x 10½", NM, $625.00 B. *Buffalo Bay Auction Co.*

Serving, metal, "Drink Coca-Cola...Delicious... Refreshing," Victorian era with girl with a glass of Coke, round, 1897, 9¼" dia., EX, $14,000.00 B.

Serving, metal, "Drink Coca-Cola," early golfing couple enjoying Coke, 1926, 10½" x 13¼", EX, $925.00 C. *Mitchell Collection.*

Serving, metal, "Drink Coca-Cola," Elaine, also known as the World War I girl with a glass of Coke, made by Stelad Signs Passic Metal Ware Company, Passaic, NJ, 1916, 8½" x 19", EX, $775.00 C. *Mitchell Collection.*

Silent flim star Faye Tincher, from Topeka, KS, was the model for the only oblong serving tray produced by Coke. She holds a bottle on the 1916 calendar.

Serving, metal, "Drink Coca-Cola," fishtail logo with birdhouse and a bottle in center, 1950s, 10½" x 13¼", EX, $115.00 C. *Mitchell Collection.*

Serving, metal, "Drink Coca-Cola," famous Johnny Weissmuller and Maureen O'Sullivan in swimsuits holding Coke in bottles. *Caution — this tray has been widely reproduced.* 1934, 13¼" x 10½" EX, $1,100.00 C. *Mitchell Collection.*

Serving, metal, "Drink Coca-Cola," French with food and Coke bottles on table, 1957, 13¼" x 10½", EX, $125.00 C. *Mitchell Collection.*

Serving, metal, "Drink Coca-Cola," Garden Girl with flare glass, oval shaped, 1920, 13¼" x 16½", EX, $925.00 C. *Mitchell Collection.*

Serving, metal, "Drink Coca-Cola," girl in swimsuit and red cap with a bottle of Coke, 1930, 10½" x 13¼", EX, $525.00 C. *Mitchell Collection.*

Model Verna Clair, whose real name is Josephine Moore, was the "Running Girl" model.

Serving, metal, "Drink Coca-Cola," girl in yellow swimsuit running on beach with bottle of Coke in each hand, 1937, 10½" x 13¼", EX, $425.00 C. *Mitchell Collection.*

Serving, metal, "Drink Coca-Cola...Have a Coke...Thirst Knows No Season," commonly known as the menu girl, tray was produced in different languages, 1950 – 1960s, 10½" x 13¼", very G, $95.00 C.

B.J. Summers.

Serving, metal, "Drink Coca-Cola," hostess woman reclining on chair arm with a glass of Coke, 1936, 10½" x 13¼", EX, $525.00 C.

Mitchell Collection.

Serving, metal, "Drink Coca-Cola," ice skater on log with a bottle of Coke, 1941, 10½" x 13¼", EX, $450.00 C. *Mitchell Collection.*

Serving, metal, "Drink Coca-Cola...in Bottles 5¢...at Fountains 5¢," with Juanita drinking Coke from a flare glass, 1906, 10½" x 13¼", EX, $2,800.00 D.

Serving, metal, "Drink Coca-Cola...'Meet Me at the Soda Fountain,' " pretty girl on telephone, 1930, 10½" x 13¼", EX, $600.00 C.
Mitchell Collection.

Serving, metal, "Drink Coca-Cola," movie star Frances Dee sitting on rail with a bottle of Coke, 1933, 10½" x 13¼", EX, $625.00 C. *Mitchell Collection.*

Serving, metal, "Drink Coca-Cola," movie star Madge Evans holding a bottle of Coke and standing beside a chair, 1935, 10½" x 13¼", EX, $525.00 C. *Mitchell Collection.*

Serving, metal, "Drink Coca-Cola...Refreshing! Delicious!" Hilda Clark at table with a bottle and a glass of Coke, 9¼" dia., EX, $7,800.00 D.

Serving, metal, "Drink Coca-Cola," pretty girl in swimsuit in chair on beach with a bottle of Coke, 1932, 10½" x 13¼", EX, $725.00 C.
Mitchell Collection.

Serving, metal, "Drink Coca-Cola," soda attendant with glasses of Coke, 1928, 10½" x 13¼", EX, $750.00 C.
Mitchell Collection.

Serving, metal, "Drink Coca-Cola," St. Louis World's Fair tray with girl at table with a glass of Coke, oval shaped, 1909, 13½" x 16½", EX, $3,000.00 C.
Mitchell Collection.

Serving, metal, "Drink Coca-Cola," two pretty women with Cokes beside a vintage car; due to the denand for metal during WWII, this was the last metal tray produced until the war ended; 1942, 10½" x 13¼", EX, $500.00 C. *Mitchell Collection.*

Serving, metal, "Drink Coca-Cola," various item in center include a bottle of Coke, French version, 1950s, 10½" x 13¼", G, $120.00 D.

Serving, metal, "Drink Coca-Cola" with flare glass being held up by a pretty young lady, 1907, 10½" x 13¼", EX, $2,750.00 C. *Mitchell Collection.*

Serving, metal, "Drink Coca-Cola," with the Afternoon Girl holding a bottle of Coke, manufactured by American Art Works, Inc., Coshoctin, Ohio, 1938, 10½" x 13¼", EX, $425.00 C. *Mitchell Collection.*

Serving, metal, "Drink Coca-Cola," woman in white fox fur with glass of Coke, 1921, 10½" x 13¼", EX, $600.00 C. *Mitchell Collection.*

Serving, metal, "Drink Delicious and Refreshing Coca-Cola," with Hilda Clark holding a flare glass, 1903, 9½" dia., NM, $3,550.00 D. *Metz Superlatives Auction.*

Serving, metal, "Drink Delicious Coca-Cola," with a King Coca-Cola girl, first rectangular tray used by Coke by American Art Works, Inc. Caution — watch for reproductions, 1909, 10½" x 13¼", EX, $1,300.00 C. *Mitchell Collection.*

Serving, metal, table with food and a bottle and glass of Coke, this one came out about the time eating in front of the television became popular, 1961, 18¼" x 13½", EX, $15.00 C. *Metz Superlatives Auction..*

Serving, metal, "Here's a Coke for You," there are three different versions of this tray, 1961, 13¼" x 10½", EX, $35.00 D.

Serving-commerative, metal, "Coca-Cola Bottling Company of the Lehigh Valley," with plant in tray center, 1981, EX, $25.00 C. *Mitchell Collection.*

Serving-commerative, metal, Canadian product with Lillian Nordica, 1968, 10½" x 13¼", EX, $85.00 C. *Mitchell Collection.*

Serving-commerative, metal, "Drink Coca-Cola," Alabama/Auburn, 1975, EX, $35.00 C. *Mitchell Collection.*

Serving-TV, metal, Coca-Cola bottles and an assortment of food, 1956, 18¼" x 13½", EX, $20.00 C.

Serving-commerative, metal, "Drink Coca-Cola in Bottles," Canadian produced in the English version, 1968, 10½" x 13¼", EX, $85.00 C.

Serving-TV, Thanksgiving theme with fall decor, 1961, 18¼" x 13½", EX, $25.00 C.

Serving-TV, metal, Duster Girl with bottle of Coke in her hand, 1970s, 10¼" x 14¼", EX, $15.00 C.

Tip, metal, "Delicious...Refreshing...Coca-Cola" with Hilda Clark holding a glass of Coke, 1903, 4" dia., EX, $2,500.00 D.

Tip, metal, "Coca-Cola" with Hilda Clark holding a glass of Coke in a silver holder, 1903, 6" dia., EX, $2,500.00 D.

Hilda Clark posed for Coca-Cola from 1899 until 1904 – 1905.

Tip, metal, "Drink Coca-Cola... Delicious! Refreshing!" Hilda Clark at table with a glass of coke, 1900, 6" dia., EX, $3,750.00 C.
Metz Superlatives Auction.

Tip, metal, "Drink a Bottle of Carbonated Coca-Cola," straight-sided paper-label bottle tilted in center, 1903, 5½" dia., EX, $5,100.00 C.

Tip, metal, "Drink Coca-Cola...Delicious and Refreshing" Hamilton King Coke girl model with a flare glass of Coke, 1913, 4¼" x 6", EX, $775.00 D.

Tip, metal, "Drink Coca-Cola...Delicious...Refreshing," Juanita drinking from a flare glass, 1900s, 4" dia., EX, $1,075.00 D.

127

Tip, metal, "Drink Coca-Cola...Relieves Fatigue 5¢," flare glass with syrup line, 1907, 4⅜" x 6⅛" EX, $825.00 C. *Collectors Auction Services.*

Tip, metal, "Drink Coca-Cola"; with Elaine, also known as the World War I girl, with a glass of Coke; 1916, 4⅜" x 6⅛", EX, $575.00 C.

Tip trays were designed to be used to return change to customers, but picked up the tip title since customers used them to leave a tip to the server.

Tip, metal, "Drink Coca-Cola...Delicious Refreshing," with Betty in white bonnet, 1914, 4⅛" x 6⅜", EX, $625.00 B.

Tip metal, "Drink Coca-Cola," St. Louis World's Fair with pretty girl with a glass of Coke, 1909, 4¼" x 6", EX, $825.00 D. *Collectors Auction Services.*

Tip, metal, "Drink Coca-Cola," the model known as the Garden Girl with a flare glass of Coke, same as the 1920 calendar, last tip tray issued in the United States, 1920, 4¼" x 6", EX, $675.00 C. *Collectors Auction Services.*

Tip, metal, "Drink Delicious Coca-Cola," with Hamilton King Coke girl in wide brim hat, 1910, 4¼" x 6", EX, $775.00 D.

Book, advertising, paper,
The Charm of Purity,
1920s, EX, $55.00 C.
Mitchell Collection.

Advertisment, news-
paper, full page for
the opening of a new
bottling plant, 1939,
F, $90.00 C. *Mitchell
Collection.*

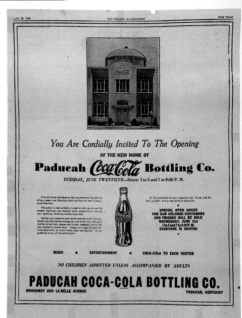

Book, children's, paper,
*Alphabet Book of Coca-
Cola,* 1928, EX, $120.00 C.
Mitchell Collection.

Book cover, paper, "America is Good...Because America is Good," U.S. map and Dwight Eisenhower on front, 1950s, EX, $20.00 C. *Mitchell Collection.*

Book cover, paper, "Bring Refreshment into Play Have a Coke," from the Peru Coca-Cola bottling Co., 1940 – 1950s, EX, $15.00 C. *Mitchell Collection.*

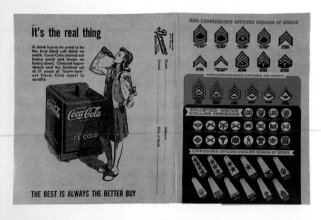

Book cover, paper, "It's the Real Thing" on back, front shows armed forces rank insigias, 1940s, EX, $35.00 C. *Mitchell Collection.*

Book cover, paper, "It's the Real Thing," with airplane identities on the front, 1940s, EX, $40.00 C. *Mitchell Collection.*

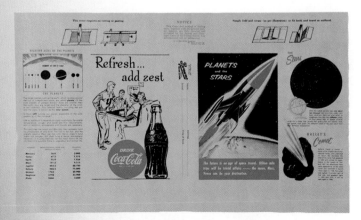

Book cover, paper, "Refresh...Add Zest," front cover has planets and space with rocket blasting off, 1960s, EX, $35.00 C. *Mitchell Collection.*

Book cover, paper, "There's Nothing Like a Coke," front cover has crossing guard, 1940s, EX, $30.00 C. *Mitchell Collection.*

Booklet, paper, "Yessir, Kit Carson Has Passed 'Em All," sliding information item with Kit Carson on front, 1950s, VG, $55.00 C. *Mitchell Collection.*

Border, corrugated paper, "Coca-Cola...Red Hot Olympics," 1990s, EX, $35.00 C. *Metz Superlatives Auction.*

Border, corrugated paper, "Enjoy Coca-Cola Classic," 6" tall, EX, $45.00 C.

Border, corrugated paper, "Diet Coke Uncapped," used to promote the 38th Grammy Awards, 97" x 12", EX, $50.00 C.

Border, corrugated paper, "Enjoy Coca-Cola Classic...Major League Baseball," EX, $40.00 C.

Border, corrugated paper, "Diet Coke," used to hide unsightly display base, EX, $35.00 C.

Border, corrugated paper, "Enjoy Coca-Cola Classic," EX, $35.00 C.

Border, corrugated paper, "Enjoy Coca-Cola" light-up Christmas truck with Santa in chair, used to hide display bases, 1996, EX, $55.00 C.

The Coca-Cola caravan truck is 64' long and has 25,000 lights.

Border, corrugated paper, "Enjoy Coca-Cola," Santa in chair, EX, $35.00 C.

Border, corrugated paper, "Enjoy Coca-Cola," with advertising for Super Bowl XXXI, 1991, EX, $40.00 C.

Border, corrugated paper, "Kick Off Your Party with Kraft Foods and Coca-Cola Products," for Super Bowl XXXV, EX, $45.00 C.

Border, corrugated paper, "The One and Only Taste," EX, $35.00 C.

Bulletin, paper, *Coca-Cola News*, third edition, scarce, 1896, 6" x 8", NM, $135.00 B. *Metz Superlatives Auction.*

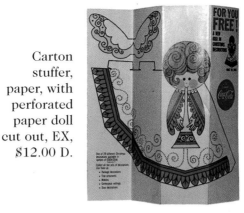

Carton stuffer, paper, with perforated paper doll cut out, EX, $12.00 D.

Check, paper, "Coca-Cola Bottling Co. No. 1" written on the Globe Bank & Trust Co., Paducah, KY, and signed by the owner and bottler, Luther Carson, 1908, EX, $110.00 C. *Mitchell Collection.*

Check, paper, "Coca-Cola Bottling Works," with bottling plant on left side of check, signed by one of the owners and written on the Paducah Banking Co. of Paducah, KY, 1915, EX, $95.00 C. *Mitchell Collection.*

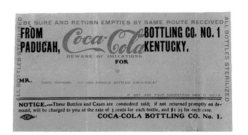

Coupon, paper, "From Paducah Coca-Cola Bottling Co. No. 1...," EX, $30.00 C. *Mitchell Collection.*

Coupon, paper, "Pause & Refresh...Drink Coca-Cola in Bottles," good for a 5¢ bottle, VG, $20.00 C.

Check, paper, "Globe Bank and Trust Co." This was signed by the Paducah, KY, bottler, Luther F. Carson; a signature other than the plant owner would reduce the value. 1907, EX, $95.00 C. *Mitchell Collection.*

Coupon, paper, "This Coupon When Returned with Empty Coca-Cola Bottle is Good for 5¢ At...," space left for vendor advertising, G, $20.00 C. *Mitchell Collection.*

Coupon, cardboard, "Save This Valuable Coupon," 1940 – 1950s, EX, $8.00 – 10.00 C. *B. J. Summers.*

Coupon, cardboard, "This Ticket is Good for ONE FREE CUP of Coca-Cola," 1940 – 1950s, EX, $8.00 – 10.00 C. *B. J. Summers.*

Low in cost; convenient to serve.
TO BE GOOD, IT MUST BE SERVED ICE COLD, BELOW 40°

Invitation, paper, Paducah, KY, new bottling plant opening, 1939, EX, $45.00 C. *Mitchell Collection.*

Coupon, cardboard, "Enjoy These 6 Bottles with Our Compliments," woman at table with a six-pack carton, 1930 – 1940s, EX, $10.00 – 15.00 C. *B. J. Summers.*

Map, paper, "Drink Coca-Cola...Delicious and Refreshing," produced by Rand McNally, 1920s, EX, $50.00 C. *Mitchell Collection.*

Coupon, cardboard, "You Are Cordially Invited to Accept This Carton Free When You Buy This One," 1950s, EX, $8.00 – 10.00 C.
B. J. Summers.

Menu sheet, paper, "Things Go Better with Coke," plastic holder, 1960s, EX, $55.00 C.
Mitchell Collection.

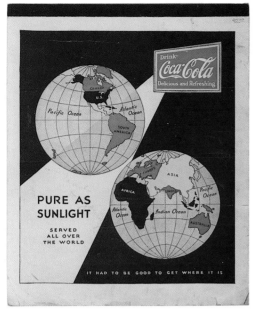

Notebook, paper, "Drink Coca-Cola...Pure as Sunlight," 1930s, VG, $35.00 C. *Metz Superlatives Auction.*

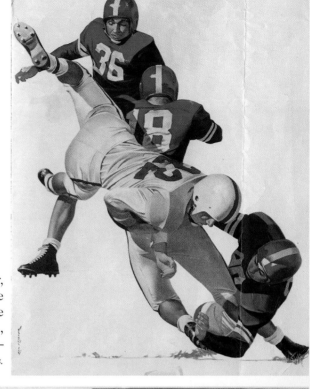

Placemat, paper, "There's Nothing Like a Coke," football scene in rear, double sided, 1960s, EX, $8.00 – 10.00 C. *B. J. Summers.*

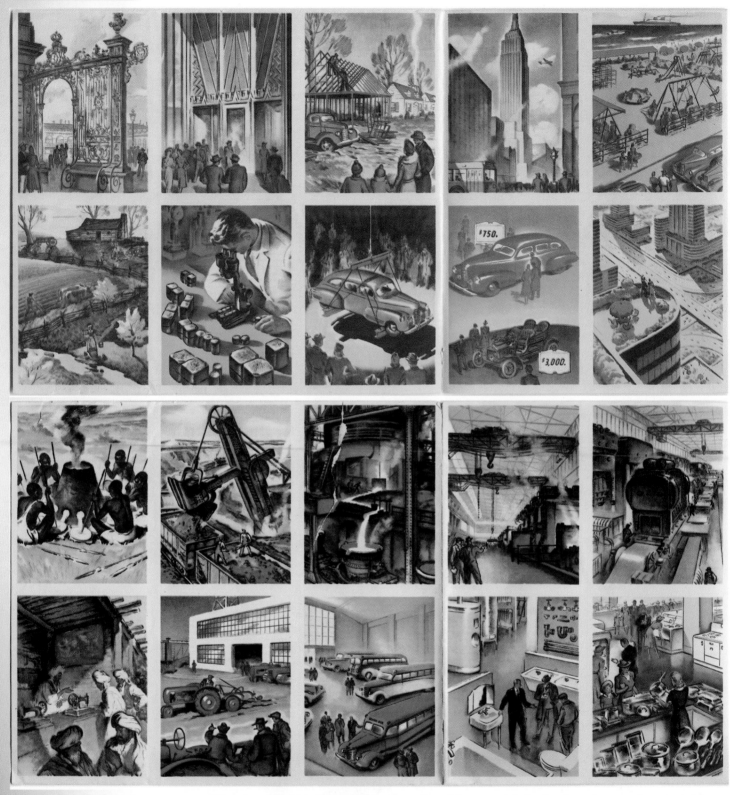

Poster pasted on sheets, paper, "Steel...a Modern Essential," educational items with fantastic colors and material for classroom use, demand seems to be slowly rising on items but is still low in comparison to other Coke advertising, 1940 – 1950s, EX, $50.00 – 75.00 C. *B. J. Summers.*

Poster, paper, "Our America...Future for Electrical Power," great instructional item with good colors and content, but demand for these remains fairly low, making them a good affordable collectible, 1940s, EX, $35.00 D. *Creatures of Habit.*

Poster, paper, "Our America...Iron and Steel" educational item, number three in four series for school, 1946, EX, $30.00 C. *Mitchell Collection.*

Profit chart, paper and cardboard, "Here's a Quick Look at Your Profit on Cartons," sliding scale for the retailer, G, $30.00 C. *Mitchell Collection.*

Safety card, paper, "Central States 1996...Safety...Pour It On!!!!" employee item, EX, $5.00 C.

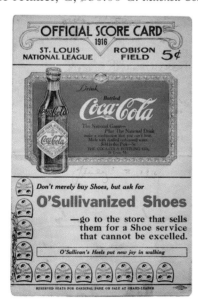

Score card, paper, official 1916 item from St. Louis National League, Robison Field, EX, $45.00 C. *Mitchell Collection.*

Score card, paper, St. Louis Cardinals souvenir item, EX, $35.00 C.

Score pad, paper, "Drink Coca-Cola Delicious and Refreshing" with a pretty woman on the front of each, 1940s, EX, $20.00 C each. *Mitchell Collection.*

Score card, paper, St. Louis Cardinals stadium vendor, "Ice-Cold Coca-Cola," EX, $30.00 C. *Mitchell Collection.*

Sheet music, paper, "Rock Me To Sleep Mother" featuring Juanita drinking from a flare glass, 1906, EX, $895.00 C. *Metz Superlatives Auction.*

Sheet Music, paper, "The Coca-Cola Girl," framed and under glass, 1927, EX, $395.00 C. *Mitchell Collection.*

Study cards, wildflower, paper, "The World Of Nature," with 20 different varieties and the original envelope, 1920s, VG, $65.00 C set. *Metz Superlatives Auction.*

Fan, solid back, bamboo, church fan donated by the Ruston, LA, Coca-Cola bottler, 1920s, EX, 145.00 C. *Mitchell Collection.*

Bamboo, "Keep Cool, Drink Coca-Cola," with Oriental scene on one side and message on other side, VG, $235.00 C.
Mitchell Collection.

Fan, solid back, bamboo, "Drink Coca-Cola...Refresh Yourself," Waycross, GA, 1950s, EX, $100.00 C. *Mitchell Collection*

Solid back, cardboard, "Buy by the Carton," from the Memphis, TN, bottler, 1930s, EX, $195.00 C.

Solid back, cardboard, "Drink Coca-Cola," featuring a yellow spotlighted bottle, wooden handle, 1930s, EX, $155.00 C.
Mitchell Collection.

Solid back, cardboard, "Drink Coca-Cola" on colored background with yellow spotlighted bottle, wooden handle, 1930s, EX, $100.00 C. *Mitchell Collection.*

Solid back, cardboard, "Drink Coca-Cola...Quality Carries On," with bottle in hand shown bursting through paper, wooden handle, 1950s, EX, $85.00 C. *Mitchell Collection.*

Solid back, cardboard, "Drink Coca-Cola...the Pause That Refreshes" with rolled paper handle, 1930s, EX, $195.00 C. *Mitchell Collection.*

Solid back, cardboard, "Drink Coca-Cola...the Pause That Refreshes" with hobbleskirt bottle, from the Martin, TN, bottler, rolled paper handle, 1940 – 1950s, EX, $125.00 C. *Mitchell Collection.*

Solid back, cardboard, "Drink Coca-Cola," with a poem named "Jackie" on the back, 1930s, EX, $225.00 C.

Solid back, cardboard, "Drink Coca-Cola," with dynamic wave logo, wooden handle, from the Coca-Cola Bottling Works of Greenwood, MS, 1960s, EX, $40.00 C.

Cardboard, "Be Prepared...Be Refreshed," young Boy Scout at box cooler with a couple of Coke bottles. This blotter crosses collectible lines — Coke, Boy Scouts, and coolers — so it will be sought after by more than just Coke collectors, 1940s, M, $350.00 B.

Cardboard, "Completely Refreshing," girl on beach with a bottle of Coke, 5¼" x 2½", EX, $35.00 B. *Collectors Auction Services.*

Cardboard, "Delicious...Wholesome... Refreshing," Canadian piece with ruler marks and protractor, this one is hard to find, 1930s, NM, $275.00 B. *Metz Superlatives Auction.*

Cardboard, "Drink Coca-Cola in Bottles... 'Good,' " with Sprite Boy in bottle cap hat, 7¼" x 3½", EX, $35.00 C.

Cardboard, "Drink Coca-Cola...Delicious and Refreshing...the Pause That Refreshes," man at soda table in striped jacket, 1930s, EX, $45.00 B. *Metz Superlatives Auction.*

Cardboard, "Drink Coca-Cola...Delicious and Refreshing...the Pause That Refreshes," with boy on bicycle and drinking a bottle of Coke, 7¼" x 3½", EX, $150.00 B. *Collectors Auction Services.*

Cardboard, "Drink Coca-Cola...Restores Energy...Strengthens the Nerves," 1926, EX, $145.00 C.

Cardboard, "Friendliest Drink on Earth," bottle in hand in front of world globe, 1956, 8" x 4", NM, $50.00 D.

Cardboard, "Good with Food...Try It," sandwich plate and bottles of Coke, 1930s, NM, $75.00 D.
Collectors Auction Services.

Cardboard, "Refresh Yo'self," old white-haired gent with a bottle of Coke, 1928, NM, $90.00 D.

Cardboard, "I Think It's Swell," pretty girl looking at a book that has a Sprite Boy ad, 1950s, G, $35.00 C.

Cardboard, "The Pause That Refreshes," pretty woman with Coke bottle seated on ground with blanket, 1934, EX, $100.00 D.

Cardboard, "The Pause That Refreshes," boy and his dog, boy is seated and enjoying a bottle of Coke and a sandwich, 1930s, NM, $105.00 D.
Metz Superlatives Auction.

Cardboard, "So Refreshing...Keep on Ice," twenties vintage couple at door of icebox with cold bottles of Coke inside, 1927, mint, $80.00 C.

Paper, "Coca-Cola...Delicious...Refreshing," scene of Piccadilly Circus London, with large Coke advertisement on the side of building, EX, $25.00 C. *Metz Superlatives Auction.*

Paper, "Coca-Cola Bottling Co., No. 1," postally used card with vignette of Coke bottling plant. The number *1* on this card refers to the first plant this bottler opened; later he opened and licensed many others. 1920s, EX, $95.00 C. *Mitchell Collection.*

Paper, "Coca-Cola," scene of the Coke pavilion at the 1964 World's Fair in New York, 1964, 5½" x 3½", EX, $30.00 C.

Paper, "Drink Delicious Coca-Cola," featuring the Hamilton King Coca-Cola girl, 1910, NM, $775.00 B. *Metz Superlatives Auction.*

Paper, "Drink Coca-Cola in Bottles" on door on new international route truck, VG, $50.00 C. *Mitchell Collection.*

"Completely refreshing"

Drink Coca-Cola

THE TASTE THAT CHARMS AND NEVER CLOYS

There's nothing so refreshing under the sun as delicious Coca-Cola, — ice-cold and tingling with the life and sparkle of real refreshment.

It has the quality of genuine goodness. Thirst asks nothing more.

THE PAUSE THAT REFRESHES

You'll welcome ice-cold Coca-Cola just as often and as surely as thirst comes. You taste its quality,—the quality of genuine goodness. Ice-cold Coca-Cola gives you the taste that charms and never cloys. You get the feel of complete refreshment, buoyant refreshment. Thirst asks nothing more.

Magazine, paper, "Drink Coca-Cola...Completely Refreshing" with bathing beauty on towel with a bottle of Coke, 1941, 7" x 10", VG, $5.00 – 15.00 C.

Almost everyone appreciates the best

...and the extra-bright refreshment of Coke brings you back so quickly.

TASTE its extra-bright tang – so bracing, so distinctive, the liveliest sparkle of them all.

FEEL its extra-bright energy, a fresh little lift that comes through in seconds.

ENJOY its extra-bright quality – the unmatched goodness that tells you "there's nothing like a Coke."

For perfect refreshment, it's always – ice-cold Coca-Cola, so pure and wholesome.

The Pause That Refreshes . . . Fifty Million Times a Day

See Eddie Fisher on "Coke Time"—NBC Television twice each week

"COKE" IS A REGISTERED TRADE-MARK. COPYRIGHT 1955, THE COCA-COLA COMPANY

Drink Coca-Cola

ICE COLD

Magazine, paper, "Drink Coca-Cola," from back page of *National Geographic*. This is one of the better ads in my opinion; it has a couple projecting the wholesome Coke image, they're in front of a highly sought-after vending machine, the Coke disc (button) is very visible, Sprite Boy is in the image, there is line promoting "Coke Time" with Eddie Fisher on television, and to remind us how good it is, there is the slogan "The Pause That Refreshes...Fifty Million Times a Day." 1955, 7" x 10", VG, $5.00 – 15.00 C.

Have a Coca-Cola = Howdy, Neighbor

...or greeting friends at home and abroad

One of the first places they head for, when they get back, is the neighborhood soda fountain and all its old associations...among them, Coca-Cola. Many places overseas, too, your American fighting man meets up with that old friend...ice-cold Coca-Cola. It's always like word from home to hear the friendly greeting *Have a "Coke"* in a strange land. Yes, around the globe, Coca-Cola stands for *the pause that refreshes*,—has become a symbol of our way of living.

In news stories, books and magazines, you read how much our fighting men cherish Coca-Cola whenever they get it. Luckily, they find Coca-Cola available in over 35 allied and neutral countries 'round the globe.

Coca-Cola —the global high-sign

It's natural for popular names to acquire friendly abbreviations. That's why you hear Coca-Cola called "Coke".

COPYRIGHT 1944, THE COCA-COLA COMPANY

Magazine, paper, "Have a Coca-Cola = Howdy, Neighbor," super WWII *National Geographic* back cover with serviceman in soda fountain relating experiences to a young man with his sister and mother, 1936, 7" x 10", VG, $5.00 – 10.00 C.

Magazine, paper, "Drink Coca-Cola...Get the Feel of Wholesome Refreshment," bottle in hand and glacier with "wet box" machine, 1936, 7" x 10", VG, $5.00 – 15.00 C.

Drink Coca-Cola ICE COLD

ICE-COLD EVERY DAY IN THE YEAR 5¢

Get the *feel* of wholesome refreshment

When days are hot—Coca-Cola is cold, ice-cold. When weather is depressing—Coca-Cola is refreshing, so refreshing. Get the *feel* of wholesome refreshment with an ice-cold Coca-Cola, and you'll make your own weather prediction: fair and much cooler.

Vol. LXX, No. 2   THE NATIONAL GEOGRAPHIC MAGAZINE   August, 1936

Magazine, paper, "So Easy to Take Home the Six-bottle Carton" with small girl on grocery counter with a vintage cardboard carrier, small black and white insert showing Mom putting the bottles in the fridge to cool, 1949, 7" x 10", VG, $5.00 – 10.00 C.

Magazine, paper, "Stretch and Refresh...Have a Coca-Cola," scene with stadium vendor at ball game, 1949, 7" x 10", VG, $5.00 – 8.00 C.

Magazine, paper, "Take Off...Refreshed," pilot and stewardess at airport fountain enjoying a Coke, notice the super hanging porcelain sign in the background, 1949, 7" x 10", VG, $5.00 – 10.00 C.

Magazine, paper, "Thru 50 years...1886 – 1936...the Pause That Refreshes," ladies in appropriate swimwear for the times and with bottles of Coke, 1936, 7" x 10", VG, $5.00 – 10.00 C.

The ad at left is from Haddom Sundblom's painting titled "Daddy's Home." The baby being held is Kay Dell Knarr.

Magazine, paper, "Thru 50 years — Making a Pause Refreshing...Drink Coca-Cola...Delicious and Refreshing," soda fountain attendants of the time 1886 – 1936, 1936, 7" x 10", VG, $5.00 – 10.00 C.

Magazine, paper "Christmas Together...Have a Coca-Cola," back cover of *National Geographic*, 1945, G, $12.00 C.

Magazine, paper, "Coca-Cola 5¢ Everywhere," front and back cover of the *Housekeeper* with front page of pretty woman drinking from a flare glass in a fountain holder, matted, framed and under glass, 1909, VG, $150.00 C.

Magazine, paper, "Coca-Cola 5¢ Everywhere," front and back cover full page makes one large ad, the *Housewife*, matted, framed and under glass, 1910, G, $190.00 C.

Magazine, paper, "Coca-Cola...at Soda
Fountains 5¢" with Lillian Nordica
with fan, a familiar pose, and a coupon
at the bottom of the page, 1904, NM,
$135.00 B.

Magazine, paper,
"Drink Coca-Cola
Delicious and
Refreshing," full
page back cover the
Railway Journal
with a glass and
bottle of Coke, and
an engineer in the
cab of an ICRR
steam engine, 1929,
8½" x 11", G,
$35.00 C.

Magazine, paper, "Even the Bubbles Taste
Better," young boy drinking from a
hobbleskirt bottle with bubbles floating
around him, 1956, VG, $15.00 C.

Magazine, paper, "We'll Trim the Tree.
Free." Christmas promotion for ornaments
with a carton of Coke, 1967, 8½" x 11", VG,
$15.00 C.

Magazine, paper "You Taste Its Quality," from *National Geographic*, pretty girl drinking from a hobbleskirt bottle, 1951, fair, $12.00 C.

YOUR HOST OF THE AIRWAVES

The Coca-Cola Company presents

EDGAR BERGEN with CHARLIE McCARTHY

CBS 8 p. m. EST every Sunday

And every day...wherever you travel, the familiar red cooler is your HOST OF THE HIGHWAYS...HOST TO THE WORKER in office and shop...HOST TO THIRSTY MAIN STREET the country over.

Magazine, paper, "Your Host of the Airways," featuring Edgar Bergen and Charlie McCarthy at a box cooler of Coke, 1950, G, $15.00 C.

The Coca-Cola Company began advertising in National Geographic in 1933. Through 1965, the company placed 188 ads in the publication. With the exception of June and October 1933, all ads were on the back cover.

Newspaper, "Coca-Cola 5¢," full page from the *Chicago Daily News*, 1908, EX, $15.00 B.

Book, advertising, paper, bottlers'
price guide for advertising items,
1944, EX, $275.00 B. *Metz Superlatives Auction.*

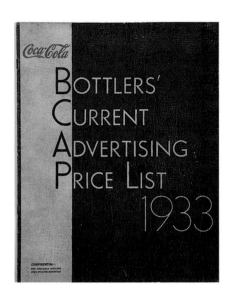

Book, advertising, paper, bottlers'
price list for Coke advertising
items, 1933, EX, $250.00 B. *Metz
Superlatives Auction.*

Book, advertising, paper, bottlers'
price list with all the advertising
signs and items available to them,
1943, EX, $235.00 B. *Metz Superlatives Auction.*

Book, advertising, paper, price list
for bottlers' advertising items,
super handy item, 1942, EX,
$235.00 B. *Metz Superlatives Auction.*

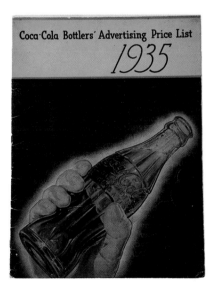

Book, advertising, paper, price
list for dealers' advertising
items, 1935, EX, $235.00 B.
Metz Superlatives Auction.

Book, advertisement, paper, 50th
anniversary price list for bottlers, 1936, EX, $350.00 B. *Metz
Superlatives Auction.*

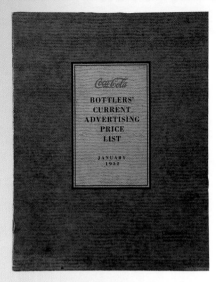

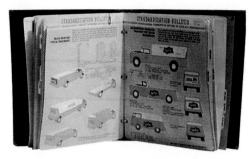

Book, advertisement, paper, special bulletins for bottlers with late-breaking up-to-date information, 1950s, G, $100.00
B. *Metz Superlatives Auction.*

Book, advertisement, paper, bottlers' current prices for advertising items, 1932, EX, $250.00 C.
Mitchell Collection.

Book, bottler, paper and vinyl, Gold Service display book for bottler use, EX, 85.00 C.

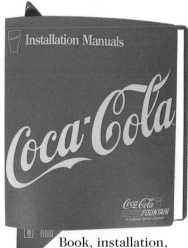

Book, history, paper, "Chronological History of the Coca-Cola Company," a very brief history of Coke and its products, VG, $35.00 C.

Book, informational, paper, "Portrait of a business...the Coca-Cola Company, a guide to the success of the Coca-Cola business, NM, $135.00 C.

Book, installation, paper and vinyl, three-ring binder with information about installing fountain stations, 1970s, NM, $215.00 C.

Book, information kit, paper, heavy stock, spiral-bound refreshment kit for displaying and merchandising effectively, NM, $275.00 C.

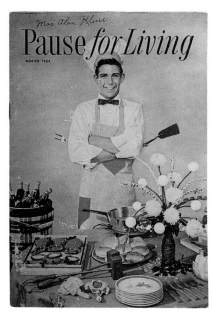

Book, magazine format, paper, "Pause for Living" with information for gracious entertaining, 1954, EX, $25.00 C.

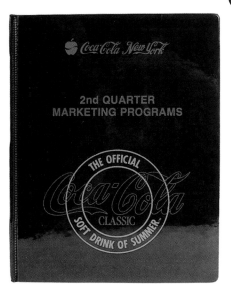

Book, marketing, paper and vinyl, binder with marketing programs for the second quarter, NM, $225.00 C.

Book, material information, paper, heavy stock for five-ring binder with information on the Cooler Radio, 1950s, EX, $80.00 C. *Mitchell Collection.*

Book, merchandising, paper and vinyl, "The Merchandising and Centennial Programs," three-ring binder full of 100th anniversary items for merchandising, 1986, EX, $275.00 C.

Book, retail sales, paper and vinyl, handbook for route salesmen to use in preparing for sales in retail stores, 1950s, EX, $35.00 C. *Metz Superlatives Auction.*

Book, supplies, paper and vinyl, Paul Flum supply catalog of items needed for advertising, point of purchase to molded fiberglass cooler in shape of older cooler, EX, $75.00 C.

Carbonation tester, metal, used before the days of premix to determine if the carbonation level was correct, EX, $725.00 D.

Display, plastic, "Coca-Cola," large hobbleskirt store attention getter, 1953, 20" high, EX, $375.00 B. *Wm. Morford Investment Grade Collectibles.*

Display, glass, large hobbleskirt aqua store display of the Christmas bottle, 6" x 20¼", NM, $350.00 B. *Wm. Morford Investment Grade Collectibles.*

Hobbleskirt, glass, "100 Years..." commemorative from the Paducah, KY, bottling company, clear, 2003, 8 oz., NM, $5.00 C. *B. J. Summer.*

Hobbleskirt, glass, six in original cardboard carton, with the countdown at one year left until the 1996 Olympics, clear, 1995, EX, $45.00 D. *Pleasant Hill Antique Mall and Tea Room/Bob Johnson.*

Hobbleskirt, glass, "Coca-Cola 50th Anniversary," gold-dipped limited production bottles on presentation bases, very unusual to find a matched pair, both still have the chain and medallion, plus the wife's bottle has the bracelet, bases are plastic and all four sides are written in gold celebrating with the bottler's name and employee and spouse, finding a matching pair adds to the collector demand and also the value, 1953, 6 oz., EX, $500.00 pair C. *B. J. Summers.*

In all, 56 bottle types were produced to celebrate the 100th anniversary of Coca-Cola.

Hobbleskirt, glass, gold-dipped 100th anniversary bottle, 1986, EX, $65.00 D.

Hobbleskirt, glass, "Coca-Cola," foreign origin, clear, 10 oz., NM, $15.00 – 25.00 C. *B. J. Summers.*

Hobbleskirt, glass, screw-on top, white lettering in English on one side and foreign on other side, bought by serviceman on overseas duty from a vending machine, Japanese, EX. $20.00 C. *Brian and Christy Kopishke.*

Hobbleskirt, glass, "Coca-Cola" in script on shoulder, plastic cap, very similar to 1920s version of this display item, smaller commemorative shown for comparison, 1960s, 20" tall, EX, $275.00 C. *B. J. Summers.*

Hobbleskirt, glass, tall display model of the Christmas 1923 bottle, in original display box with the original tag around the neck of the bottle with instructions for filling, clear, 1930s, 20" tall, EX, $750.00 B. *Metz Superlatives Auction.*

The design and shape of the hobbleskirt bottle is so unique that it has its own registered trademark.

Hobbleskirt, glass, with white lettering on screw top, Canadian, 40 oz., EX, $40.00 D.

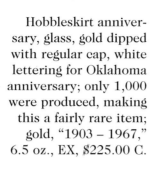

Hobbleskirt anniversary, glass, gold dipped with regular cap, white lettering for Oklahoma anniversary; only 1,000 were produced, making this a fairly rare item; gold, "1903 – 1967," 6.5 oz., EX, $225.00 C.

Hobbleskirt special occasions, glass, gold dipped, embossed lettering with regular cap, made for special events for bottlers' use, gold, 6 oz., EX, $85.00 C. *Metz Superlatives Auction.*

Hobbleskirt, rubber, display advertising piece, 1940s, 43" tall, G, $850.00 B. *Metz Superlatives Auction.*

Hobbleskirt commemorative, glass, "Root" reissue of the original 1915 bottle; the reissue is marked on the bottom, but the originals were not marked; only 5,000 made, clear, 1965, EX, $495.00 C. *Mitchell Collection.*

When collecting hobbleskirt bottles it helps to be aware that there are five classes:

1) *Pat'D Nov. 16, 1915, known as the Thanksgiving bottle, produced 1917 – 1928*
2) *Pat'D Dec. 25, 1923, known as the Christmas bottle, produced 1928 – 1938*
3) *Pat'D 105529, produced from 1938 to 1951*
4) *U.S. Patent office 6 oz., produced 1951 – 1958*
5) *U.S. Patent Office 6½ oz., produced 1958 – 1965*

Hobbleskirt commemorative, glass, Super Bowl 2000, in original carton, 2000, 8 oz., NM, $95.00 C.

Hobbleskirt miniature, glass, perfume bottle and stopper, *reproductions exist,* clear, 1930s, EX, $85.00 C.

154

Jug, stoneware, "Coca-Cola," with paper label, 1910, ½ gal., VG, $4,300.00 B. *Metz Superlatives Auction.*

Jug, ceramic, with paper label used to ship syrup, this shoulder jug with cork stopper is extremely difficult to find, *reproductions exist in abundance,* creme and brown, 1900s, 1 gal., VG, $2,600.00 B. ($3,400.00 D if EX). *Metz Superlatives Auction.*

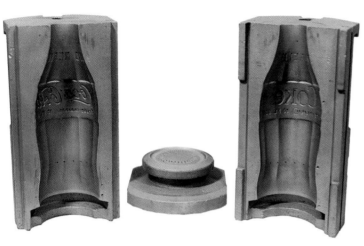

Mold, hobbleskirt, iron, made for the 10 oz. no-return bottle, EX, $525.00 C.

Premix, glass, used in early bottling process, green, 1920s, 2¼" x 7¾", EX, $95.00 C.

Seltzer, glass, "Coca-Cola Bottling Company...Cairo, Illinois." Another great example of a Cairo bottle, and contrary to most thinking, this one is scarcer than the Ritz Boy Cairo seltzer. Some calcium deposit on inside of bottle that could be cleaned, and a good clean metal top. 1940 – 1950s, EX, $575.00 C. *B. J. Summers.*

Refrigerator, glass, "Compliments Coca-Cola Bottling Co.," water bottle with green glass and advertising on front, EX, $125.00 – 145.00 C. *Mitchell Collection.*

Seltzer, glass and metal, "Coca-Cola Bottling Company, Bradford, PA," good strong clear acid etching, dark blue, EX, $455.00 C.

Seltzer, glass and metal, "Coca-Cola Bottling Company, Bradford, PA," acid etched, light aqua, EX, $285.00 C.

Many people collect Coke bottles by size, design, color, or — my area of interest — by city. At the time of this writing, I need seven more bottlers to complete my KY bottlers collection.

Seltzer, glass and metal, "Coca-Cola Bottling Works... Clearfield, PA," EX, $165.00 C.

Seltzer, glass, "Property of Cairo, Illinois Coca-Cola Bottling Co.," with Ritz Boy carrying a bottle on a tray, good cap with very little metal distress and a good strong bottle label. This bottler, now out of business, was related to Luther Carson, who founded and operated the Paducah, KY, bottling plant, and the factory (Cairo) obtained its license through the Paducah plant. 1940 – 1950s, EX, $450.00 C. *B. J. Summers.*

Seltzer, glass and metal, "Northern Coca-Cola Bottling Works, Inc., Messena, N.Y.," EX, $245.00 C.

Straight sided, glass, Biedenharm Candy Co., Vicksburg, MS, Hutchison. Same slug-plate-style letter as found on his 1900s bottles, aqua, 1890s, EX, $985.00 C. *Note: The Hutchison bottle was invented by Charles Hutchison. It was sealed with a wire-looped stopper that, when hit to open, resulted in a distinctive pop, thereby giving rise to the term soda pop.*

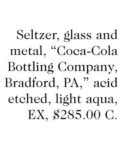

The first bottles to contain the carbonated Coca-Cola weren't labeled with the Coca-Cola name, but marked "Biedenharm Candy Co." and were bottles previously used for other flavors, these were thick walled "Hutch Bottles."

Straight sided, glass, Biedenharm Candy Co., Vicksburg, MS, lettering arranged in slug-plate fashion on body of bottle, aqua, 1900s, EX, $450.00 C – 950.00 C.

Straight sided, glass, block print in circle on front of bottle from Sedalia, MO, aqua, 6½", EX, $65.00 C.

Straight sided, glass, block print on shoulder and large size for the period, green, 32 oz., EX, $115.00 C.

Straight sided, glass, block print on shoulder, from Raton, NM, aqua, 6 oz., EX, $65.00 C.

Straight sided, glass, "Coca-Cola...Bottling Co. No. 1...Trade Mark Registered...Paducah, KY," very good slug plate with good embossing, all seams are raised and pronounced, light green, 1903 – 1915, 6.5 oz., EX, $500.00 C.

B. J. Summers.

Straight sided, glass, "Coca-Cola" embossed script on base, extremely unusual shoulder with steep pitch, clear, EX, $115.00 C.

Straight sided, glass, "Coca-Cola" in block print on base, with fluted sides, clear, 7 oz., EX, $65.00 C.

Straight sided, glass, "Coca-Cola" in script embossed in center with embossed border, aqua, 1910s, 6 oz., VG, $175.00 C.

Straight sided, glass, "Coca-Cola" in script on shoulder, Verner Springs Water Co., Greenville, SC, 1910s, 9" tall, VG, $75.00 C.

Straight sided, glass, "Coca-Cola" in script inside of double diamonds, from Toledo, OH, light amber, 1900 – 1910, 6 oz., EX, $195.00 C.

Straight sided, glass, "Coca-Cola" in script on base, "Bottling WKS 2nd Registered" on base in block print, light amber, 1910s, 6.5 oz., EX, $145.00 C.

Straight sided, glass, "Coca-Cola" in script on shoulder, no location listed, light amber, 1910s, 6 oz., EX, $135.00 C.

Straight sided, glass, "Coca-Cola" on bottom edge of base, "This bottle our private property and protected by registration under Senate Bill No. 130 approved June 7th, 1911," Dayton, OH, light amber, 1900 – 1910, 6 oz., EX, $275.00 C.

Straight sided, glass, "Coca-Cola" inside arrow circle, Louisville, KY, light amber, 1910s, 6 oz., EX, $195.00 C.

Straight sided, glass, "Coca-Cola" label under glass syrup container with metal cap, 1920s, EX, $700.00 C.
Mitchell Collection.

Straight sided, glass, "Coca-Cola" on base in script, no location named, light amber, 1910s, 6 oz., EX, $135.00 C.

Straight sided, glass, "Coca-Cola" on front, no location listed, medium amber, 1910s, 6 oz., EX, $125.00 C.

Straight sided, glass, "Coca-Cola" on shoulder of bottle with vertical arrow, "Cincinnati, Ohio" in block printing on base, light amber, 1910s, 6 oz., EX, $195.00 C. *Collectors Auction Services.*

Straight sided, glass, first generation throw-away bottle with embossed diamond, inside is embossed bottle and block "Coke," still full, clear, 1960s, 10 oz., NM, $45.00 C.

Straight sided, glass, Hutchison-style bottle for the 75th National Convention anniversary, fairly difficult to locate, light aqua, 1961, EX, $295.00 C.

Straight sided, glass, "Property of Coca-Cola Bottling Co., La Grange, Texas" in block print on front of body, with embossed ribbon around shoulder; probably didn't have Coke, but another flavor produced by the Coca-Cola bottler; aqua, 6 oz., EX, $75.00 C. *Mitchell Collection.*

Straight sided commemorative, glass, "Kentucky Leadership Center, Developing Leaders for Kentucky's Youth," 4-H, clear, 1986, 10 oz., EX, $50.00 C.

The 10 oz. tall commemorative bottle was phased out in 1992 in favor of an 8 oz. hobbleskirt bottle.

Straight sided commemorative, glass, "Tri-State Area Council Boy Scouts of America," green, 1953, EX, $265.00 C. *Mitchell Collection.*

159

Straight sided commemorative, glass, 75th anniversary bottle, with painted facsimile of paper label, clear, 1978, 10 oz., EX, $15.00 – 20.00 C.

B. J. Summers.

Straight sided commemorative, glass, "The Cola Clan...Mid South," made bottle for the third annual Septemberfest in Elizabethtown, KY, clear, 1979, 10 oz., EX, $30.00 C.

B. J. Summers.

Straight sided, glass, "Coca-Cola Bottling Co.," Decatur, large *S* embossed up the body of the bottle, aqua, 9 oz., VG, $65.00 C.

Straight sided, glass, "Registered... Coca-Cola...Bottling Co...To Be Returned to Paducah, KY," clear, 1903 – 1915, 6.5 oz., EX, $85.00 C.

B. J. Summers.

Straight side, glass, Biedenharm Candy Co., Vicksburg, MS, with the script "Coca-Cola" embossed on the edge of the base, aqua, 1905, EX, $525.00 C.

Collectors Auction Services.

Syrup, glass, "Coca-Cola," with paper label, metal screw-on cap, 1960s, one gal., EX, $12.00 C.

B. J. Summers.

Syrup, glass, "Drink Coca-Cola" inside etched wreath, metal cap, 1910s, EX, $600.00 C.

Syrup, glass, "Drink Coca-Cola" on label, metal cap, 1920s, EX, $400.00 C.

Syrup keg, wooden with paper label on end, 1930s, 5 gal., F, $125.00 C. *Metz Superlatives Auction.*

Contour, metal, with hobbleskirt bottle on outside, produced to feel like a hobbleskirt bottle, trial issue that didn't work, 1990s, 12 oz., EX, $9.00 C.

Diamond, metal, full-length diamond with bottle in center of diamond, 12 oz., EX, $110.00 D.

Dynamic wave, waxed paper, "Coca-Cola" on front, prototype that was never put into production, metal top and bottom, 12 oz., EX, $175.00 C.

Dynamic wave, metal, NCAA Final Four commerative 16 oz. can and pin set, 1994, EX, $20.00 B. *Metz Superlatives Auction.*

Dynamic wave, steel, "Coca-Cola Light" pop-top lid, bought from vending machine by U.S. serviceman on overseas duty, never opened, Japanese, 250 ml., EX, $25.00 C.

Brian & Christy Kopischke.

Straight sided, metal, "Coca-Cola" circle label, syrup can for cruise ship use only, red and white, 1940s, 1 gal., G, $250.00 B. *Metz Superlatives Auction.*

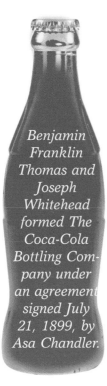

Benjamin Franklin Thomas and Joseph Whitehead formed The Coca-Cola Bottling Company under an agreement signed July 21, 1899, by Asa Chandler.

Straight sided, metal, paper label syrup can, red and white, 1940s, 1 gal., EX, $350.00 D.

163

Bell, glass, "Drink Coca-Cola," clear, 1940 – 1960s, EX, $20.00 C. *Mitchell Collection.*

Bell, pewter, "Coca-Cola," scarce, 1930s, EX, $375.00 B. *Metz Superlatives Auction.*

Bell, glass, "Enjoy Coke," set of four different sizes, 1960 – 1970s, EX, $25.00 D.

Bell anniversary, glass, presented to John W. Boucher, 1936, NM, $375.00 B. *Metz Superlatives Auction.*

Bell, glass, "Drink Coca-Cola 5¢," acid-etched arrow and syrup line, 1912 – 1913, EX, $875.00 B. *Metz Superlatives Auction.*

Flare, glass, "Drink Coca-Cola," etched syrup line, clear, 1910s, EX, $500.00 C. *Mitchell Collection.*

Modified flare, glass, "Coca-Cola," clear, 1926, EX, $250.00 C. *Mitchell Collection.*

Glass holder, metal, "Coca-Cola," new, EX, $25.00 C. *Mitchell Collection.*

Glass holder, "Coca-Cola," silver, 1900, VG, $2,400.00 B. *Metz Superlatives Auction.*

Creamer, "Drink Coca-Cola" matches sugar bowl, red on white, 1930s, VG, $350.00 C. *Mitchell Collection.*

Nut dish, "Coca-Cola," different world scenes, 1960s, 11½" x 11½", EX, $145.00 C.

Sandwich plate, "Drink Coca-Cola...Good with Food," scalloped edge, Wellsville China Co., white, 1940 – 1950s, 7½" dia., VG, $750.00 B. *Metz Superlatives Auction.*

Sandwich plate, "Drink Coca-Cola...Refresh Yourself," bottle and glass in center, 1930s, 8¼" dia., NM, $1,200.00 B. *Metz Superlatives Auction.*

Sandwich plate, "Drink Coca-Cola...Refresh Your-self," bottle and glass in center, Knowles China Co., 1931, 8¼" dia., NM, $775.00 B. *Metz Superlatives Auction.*

Sugar bowl, Drink Coca-Cola...Refresh Yourself," complete with lid that's most often missing, red on white, 1930s, M, $395.00 C. *Mitchell Collection.*

Metal, Western Coca-Cola Bottling Co., dark-haired beauty in a reflective pose, Coke advertising is in small print on the reverse side of the tray. Probably designed for the saloon trade; the subject matter could have been considered risqué for the time. 1908 – 1912, 9⅞" dia., 16" sq. with frame, EX, $425.00 C.

Metal, Western Coca-Cola Bottling Co., dark haired lady with a very low drape pose, 1908 – 1912, 9⅞" dia., 16" sq. in frame, EX, $450.00 C.

Metal, Western Coca-Cola Bottling Co., dark-haired lady with red cap, 1908 – 1912, 9⅞" dia., 16" sq. in frame, EX, $475.00 C.

Metal, Western Coca-Cola Bot-tling Co., dark-haired woman with yellow cap, 1908 – 1912, 9⅞" dia., 16" sq. in frame, EX, $425.00 C.

Due to the questionable nature of these plates, the Coca-Cola advertising is located on the back side.

Metal, Western Coca-Cola Bottling Co., pretty brunette with a red scarf in her hair and holding a pink rose, 1908 – 1912, 9⅞" dia., 16" sq. in frame, EX, $500.00 C.

Metal, Western Coca-Cola Bottling Co., dark-haired beauty with very revealing pose for the times, 1908 – 1912, 9⅞" dia., 16" sq. in frame, EX, $450.00 C.

Metal, Western Coca-Cola Bottling Co., risqué drape pose of a pretty red-headed woman, 1908 – 1912, 9⅞" dia., 16" sq. in frame, EX, $500.00 C.

Metal, Western Coca-Cola Bottling Co., with long-haired beauty in a drape with her head turned. These were produced in a shadow box–type frame; however, few of the frames seem to exist today. 1908 – 1912, 9⅞" dia., EX, $495.00 D.

Metal, Western Coca-Cola Bottling Co., topless long-haired beauty, this is the one everyone is after, a very popular plate, double the value shown if the original shadow box is still with the plate, 1908 – 1912, 9⅞" dia., 16" sq. in frame, EX, $1,200.00 C.

Metal, Western Coca-Cola Bottling Co., young auburn-haired beauty with red adornment in her hair, 1908 – 1912, 9⅞" dia., 16" sq. in frame, EX, $450.00 C.

Pocket, cardboard, "Drink Coca-Cola in Bottles," folding in shape of cat's head, 1920s, EX, $895.00 C. *Mitchell Collection.*

Pocket, celluloid, "Drink Coca-Cola," featuring Elaine with a straight sided paper label bottle in her hand, 1916, 1¾" x 2¾", G, $225.00 B. *Metz Superlatives Auction.*

Pocket, celluloid, "Drink Delicious Coca-Cola" featuring the Hamilton King Coca-Cola girl, 1911, 1¾" x 2¾", F, $195.00 B. *Metz Superlatives Auction.*

Pocket, celluloid, "Drink Coca-Cola," with one of the Hamilton King Coke girls, 1910, 1¾" x 2¾", EX, $375.00 B. *Metz Superlatives Auction.*

Pocket, celluloid, "Wherever You Go You Will Find Coca-Cola at All Fountains 5¢," round, 1900s, G, $950.00 C. *Mitchell Collection.*

Wall, glass and metal, "Drink Coca-Cola in Bottles," with silhouette girl at bottom and thermometer on left side, 1939, 10" x 14¼", VG, $850.00 B. *Metz Superlatives Auction.*

Wall, glass and wood, "Drink Coca-Cola in Bottles...Coca-Cola Bottling Co. ...Madisonville, KY," arched top, 1920 – 1930s, 8" x 17½", G, $600.00 C. *Mitchell Collection.*

Desk, metal, "Drink Coca-Cola," scale measurement in both Celsius and Fahrenheit, 1940s, VG, $55.00 C. *Mitchell Collection.*

Metal, metal, "Drink Coca-Cola," die-cut double-bottle gold version, 1942, 7" x 16", EX, $525.00 C. *Mitchell Collection.*

Wall, card-board, "Drink Coca-Cola," retailers' reference for regulator settings according to air temperature, 1960s, VG, $75.00 C. *Mitchell Collection.*

Wall, Masonite, "Drink Coca-Cola...Thirst Knows No Season," bottle with tilted scale, 1940s, 6¾" x 17", EX, $500.00 C. *Mitchell Collection.*

Wall, metal and glass, "Drink Coca-Cola in Bottles," round dial type reading, 1950s, 12" dia, EX, $250.00 B. *Metz Superlatives Auction.*

Wall, metal and glass, "Enjoy Coca-Cola," round dial-type reading, 1960s, 12" dia., EX, $155.00 B. *Metz Superlatives Auction.*

Wall, metal and glass, "Drink Coca-Cola...Sign of Good Taste," a round Robertson scale, white on red, 1950s, 12" dia., EX, $150.00 C. *Mitchell Collection.*

Wall, metal and plastic "Things Go Better with Coke," round Pam with dial type scale reading, 1950s, 12" dia., NM, $250.00 B. *Metz Superlatives Auction.*

Wall, metal, "Buvez Coca-Cola...La Soif N'a Pas de Saison," French Canadian with silhouette girl at bottom, 1940s, 5¾" x 18", G, $300.00 C.

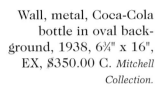

Wall, metal, "Buvez Coca-Cola," with bottle and scale reading, 6" x 16", NM, $350.00 B. *Metz Superlatives Auction.*

Wall, metal, Coca-Cola bottle in oval background, 1938, 6¾" x 16", EX, $350.00 C. *Mitchell Collection.*

Wall, metal, "Coca-Cola," die-cut bottle with scale in main body of piece, 1956, 5" x 17", NM, $160.00 B. *Metz Superlatives Auction.*

Wall, metal, "Coca-Cola," die-cut embossed 1923 Christmas bottle, 1931, VG, $210.00 B. *Metz Superlatives Auction.*

Wall, metal, "Coca-Cola," embossed Spanish bottle on background, 1950s, 6" x 18", EX, $150.00 B. *Metz Superlatives Auction.*

Wall, metal, "Coca-Cola" gold bottle with scale type reading in center of bottle body, 1956, 2¼" x 7½", NM, 75.00 C.

Wall, metal, "Drink Coca-Cola...Be Really Refreshed," round dial with fishtail logo in center, 1959, 12" dia., NM, $600.00 B. *Metz Superlatives Auction.*

170

Wall, metal, "Drink Coca-cola Delicious and Refreshing" with silhouette girl at bottom of scale, 1930s, 6½" x 16", EX, $500.00 C. *Mitchell Collection.*

Wall, metal, "Drink Coca-Cola in Bottles...Quality Refreshment," button at top and scale-type reading, 1950s, EX, $225.00 C. *Mitchell Collection.*

Wall, metal, "Drink Coca-Cola in Bottles...Serve Coke at Home," embossed with Art Deco styling, 1948, 9" tall, EX, $165.00 C. *Collectors Auction Services.*

Wall, metal, "Drink Coca-Cola in Bottles," with notations for oil, grease, and battery, from Dyersburg, TN bottler, 1940s, VG, $55.00 C. *Mitchell Collection.*

Wall, metal, "Drink Coca-Cola...Sign of Good Taste," known as the cigar thermometer due to the shape, good working scale, red and white, 1950s, 8" x 30", EX, $575.00 B. *Wm. Morford Investment Grade Collectibles.*

Wall, metal, "Drink Coca-Cola...Sign of Good Taste...Refresh Yourself," because of the design this is known as the cigar thermometer, 1950s, 8" x 29", EX, $450.00 C.

Wall, metal & plastic "Drink Coca-Cola," Pam dial-type scale with red center and green outside ring, 1950s, 12" dia., EX, $475.00 B. *Metz Superlatives Auction.*

Wall, plastic "Drink Coca-Cola," prototype with square numbers, 15" sq., EX, $650.00 B. *Metz Superlatives Auction.*

171

Wall, porcelain, "Drink Coca-Cola...Coke Refreshes," vertical scale in center, 1940s, 8" x 36", F, $750.00 B. *Metz Superlatives Auction.*

Wall, porcelain, "Drink Coca-Cola...Thirst Knows No Season," Canadian green version with silhouette girl at bottom, 1940s, 5¾" x 18", M, $1,700.00 B. *Collectors Auction Services.*

Wall, plastic, "Enjoy Coca-Cola," with vertical scale, message panel at bottom, 1960s, 7" x 18", G, $45.00 C.

Wall, plastic, "Enjoy TAB," vertical scale with message panel at bottom, 1960s, 7" x 18", EX, $65.00 C. *Mitchell Collection.*

Wall, porcelain, "Drink Coca-Cola...Thirst Knows No Season," Canadian, with silhouette girl at bottom, 1942, 5¾" x 18", VG, $450.00 B. *Metz Superlatives Auction.*

Wall, wooden, "Drink Coca-Cola 5¢...Delicious Refreshing," vertical scale, 1905 – 1910, 5" x 21", VG, $525.00 B. *Wm. Morford Investment Grade Collectibles.*

Wall, wooden, "Drink Coca-Cola in Bottles...," vertical scale, from V. O. Colson Co., Paris, IL, 1910s, VG, $725.00 C. *Mitchell Collection.*

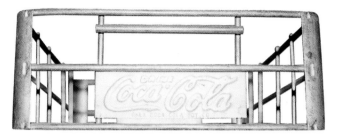

Case, aluminum, "Drink Coca-Cola" on ends, 1940s, 24 bottle, EX, $55.00 C.

Case, 24-bottle, wood, "Refresh Yourself...Drink Coca-Cola in Bottles," very early case with dove-tailed joints, 1920s, EX, $295.00 C.

Case, metal, "Drink Coca-Cola" metal case carrier with wire handles, 1950 – 1960s, G, $95.00 C. *Metz Superlatives Auction.*

Display rack, cardboard, "Drink Coca-Cola...Take Home a Carton," multiple-level store unit, 1930s, VG, $725.00 B. *Metz Superlatives Auction.*

Case, metal, "Coca-Cola," polished aluminum case with rounded corners, 1940 – 1950s, 24 bottles, EX, $140.00 B. *Metz Superlatives Auction.*

Display rack, metal and wire, "Drink Coca-Cola" disc with three tiers for cartons, unusual and difficult to find, 1940s, F, $290.00 B. *Metz Superlatives Auction.*

Display rack, cardboard, "Shop...Coca-Cola...Here," carton unit for store use, 1950s, 14" x 20" x 8", EX, $235.00 B. *Metz Superlatives Auction.*

Display rack,
metal and wire,
"Drink Coca-
Cola...Take
Enough Home,"
fold-out wire
body for store
use with metal
courtesy panel
at top, EX,
$175.00 C.
Patrick's Collectibles.

Display rack, metal
and wire, "Take Some
Coca-Cola Home
Today," wire body
with top courtesy
panel and metal
wheels on bottom,
EX, $295.00 C.

Display rack, metal,
"Coca-Cola...6 bottles
25¢," early and hard-to-
find store fixture, 1930s,
NM, $825.00 B. *Metz
Superlatives Auction.*

Display rack, metal, "Drink
Coca-Cola...Regular size," store
use for several cartons, spring
loaded shelves for easy use and
storage, 1960s, EX, $100.00 B.
Metz Superlatives Auction.

Display rack,
metal, "Place
Empties
Here...Thank
You," three-case
store rack for
placement beside
a vending
machine, G,
$425.00 C.

Display rack, metal,
"Drink Coca-Cola"
courtesy panel at
top, 1940 – 1950s,
47" tall, EX, $225.00
B. *Metz Superlatives Auction.*

Display rack, metal,
"Take Home a
Carton...Coca-Cola."
store carton display,
round message panel
at top, 1930s, 55" tall,
VG, $500.00 B. *Metz
Superlatives Auction.*

Display rack, metal, "Things Go Better with Coke," miniature salesman' sample with cases of miniature bottles, 1960s, NM, $2,200.00 B. *Metz Superlatives Auction.*

Six pack, aluminum, Coca-Cola...Delicious...Refreshing," slanted top, wire handle, separate bottle compartments, 1950s, EX, $85.00 C. *Mitchell Collection.*

Six-pack, aluminum, "Coca-Cola" embossed on sides, rolled metal handle, 1940 – 1950s, EX, $95.00 C. *Mitchell Collection.*

Six-pack, aluminum, "Drink Coca-Cola" embossed and painted on sides, rolled wire handle with wooden grip, 1950s, EX, $135.00 C. *Mitchell Collection.*

Six-pack, cardboard, "6 for 25¢," 1939, EX, $95.00 C. *Mitchell Collection.*

Six-pack, aluminum, "Drink Coca-Cola...King Size," lettered on sides, wire handle, 1950s, EX, $125.00 C. *Mitchell Collection.*

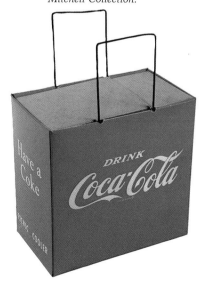

Six-pack, cardboard, "Drink Coca-Cola," straight-sided box with wire handles, 1956, EX, $140.00 C. *Mitchell Collection.*

Six-pack, cardboard, "Season's Greetings...Drink Coca-Cola," with Christmas motif, 1930 – 1940s, VG, $75.00 C. *Mitchell Collection.*

Six-pack, wood, "Pause...Go Refreshed," wire handle with wood grip and wood bottle compart- ments, wings under message on carton end, 1930s, EX, $450.00 B. *Metz Superlatives Auction.*

Six-pack, cardboard, "Six Bottles...Coca-Cola...Serve Ice Cold," 1930s, EX, $165.00 C. *Mitchell Collection.*

Six-pack, cardboard, "Six bottles...Coca-Cola...Serve Ice Cold," with pull-up handle, 1930s, EX, $145.00 C. *Mitchell Collection.*

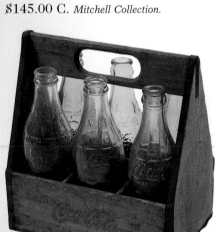

Six-pack, wood, "Drink Coca- Cola" on sides, wire handle with round wooden grip, 1930 – 1940s, EX, $120.00 C. *Mitchell Collection.*

"Serve Ice Cold" first used in 1931.

Six-pack, wooden, "Drink Coca- Cola in Bottles," wooden cut-out handle, 1940s, EX, $175.00 C. *Mitchell Collection.*

Six-pack, wooden, "Drink Coca-Cola" on sides, bent wood with round- ed corners and flat wooden handle, 1940s, VG, $165.00 C. *Mitchell Collection.*

Stadium vendor, metal, "Drink Coca-Cola," backpack with premix device and cup holder, white on red, 1950 – 1960s, G, $525.00 B. *Metz Superlatives Auction.*

Stadium vendor, metal, "Drink Coca-Cola," metal holder with curved side toward vendors body, insu- late, with canvas carrying strap, original opener on end, 1940 – 1950s, VG, $350.00 C. *Mitchell Collection.*

Chest, cardboard, "Drink Coca-Cola in Bottles," salesman's sample, 1940 – 1950s, G, $195.00 C.
Mitchell Collection.

The first standardized cooler made especially for Coca-Cola was produced by Glascock Brothers in 1929, and the cost to bottlers was $12.50.

Chest, cardboard, "Drink Coca-Cola," Westinghouse WE-6 salesman's sample, 1940 – 1950s, 4⅜" x 4" x 3", G, $475.00 C.
Mitchell Collection.

Chest, metal, "Drink Coca-Cola," salesman sample of Westinghouse standard wet box with case storage under box, complete with opener and cap catcher, EX, $2,400.00 C.
Mitchell Collection.

Chest, metal, "Drink Coca-Cola," Cavalier wet box with fold in the middle top and storage space for cases under box, EX, $750.00 D – 995.00 C.

Chest, metal, "Drink Coca-Cola Ice Cold," lift-top bottle opener with cap catcher, will cool two cases. Has no vending device, so it's an honor-system machine. 1940 – 1950s, 18½" x 18½" x 40¼", EX, $1,595.00 D – 2,000.00 C.

Picnic, metal, "Drink Coca-Cola," Acton-produced unit still with original box, metal swing handle, tray is still inside, 1950 – 1960s, 17" x 12" x 19", EX, $395.00 C.

Chest, wood and zinc, "Help Yourself...Drink Coca-Cola...Deposit in Box 5¢," very early lined box with side handles and hinged top, red on yellow, 1920s, VG, $325.00 B. *Metz Superlatives Auction.*

When Westinghouse introduced its line of coolers in 1934, the Glascock coolers' popularity began to diminish.

Picnic, metal, "Drink Coca-Cola," airline with round metal handle on top, 1950s, G, $325.00 B. *Metz Superlatives Auction.*

Picnic, metal, "Drink Coca-Cola" Cavalier in original box, in unused condition, 1950s, NM, $275.00 B. *Metz Superlatives Auction.*

Picnic, metal, "Drink Coca-Cola in Bottles," with swing-type handle and lock, removable top, white on red, 1950s, VG, $145.00 C. *Mitchell Collection.*

Picnic, metal, "Drink Coca-Cola," junior stainless steel with removeable lid and swing handle lock, 1950s, 12" x 9" x 14", EX, $650.00 B. *Metz Superlatives Auction.*

Picnic, metal, "Drink Coca-Cola in Bottles," large with message on front, wire handles on each side, opener on one side at handle, hinged lift top, G, $135.00 C.

Picnic, metal, "Drink Coca-Cola," stainless look with swing handle and lock, six-pack size, EX, $425.00 B. *Metz Superlatives Auction.*

Picnic, metal, "Drink Coca-Cola," unusual round design with decal on outside and zinc liner inside, white on red, 1940s, 8" x 9", VG, $250.00 B. *Metz Superlatives Auction.*

Picnic, metal, "It's the Real Thing...Drink Coca-Cola," dynamic wave logo, wire handles on side with opening top, white on red, 1960s, 18" x 13" x 16½", G, $185.00 D. *Patrick's Collectibles.*

Picnic, metal, bottle-in-hand decal, bail-type handle, 1940s, 8" x 12" x 13", EX, $100.00 B. *Metz Superlatives Auction.*

Picnic, vinyl, "Coke Adds Life to Everything Nice," zip top, red and white, 1960 – 1970s, 13" x 13" x 9", EX, $45.00 C.

Picnic, stainless steel, "Drink Coca-Cola," airline cooler with top embossed "Northwest Airlines," unusual in the short body height, good top handle with snap-down locks, stainless steel, 1940 – 1950s, 9½" tall, EX, $750.00 B. *Metz Superlatives Auction.*

The Glascock Brothers Mfg. Co of Muncie, IN, produced many of the early coolers that are so collectible today. One was a portable unit that resembled the Standard model fitted on a three-wheel dolly.

179

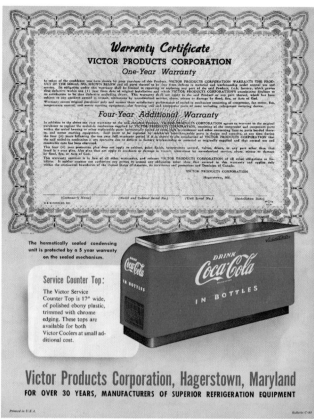

INTRODUCING *Victor* Counter Coolers FOR COCA-COLA

Available in two big sizes—31 and 45 case capacity. These famous Victor Dry Counter Coolers are made especially for bottlers of Coca-Cola*... the last word in self-service merchandisers. Think of it! The Victor Model C-31, pictured above, occupies only 15.2 square feet of floor space and its capacity is 31 cases.

For use in any location—either self-service or under the counter. Can be used as a counter when equipped with service counter

top. Removable, rust-proof, heavy wire dividers can be adjusted to accommodate any storage arrangement. Meets all health codes. Glide-back lids permit instant service and easy access to each section. Victor Counter Coolers for Coca-Cola are equipped with hermetically sealed condensing units protected by five year warranty on the sealed mechanism.

MODEL C-31

*"Coca-Cola" and its abbreviation "Coke" are the registered trademarks which distinguish the product of The Coca-Cola Company.

DESIGNED FOR *Greater Sales* ... CONSTRUCTED FOR LONG, *Service-Free Life!*

Warranty Certificate
VICTOR PRODUCTS CORPORATION
One-Year Warranty

Four-Year Additional Warranty

The hermetically sealed condensing unit is protected by a 5 year warranty on the sealed mechanism.

Service Counter Top: The Victor Service Counter Top is 17" wide, of polished ebony plastic, trimmed with chrome edging. These tops are available for both Victor Coolers at small additional cost.

Victor Products Corporation, Hagerstown, Maryland
FOR OVER 30 YEARS, MANUFACTURERS OF SUPERIOR REFRIGERATION EQUIPMENT

Printed in U.S.A.

Victor Dry Counter Coolers for COCA-COLA

furnish ample reserve stock where you need it most ... IN THE COOLER!

SPECIFICATIONS

Cooling Capacity: Model C-31, thirty-one cases of Coca-Cola. Model C-45, forty-five cases of Coca-Cola.

Outside Dimensions: Model C-31: 75½" wide, 29" deep, 40" high. Model C-45: 98½" wide, 29" deep, 40" high.

Exterior Shell: Heavy gauge cold rolled steel, bonderized against rust for perfect finish and long life.

Interior Shell: Heavy gauge galvanized steel; resists rust, cleans easily.

Insulation: High efficiency Fiberglas 3 inches thick; keeps temperatures and operating costs down.

Compressor: Model C-31, hermetically sealed Tecumseh unit, Model C-45, ⅓ H.P. hermetically sealed Tecumseh unit. (Service cord is not furnished with ⅓ H.P. units. Electrical connection to junction box is required to comply with Underwriters, CSA and local codes.)

Cooling Coil: Oversize, self-defrosting finned coil, forced convection type; gives rapid heat removal.

Fan Motor: Lifetime oiled heavy duty motor, directly connected to four blade fan, forces a constant stream of cold air over each bottle ... cooling top bottles FIRST. Fan motor 110 volt, 60 cycle, single phase current.

Lids: Disappearing lids glide on tempered brass track; allow full use of cooler during rush periods.

Dividers: Removable, rust-proof, heavy wire dividers can be adjusted to provide the desired size storage compartment in each section. Facilitates proper rotation of stocks during peak output of sales.

Apron: Stainless steel apron on service side prevents cabinet from being marred by bottles and cases; gives protection at point of greatest use.

Crown Catcher: Special removable crown catchers at each end of cabinet. Large capacity, leak-proof crown containers can be emptied in a jiffy ... no mess on floor.

Kick Plate: Black enamel inset around base gives greater comfort to both dealers and customers; prevents finish from being scratched.

Drain: ¾" drain outlet—plus directional elbow—in left hand front end makes cabinet easy to clean and keep clean.

Approximate Shipping Weight When Crated: Model C-31, 680 lbs. Model C-45, 825 lbs.

Warranty: 5 year warranty.

Counter Tops: Additional accessory—constructed of heavy plywood covered with Formica and trimmed in chrome edging.

All specifications and descriptions are subject to change without notice.

OUTSTANDING FEATURES

★ Exclusive Victor design, controlled forced air cooling system chills top bottles first and unbelievably fast.

★ Lids glide back. No lifting strain. Easy access to bottles with greatest chill exposure.

★ Unmatched temperature recovery after loading warm bottles.

★ Super cooling capacity, assuring efficient normal operation *even in prolonged high temperatures.*

★ Big capacity per square foot of floor space.

★ Designed for merchandising. Increases impulse buying at point of sale.

- Stainless Steel Apron Protects Point of Greatest Use
- Heavy Gauge Cold Rolled Steel Bonderized
- Heavy Fiberglas Insulation
- Coldest Bottles Always on Top
- Two Crown Pullers
- Glide Back Lids
- Two Removable Crown Catchers
- Recessed Kick Plate
- Baked on Enamel Finish
- Sealed Compressor Protected by a 5 Year Warranty
- Model C-45 45 Case Capacity
- Model C-31 31 Case Capacity (See Cover)

Retailer leaflet, paper, "Drink Coca-Cola in Bottles" shown on coolers in pictures, informational material for retailer about the Victor C-31, at one time a very popular machine in lunchrooms, four pages, 1950s, 8½" x 11", EX, $25.00 C.

Selling aid, plastic, salesman's sample for route salesman, EX, $195.00 C. *Mitchell Collection.*

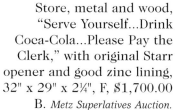

Store, metal and wood, "Serve Yourself...Drink Coca-Cola...Please Pay the Clerk," with original Starr opener and good zinc lining, 32" x 29" x 2¼", F, $1,700.00 B. *Metz Superlatives Auction.*

Store, metal, "Drink Coca-Cola," Glascock junior complete with cap catcher, which is a hard-to-locate item, 1929, EX, $2,200.00 C, *Mitchell Collection.*

Store, metal, "Buvez Coca-Cola," foreign with fish-tail design logo and two center-hinge top-opening lids that expose the Cokes in one large compart-ment, 42" x 35" x 27", G, $275.00 B – 350.00 C.

Store, metal, "Drink Coca-Cola." Two-piece unit — top is picnic cooler and bottom is designed to sit on the floor and accept the top. 1950s, 17" x 12" x 39", EX, $3,100.00 B. *Metz Superlatives Auction.*

Store, metal, "Drink Coca-Cola," Westinghouse salesman's sample of wet box, red and white, EX, $2,750.00 D.

Store, metal, salesman's sample of Glascock junior, with the original carrying case, all four side panels with the "Drink Coca-Cola" logo, next to impossible to find in this shape with the original case, 1929, EX, $28,000.00 B. *Metz Superlatives Auction.*

Store, metal, "Ice Cold Coca-Cola Sold Here," floor model with embossed hobbleskirt bottle beside message, on rollers for ease of movement, lift top, 29" x 32½" x 22", VG, $950.00 B. *Metz Superlatives Auction.*

Store, wood and plastic, "Drink Coca-Cola," salesman's sample of counter dispenser, still with original carrying box, 1960S, 4½" x 6½" x 6¼", EX, $2,500.00 B. *Metz Superlatives Auction.*

Store, metal, "Serve Yourself...Drink Coca-Cola...Please Pay Cashier," salesman's sample Glascock, complete with miniature cases of bottles on storage rack beneath wet box, NM, $2,300.00 C. *Mitchell Collection.*

Store, wood and zinc, "Drink Coca-Cola Delicious Refreshing," wet box with zinc-lined inside, 1920s, 38" x 20" x 35", F, $950.00 B. *Metz Superlatives Auction.*

Dispenser, metal, "No-Drip Protectors...Keeps Your Hands and Clothing Dry," self-serve dispenser, 1930s, 4½" x 8" x 2¼", EX, $100.00 – 145.00 C. *Metz Superlatives Auction.*

Dispenser, metal, with two original sleeves and original box with mounting instructions, not marked, 6½" x 5", EX, $170.00 B. *Autopia Advertising Auctions.*

Paper, "Drink Coca-Cola...Delicious and Refreshing...a Great Drink...with Good Things to Eat," couple cooking outside and enjoying a bottle of Coke, 1930 – 1940s, 3¾" x 6½", EX, $10.00 – 14.00 C. *B. J. Summers.*

Paper, "Drink Coca-Cola...So Refreshing with Food," woman with cafeteria tray and a bottle of Coke, 1932, VG, $15.00 – 25.00 C. *Mitchell Collection.*

Paper, "Drink Coca-Cola Delicious and Refreshing...Makes a Light Lunch Refreshing," man and woman at lunch counter, 1940s, EX, $15.00 – 20.00 C.

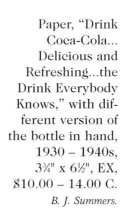

Paper, "Drink Coca-Cola... Delicious and Refreshing...the Drink Everybody Knows," with different version of the bottle in hand, 1930 – 1940s, 3¾" x 6½", EX, $10.00 – 14.00 C. *B. J. Summers.*

Paper, "Every Bottle Refreshes...Drink Coca-Cola," 1930 – 1940s, 3¾" x 6½", EX, $6.00 – 8.00 C.
B. J. Summers.

Paper, "It's the Real Thing" pretty lady with bottle of Coke, 1920 – 1930s, 3¾" x 6½", EX, $8.00 – 12.00 C. *B. J. Summers.*

Paper, "Now...You Can Buy a Guaranteed Glass — the Distinctive Coca-Cola Glass," hand holding a full Coke glass, EX, $15.00 – 20.00 C. *Metz Superlatives Auction.*

Paper, "Our Sandwiches...Delicious with Ice Cold Coca-Cola," hobbleskirt bottle and sandwich, 1931, EX, $25.00 – 40.00 C. *Mitchell Collection.*

Paper, "Quality Carries on...Drink Coca-Cola," bottle in hand, 1930 – 1940s, 3¾" x 6½", EX, $8.00 – 12.00 C.
B. J. Summers.

Paper, "Take Home a Carton...So Easy to Serve at Home," cardboard six-pack, six for 25¢, 1930 – 1940s, 3¾" x 6½", EX, $10.00 – 15.00 C. *B J. Summers.*

Changer, metal, "Drink Coca-Cola...Serve Yourself," made by Vendo Co., with 1938 and 1940 dates, 1940s, 8" x 8½" x 4½", VG, $125.00 – 150.00 C.

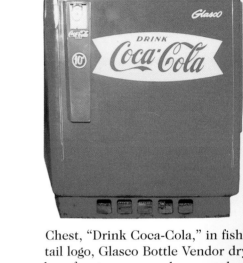

Chest, "Drink Coca-Cola," in fishtail logo, Glasco Bottle Vendor dry box, front opener and cap catcher, slider top, Muncie, IN, 1960s, 35½" x 20" x 40", EX, $950.00 – 1,250.00 D.

Chest, metal, "Coca-Cola," decal lettering, lift-top lid, bottle opener and cap catcher, 32" x 18" x 41", F, $700.00 D.

Chest, metal, "Drink Coca-Cola," Cavalier C-27 with lift top and star handle, sought after in part because of the size, white on red, 1940 – 1950, 18" x 22" x 41", EX, $1,400.00 B. *Metz Superlatives Auction.*

Chest, metal, "Drink Coca-Cola...Ice Cold," Westinghouse ten-case master, top lid hinges in the middle and lifts from both ends, 1950s, 30½" x 36" x 45", NM, $1,850.00 D. *Patrick's Collectibles.*

Chest, metal, "Drink Coca-Cola in Bottles...Ice Cold," Vendo #23, also known as the spin top, found in standard and deluxe models (depends on top and other colors), 1950s, 24" x 36" x 21", EX, $1,395.00 D – 1,695.00 D.

The Vendo Company introduced its coin changer shortly following WWII due to the huge demand for nickels for vending machines.

Coin changer, metal, "Have a Coke," Vendo coin changer with keys, sign on this one is a reproduction, EX, $625.00 B. *Metz Superlatives Auction.*

Cooler, chest, plastic, "Drink Coca-Cola in Bottles," plastic store POP display, built to resemble a Vendo V-81, EX, $375.00 D.

Upright, metal, "Drink Coca-Cola in Bottles," Vendolator 72, lettering is embossed, dispenses 72 bottles, precools six, double drop chute, paddle handle, 1950s, 25" x 58" x 15", G, $1,800.00 C.

Upright, metal, "Drink Coca-Cola in Bottles," Vendo V-39, very desirable machine due to its small size, also fairly common and easy to find, 1940 – 1950s, 27" x 58" x 16", NM, $2,995.00 D.
Patrick's Collectibles.

Upright, metal, "Drink Coca-Cola in Bottles," Vendo V-81, a much sought-after machine for home use mostly due to its size and eye appeal, 1950s, 27" x 58" x 16", VG, $1,500.00 C.
Mike and Debbie Summers.

Upright, metal, "Drink Coca-Cola in Bottles," Westinghouse model 42T, sides embossed with "Here's a Coke for You," single drop chute, will hold 42 bottles, 1950s, 25" x 20" x 53½", EX, $2,295.00 D. *Riverside Antique Mall.*

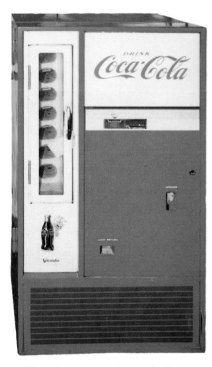

Upright, metal, "Drink Coca-Cola," Vendo HA56-B, front opening see through door, 1960s, EX, $795.00 D. *Riverside Antique Mall.*

Upright, metal, "Drink Coca-Cola," Vendolator Dual 27, dispenses 27 bottles, successor to the tabletop machine, 1950s, 25½" x 52" x 17½", NM, $2,295.00 D. *Patrick's Collectibles.*

Upright, metal, Vendo #44, "Drink Coca-Cola," two tone with white top and red bottom, 1950s, 16" x 57½" x 15½", NM, $2,400.00 B – 275.00 C, *Metz Superlatives Auction.*

Bottle, Bakelite, "Drink Coca-Cola," shaped like a hobbleskirt bottle, made by Crosley, Cincinnati, 1930s (1931 – 1934), 7½" dia. x 24" tall, EX, $5,500.00 B. *Metz Superlatives Auction.*

Bottle, plastic, "Enjoy Coca-Cola," AM-FM in shape of hobbleskirt bottle, 1970s, EX, $45.00 C. *Mitchell Collection.*

Can, plastic, "Enjoy Coca-Cola" and dynamic wave, 1970s, EX, $50.00 C. *Mitchell Collection.*

Cooler, plastic and metal, "Coca-Cola Refreshes You Best," an extremely hard-to-locate item, designed to resemble an airline cooler, top lifts to reveal controls, 1950s, G, $3,800.00 B. *Metz Superlatives Auction.*

Store cooler, plastic, "Drink Coca-Cola." In shape of the lift top cooler, this is probably the most sought-after radio for collectors. Prices will vary greatly on this item — I've seen them sell for a couple of hundred to a couple of thousand, price is usually dictated by the type of sale and, of course, the condition. There are new versions of this on the market, just remember the new ones have FM. White on red, 1950s, VG, $975.00 C.

Store cooler, plastic, "Drink Coca-Cola," small version that is a crystal radio. If all pieces and instructions are present, add approximately 40% to the price given. EX, $235.00 C. *Mitchell Collection.*

Vending machine, plastic, "Coke," upright machine, 1980s, EX, $95.00 C. *Mitchell Collection.*

Vending machine, plastic, "Drink Coca-Cola," upright design with left-hand see-through door, 1960s, G, $165.00 C.
Mitchell Collection.

Radio, vending machine, plastic, "Drink Coca-Cola," upright machine with double drop chute, F, $200.00 C.
Mitchell Collection.

Vending machine, plastic, "Enjoy Coca-Cola," upright design with dynamic wave panel at top, 1970s, EX, $135.00 C. *Mitchell Collection.*

Vending machine, plastic, "Enjoy Coke," upright design with vertical dynamic wave panel and push-button selectors on right, 1970s, EX, $135.00 C.
Mitchell Collection.

Counter, metal and glass, "Drink Coca-Cola...Lunch with Us," square clock face at left of message panel, 1940 – 1950s, 19½" x 5" x 9", EX, $950.00 D.

Anniversary, glass and metal, "Drink Coca-Cola" in center of clock face, small miniature bottles on bottom movements, covered by clear glass dome, 1950s, 3" x 5", EX, $975.00 C. *Mitchell Collection.*

Boudoir, leather, "Drink Bottled Coca-Cola...So Easily Served," shaped like a straight-sided bottle, gold lettering, 1910, 3" x 8", VG, $1,500.00 B. *Metz Superlatives Auction.*

Counter, metal and glass, "Drink Coca-Cola Please Pay When Served," with clock at left of message panel, 1950s, 19¼" x 9" x 5", EX, $800.00 C.

Counter, metal and glass, "Pause...Drink Coca-Cola" with Art Deco influence and great crinkle paint, large round clock at top, "Drink Coca-Cola" message panel below, rare piece, 1930s, EX, $5,700.00 C. *Mitchell Collection.*

Counter, metal and glass, "Drink Coca-Cola...Serve Yourself," light-up with clock to left of message panel, 1950s, 20" x 9", EX, $925.00 C. *Note: There were several versions of this clock produced. All are very desirable.*

Desk, china, "Coca-Cola" in red on face, rare and scarce, given to some of the better soda fountains, G, $3,500.00 C.
Mitchell Collection.

Desk, celluloid, "Drink Coca-Cola...," featuring Hilda Clark and round clock dial at lower left, 1901, 5½" x 7¼", EX, $9,000.00 C.

Desk, leather, "Drink Coca-Cola in Bottles" with gold lettering and gold hobbleskirt bottle at lower left and right, rare item, 1910, 4⅓" x 6", EX, $1,400.00 C.

Desktop, metal, "Drink Coca-Cola," German-made brass-case travel clock, 1960s, 3" x 3", EX, $145.00 C. *Mitchell Collection.*

Outside mount, metal, glass and neon, "Drink Coca-Cola...Sign of Good Taste," arched banner from nine to three, 1950s, 36" dia., NM, $1,550.00 B. *Metz Superlatives Auction.*

Wall, composition, "Coca-Cola...the Ideal Brain Tonic," Baird Clock Co., 1891 – 1895, 24" tall, EX, $5,300.00 D.

Wall, metal and wood, "Drink Coca-Cola in Bottles," with extended wings sporting the Sprite Boy decal, 1951, EX, $1,200.00 C.

Wall, metal and glass, "Drink Coca-Cola in Bottles," with tilted bottle at top, 1930s, 20" dia., G, $775.00 C. *Mitchell Collection.*

Wall, metal and glass, "Drink Coca-Cola," electric made by Swihart, 1960s, 8" x 6½" unusual, EX, $350.00 B. *Metz Superlatives Auction.*

Wall, metal and glass, "Drink Coca-Cola," in center red dot, 14½" dia., EX, $575.00 C.

Wall, metal and glass, "Drink Coca-Cola" in red fishtail logo on white background, usually seen in the red and green version, 1960s, M, $550.00 B. *Metz Superlatives Auction.*

Wall, metal and glass, "Drink Coca-Cola," light up by Modern Advertising Company, Brooklyn, NY, 1950s, 24" dia., EX, $550.00 B. *Metz Superlatives Auction.*

Wall, metal and glass, "Drink Coca-Cola" with center fishtail logo, green background, NOS, 1960s, EX, $325.00 C.

Wall, metal and glass, "Drink Coca-Cola," with silhouette girl in spotlight at bottom, 1930 – 1940s, 18" dia., VG, $775.00 B. *Metz Superlatives Auction.*

Wall, metal and plastic, "Drink Coca-Cola...Roller Skate for Fun," 1950s, 25" x 55", EX, $500.00 B. *Metz Superlatives Auction.*

Wall, metal and plastic, "Drink Coca-Cola," red and white face, EX, $495.00 C. *Mitchell Collection.*

Wall, metal and plastic, "Things Go Better with Coke," 16" x 16", EX, $105.00 D.

Wall, metal and wood, "Coca-Cola," round red dot Telechron clock with wings, 36", VG, $500.00 C. *Mitchell Collection.*

Wall, metal and glass, neon, "Drink Coca-Cola," in center with spotlight bottle at bottom, green wrinkle paint on outside, 1930s, 16" x 16", EX, $825.00 B. *Metz Superlatives Auction.*

Wall, metal and wood, "Drink Coca-Cola" in red center dot, with metal on wood wings, 1950s, 17½" dia., EX, $350.00 C.

Wall, metal and glass, "Coca-Cola," unusual bronze electric with original plastic cover over the hands, not easily found, 1940 – 1950s, EX, $650.00 B. *Metz Superlatives Auction.*

Wall, metal and glass, neon, "Ice Cold Coca-Cola" with spotlight silhouette girl at bottom of circle, 1940s, 18" x 18", VG, $1,600.00 B. *Metz Superlatives Auction.*

Wall, plastic, "Drink Coca-Cola," dynamic wave at bottom, 1970s, EX, $20.00 D.

Wall, plastic, "Enjoy Coca-Cola" in lower panel containing dynamic wave, 1970s, EX, $40.00 B. *Metz Superlatives Auction.*

Wall, wood and glass, "Coca-Cola in Bottles," Gilbert pendulum, 1930s, VG, $1,200.00 B. *Metz Superlatives Auction.*

Wall, wood and glass, "Drink Coca-Cola in Bottles," wood frame, glass front with red message circle in center of face, 1939, 16" x 16", G, $250.00 D.

Wall, wood and glass, "Drink Coca-Cola" on well-worn face, Gilbert regulator, 1910, EX, $6,000.00 B. *Metz Superlatives Auction.*

Wall, wood and glass, "In Bottles," Gilbert regulator that hung in many bottlers offices. This one hung in the old location of the Paducah Coca-Cola Bottling Co. office on Jackson St. This clock has only had three owners since the early removal from the Coke office. 1920 – 1930s, EX, $2,100.00 C. *Mitchell Collection.*

Wall, wood and glass, Ingram regulator, 1905, VG, $950.00 B. *Metz Superlatives Auction.*

Wall, wood, "Drink Coca-Cola," Welch octagon schoolhouse, 1901, EX, $1,800.00 D.

Wall; wood, glass, and composition; "Drink Coca-Cola 5¢ Delicious Refreshing," Baird Clock Co., 15-day movement, 1896 – 1899, EX, $6,725.00 C.

Handheld, metal and Bakelite, bottle opener and can opener combination, 1950s, EX, $65.00 D.

Handheld, metal and plastic, "50th Anniversary Coca-Cola in Bottles," EX, $60.00 C. *Mitchell Collection.*

Handheld, metal, "50th Anniversary," bottle shaped with opener on bottom of bottle, Nashville, TN, 1952, EX, $105.00 C. *Mitchell Collection.*

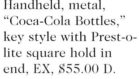

Handheld, metal and plastic, "75th Anniversary...Coca-Cola...Coca-Cola Bottling Co., Columbus, Ohio," 1970s, EX, $20.00 C. *Mitchell Collection.*

Handheld, metal and plastic, "Buvez Coca-Cola," red on plastic handle, foreign, EX, $5.00 – 10.00 D. *Collectors Auction Services..*

Handheld, metal, bottle shaped with end opener, EX, $50.00 C.

Handheld, metal, "Coca-Cola," wishbone style, 1900s, EX, $125.00 D.

Handheld, metal, "Coca-Cola Bottles," key style with Prest-o-lite square hold in end, EX, $55.00 D.

Handheld, metal, bottle shaped, 1950s, EX, $150.00 C. *Metz Superlatives Auction.*

Handheld, metal, "Drink Coca-Cola in Bottles," 1920 – 1940s, EX, $20.00 D. *Mitchell Collection.*

Handheld, metal, "Drink Bottled Coca-Cola," saber shaped, 1920s, EX, $200.00 D.

Handheld, metal, "Drink Coca-Cola," key shaped with cap likeness at top, 1920 – 1950s, F, $40.00 C. *Mitchell Collection.*

Handheld, metal, "Drink Coca-Cola in Sterlized Bottles," lollipop shaped, 1930s, EX, $115.00 C. *Mitchell Collection.*

Handheld, metal, "Drink Coca-Cola," nail puller from the Piqua Coca-Cola Bottling Co., 1960s, EX, $100.00 C. *Mitchell Collection.*

Handheld, metal, "Drink Coca-Cola in Bottles," brass, key design with the Prest-o-lite valve hole, 1910s, EX, $125.00 D. *Mitchell Collection.*

Handheld, metal, "Glascock Bros. Mfg. Co., Coca-Cola Quality Coolers," opener on one end and capper on other end, 1919 – 1920s, EX, $110.00 D.

Handheld, metal, used over the top, several versions exist, 1940s, EX, $35.00 C. *Mitchell Collection.*

Handheld, metal, hand formed, several versions exist, 1930s, EX, $30.00 C. *Mitchell Collection.*

Handheld, metal, "Have a Coke," beer-type opener, EX, $8.00 C. *Mitchell Collection.*

Handheld, metal, "Drink Coca-Cola," straight, 1910 – 1950s, EX, $35.00 – 40.00 C. *Mitchell Collection.*

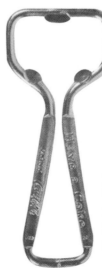

Handheld, metal, "Have a Coke," 1950 – 1960s, EX, $15.00 C. *Mitchell Collection.*

Handheld, metal, spoon opener, 1920s, 7½" long, EX, $125.00 C. *Mitchell Collection.*

Wall mount, "Drink Coca-Cola," with original box, "The Starr 'X' manufactured...by Brown Manufacturing Co.," 1940 – 1980s, EX, $35.00 D. *Mitchell Collection.*

Wall mount, metal, corkscrew, 1950s, EX, $45.00 C. *Mitchell Collection.*

Wall mount, metal, "Drink Coca-Cola," 1930s, EX, $15.00 C. *Mitchell Collection.*

Wall mount, metal, "Drink Coca-Cola," known as bent metal opener, 1950s, EX, $25.00 C. *Mitchell Collection.*

Wall mounted, corkscrew, 1920s, EX, $85.00 C. *Mitchell Collection.*

"Coca-Cola Bottling Company," one
blade and opener, 1910s, EX, $350.00 C.
Mitchell Collection.

"The Coca-Cola Bottling Co....Kaster and
Co., Germany," blade and corkscrew
(many reproductions), 1905 – 1915, EX,
$450.00 C. *Mitchell Collection.*

"Drink Coca-Cola in bottles," blade
and corkscrew, 1930s, EX, $145.00 C.
Mitchell Collection.

"Drink Coca-Cola," two
blade, G, $45.00 C. *Mitchell
Collection.*

"Enjoy Coca-Cola," single blade and nail file,
1960s, EX, $35.00 C. *Mitchell Collection.*

"Enjoy Coca-Cola," two blades
with metal handle, EX, $30.00 C.
Mitchell Collection.

In the early years of Coca-Cola, most bottlers operated only in the summer months, when demand for their product was high.

Bulb handle, wood and metal, "Coca-Cola" painted in black on handle, 1920s, VG, $65.00 C. *Mitchell Collection.*

Round handle, wood and metal, bottle opener in handle end, "Coca-Cola in bottles" in red painted lettering on handle, 1930 – 1940s, EX, $40.00 – 45.00 C. *Mitchell Collection.*

Round handle, wood and metal, bottle opener on end of handle, "Drink Coca-Cola in Bottles" in black on handle, 1920 – 1930s, EX, $50.00 C. *Mitchell Collection.*

Round handle, wood and metal, "Enjoy Coca-Cola," in painted red lettering on handle, 1960s, EX, $12.00 – 15.00 C.
Mitchell Collection.

Square handle, wood and metal, "Coca-Cola in Bottles...Ice-Coal...Phone 87," in painted black lettering on handle, 1930 – 1940s, EX, $35.00 C. *Mitchell Collection.*

Desk, ceramic, "Part-
ners...Coca-Cola" with
facsmile of baseball in
circle, 1950s, 7¼" sq.,
EX, $85.00 B. *Metz
Superlatives Auction.*

Tabletop, Bakelite and metal, match pull
from top of bottle, easily the most sought
after of all Coke ashtrays, 1940s, EX,
$1,200.00 – 1,800.00 C. *Mitchell Collection.*

Tabletop, ceramic and plastic,
"Drink Coca-Cola" logo in
bowl, miniature bottle on edge,
from Canadian bottler, 1950s,
EX, $250.00 B. *Metz Superlatives
Auction.*

Tabletop, glass, "Coca-Cola Bottling,
Company...Dickson, Tennessee,
Coca-Cola...Jerry Humphrey's," with
four cigarette groves, $20.00 – 25.00
C. EX, $25.00 C. *Mitchell Collection.*

Tabletop, glass, "Disfrute Coca-
Cola" with dynamic wave logo,
1970s, EX, $5.00 – 8.00 D.

Tabletop, metal,
"50th Anniversary"
embossed with bot-
tle and lettering,
Bronze, 1950s, EX
$75.00 – 85.00 C.
Mitchell Collection.

Tabletop, glass, set of four different shapes, ruby red glass, price is highest if box is still with set, 1950s, EX, $450.00 – 700.00 C. *Mitchell Collection.*

Tabletop, metal and plastic, bottle lighter in center with six cigarette grooves, 1950s, EX, $175.00 – 300.00 C. *Mitchell Collection.*

Tabletop, metal, "Enjoy Coca-Cola" molded cigarette holders and lettering with dynamic wave logo, EX, $35.00 – 40.00 C. *Mitchell Collection.*

Tabletop, metal, "Drink Coca-Cola...High in Quick Energy...Low in Calories," scenes of sports in bowl, 1950s, EX, $30.00 – 35.00 C. *Mitchell Collection.*

201

Pocket, metal and plastic, in shape of bottle, fairly common, 1950s, M, $45.00 C. *Mitchell Collection.*

Pocket, metal, "Drink Coca-Cola," 1950s, EX, $35.00 – 45.00 C. *Mitchell Collection.*

Pocket, metal, "Drink Coca-Cola," musical when lit, 1970s, EX, $225.00 – 250.00 C. *Mitchell Collection.*

Tabletop, Bakelite, pen holder and miniature bottle, 1950s, EX, $185.00 – 245.00 C. *Mitchell Collection.*

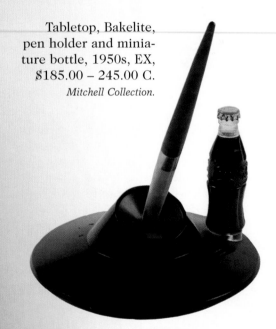

Tabletop, metal, "Coke," can shaped with dynamic wave contour, 1960 – 1970s, M, $45.00 – 55.00 C. *Mitchell Collection.*

Tabletop, metal, "Enjoy Coca-Cola," in shape of Coke can with diamond on front, 1960s, EX, $45.00 – 65.00 C. *Mitchell Collection.*

Holder, table top, metal, "Drink Coca-Cola...Be *Really* Refreshed!" holder for match books. Books could be pulled out from the bottom and refilled from the top. 1959, EX, $195.00 – 245.00 C. *Mitchell Collection.*

Matchbook, "50th Anniversary," 1936, EX, $15.00 – 20.00 C. *Mitchell Collection.*

Matchbook, "Coolers for Bottlers of Coca-Cola," G, $8.00 – 10.00 C. *Mitchell Collection.*

Matchbook, "Compliments...The Coca-Cola Bottling Co....Fulton, KY...Telephone 447," EX, $12.00 – 20.00 C. *Mitchell Collection.*

Matchbook, "A Distinctive Drink in a Distinctive Bottle," 1922, EX, $125.00 – 140.00 C. *Mitchell Collection.*

Matchbook, "Drink Coca-Cola," mock-up of Westinghouse vending machine, EX, $90.00 – 115.00 C.

Matchbook, "Have a Coke," 1950s, VG, $5.00 – 10.00 C. *Mitchell Collection.*

Matchbook, "King Size Coke," 1959, VG, $10.00 – 15.00 C. *Mitchell Collection.*

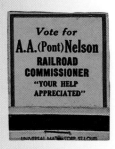

Matchbook, "Vote for A.A. Nelson, Railroad Commissioner," VG, $8.00 – 12.00 C.
Mitchell Collection.

Matchbook, "The 1982 World's Fair," 1982, EX, $8.00 – 12.00 C.
Mitchell Collection.

Matchbook, "World's Fair New York," 1964, VG, $15.00 – 20.00 C.
Mitchell Collection.

Match safe, pocket, porcelain, "Compliments of Coca-Cola Bottling Co....Union City, Tenn," combination safe and striker, 1930s, EX, $300.00 – 400.00 C.
Mitchell Collection.

Wall hung, metal, "Drink Coca-Cola in bottles...Coca-Cola Bottling Co.," 1940s, fair, $375.00 – 435.00 C.
Mitchell Collection.

Wall hung, porcelain, "Drink Coca-Cola Strike Matches Here," 1939, NM, $400.00 B. *Metz Superlatives Auction.*

"Drink Coca-Cola in bottles" first used in 1910.

Paper, "Drink Coca-Cola" on one side and advertising for the
37th American Legion Convention in Miami, FL,
Oct. 10 – 13, 1955, on the other. VG, $40.00 – 45.00 C.

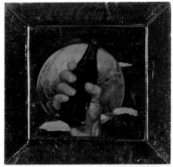

Paper foil, "Drink
Coca-Cola Ice
Cold," bottle in
hand, M, $8.00 –
12.00 C. *Mitchell
Collection.*

Paper foil, "Drink
Coca-Cola Ice Cold,"
party tray with bot-
tles of Coke, M,
$8.00 – 12.00 C.
Mitchell Collection.

Paper foil, "Drink
Coca-Cola Ice
Cold," street car
scene, mint, $8.00 –
12.00 C. *Mitchell Col-
lection.*

Paper foil, "Drink
Coca-Cola Ice Cold,"
woman being offered a
bottle of Coke, M,
$8.00 – 12.00 C.
Mitchell Collection.

From left:
Paper, "Please Put Empties in the
Rack" with bottle being placed in
bottle rack, EX, $10. 00 – 12.00 C.

Paper, "Things Go Better with
Coke" in square outline inside of
circle, EX, $10.00 – 12.00 C.

Paper, "Things Go Better with
Coke," scalloped edges, mint,
$8.00 – 12.00 C. *Mitchell Collection.*

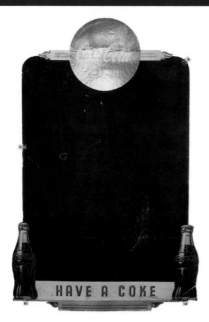

Wall hung, cardboard, "Drink Coca-Cola...Sign of Good Taste," bottle on each side of message panel, 1959, 19" x 28", NM, $250.00 B. *Metz Superlatives Auction.*

Wall hung, cardboard, "Have a Coke," button at top and double bottles at bottom, 1940s, VG, $225.00 – 255.00 C.

Wall hung, cardboard, wood and metal, "Drink Coca-Cola," with divided bottom message panel under the headings "6½ oz. size" and "12 oz. King Size," 1950s, 25" x 15", G, $175.00 B. *Metz Superlatives Auction.*

Wall hung, metal, "Coca-Cola...Sign of Good Taste," painted fishtail logo at top of chalkboard, 1959, 19½" x 28", G, $135.00 – 175.00 C.

Wall hung, metal, "Drink Coca-Cola...Be Refreshed...Have a Coke," chalkboard design, Canadian product, 1950s, EX, $325.00 – 375.00 C. *Metz Superlatives Auction.*

Wall hung, metal, "Drink Coca-Cola," bottle with tag-type panel at top of message area, chalkboard design, EX, $200.00 – 275.00 D. *Riverside Antique Mall.*

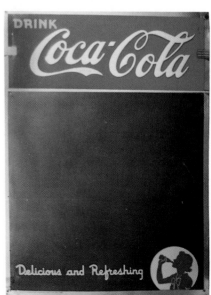

Wall hung, metal, "Drink Coca-Cola Delicious and Refreshing," with silhouette girl in lower right corner, American Art Works, Inc., Coshocton, Ohio, 1940s, 19¼" x 27", EX, $275.00 – 400.00 D. *Riverside Antique Mall.*

Wall hung, metal, "Drink Coca-Cola in Bottles" button in center, 1950s, 60" x 14", NM, $2,300.00 B. *Metz Superlatives Auction.*

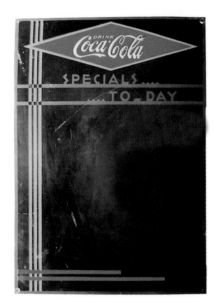

Wall hung, metal, "Drink Coca-Cola...Enjoy That Refreshing New Feeling," top fishtail design on painted background, NM, $375.00 – 450.00 B. *Metz Superlatives Auction.*

Wall hung, metal, "Drink Coca-Cola...Specials To-day," chalkboard design, 1932, EX, $450.00 – 500.00 D. *Riverside Antique Mall.*

Wall hung, metal, "Drink Coca-Cola...Specials To-day," diamond logo at top, chalk board design, 1931, EX, $300.00 – 450.00 D. *Riverside Antique Mall.*

Wall hung, metal, "Specials to-day...Drink Coca-Cola...Refresh Yourself" with bottle and straw in lower right hand corner, 1930s, VG, $325.00 B. *Metz Superlatives Auction.*

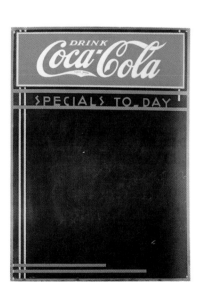

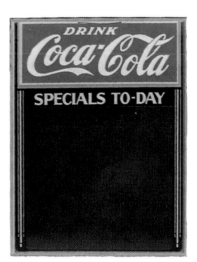

Wall hung, metal, "Drink Coca-Cola...Specials To-day," message panel at top, 1930s, G, $185.00 – 225.00 C. *Metz Superlatives Auction.*

Wall hung, metal, "Drink Coca-Cola...Specials To-day," product panel at top, chalkboard design, Canadian, difficult to locate, 1938, 17" x 24", NM, $650.00 B. *Metz Superlatives Auction.*

Wall hung, plastic, "Drink Coca-Cola...Delicious with Food," fishtail logo, still in original box, 1960s, 57" x 16", NM, $1,000.00 B. *Metz Superlatives Auction.*

Wooden Kay Displays signs were made during WWII to conserve metal.

Wall hung, plywood, "Drink Coca-Cola...Menu," double rack of menu strips with bottle in center, Kay Displays, 1930s, 36" x 26", G, $375.00 B. *Metz Superlatives Auction.*

Wall hung, wood, "Drink Coca-Cola," panel at top of menu strips, Kay Displays, 1930 – 1940s, 20" x 37", G, $335.00 – 375.00 C. *Metz Superlatives Auction.*

Wall hung, wood and metal, "Drink Coca-Cola" button at bottom, slide menu strips, 1940s, EX, $650.00 B. *Metz Superlatives Auction.*

Wall hung, wood and metal, "Coca-Cola," Kay Displays, 1940s, F, $550.00 B. *Metz Superlatives Auction.*

Wall hung, wood and metal, "Drink Coca-Cola in Bottles," slide-type menu slots with 16" dia. button at top, Kay Displays, 17" x 29", EX, $525.00 B. *Metz Superlatives Auction.*

Wall hung, wood and metal, "Drink Coca-Cola," metal slide menu strips, fishtail logo at top, 1950s, VG, $250.00 – 300.00 C. *Mitchell Collection.*

Wall hung, wood and metal, "Drink Coca-Cola" panel at bottom, slide-type menu strips, 1940s, EX, $675.00 – 800.00 C. *Mitchell Collection.*

Bar, metal, "Coke Adds Life..." unusual black background color, 1970 – 1980s, NM, $75.00 B. *Metz Superlatives Auction.*

Bar, metal, "Drink Coca-Cola delicious refreshing," silhouette girl in yellow spotlight on left side of bar, 1939, 28" x 3½", NM, $500.00 B. *Metz Superlatives Auction.*

Bar, metal, "Drink Coca-Cola...Refresh Yourself...in Bottles," reverse side "Thanks — Call Again," G, $375.00 – 425.00 C.

Bar, porcelain, "Buvez Coca-Cola Glace," Canadian, 31" x 3½", EX, $75.00 – 150.00 C. *Metz Superlatives Auction.*

Bar, porcelain, "Coke Is It!" dynamic wave logo, 1970s, NM, $95.00 B. *Metz Superlatives Auction.*

Bar, porcelain, "Drink Coca-Cola...Ice Cold...in Bottles," 1940 – 1950s, 30" wide, M, $1,000.00 B. *Metz Superlatives Auction.*

Bar, porcelain, "Ice Cold Coca-Cola in Bottles," 1930s, 30" x 2½", NM, $300.00 B. *Metz Superlatives Auction.*

Bar, porcelain, "Ice Cold Coca-Cola in Bottles," reverse side has "Thank You, Call Again," 1930s, 25" x 3¼" NM, $475.00 B. *Metz Superlatives Auction.*

Bar, porcelain, "Refreshing Coca-Cola New Feeling," 1950 – 1960s, EX, $195.00 – 235.00 C. *Mitchell Collection.*

Bar, porcelain, "Take Some Coca-Cola Home Today," 1950s, 34" long, NM, $525.00 B. *Metz Superlatives Auction.*

Flat plate, porcelain, "Prenez un Coca-Cola," unusual foreign design in horizontal version, 6½" x 3¼", NM, $120.00 B. *Metz Superlatives Auction.*

Flat plate, porcelain, "Merci Revenez Pour un Coca-Cola," French, 3½" x 13½", NM, $160.00 B. *Metz Superlatives Auction.*

Flat plate, porcelain, "Thanks Call Again for a Coca-Cola," Canadian, 3½" x 13½", NM, $325.00 B. *Metz Superlatives Auction.*

Flat plate, porcelain, "Come in! Have a Coca-Cola," Canadian, 4" x 11½", NM, $320.00 B. *Metz Superlatives Auction.*

Flat plate, porcelain, "Pull...Refresh Yourself...Drink Coca-Cola," matching "Push...," 1950s, 4" x 8", EX, $450.00 – 725.00 D.

Flat plates, metal, "Push...Drink Coca-Cola...Be Really Refreshed," matching "Pull...," vertical fishtail logo, great pair not seen very often, 1960s, NM, $875.00 B. *Metz Superlatives Auction.*

Handle, aluminum, "Drink Coca-Cola," in shape of bottle, 1930s, NM, $275.00 – 300.00 D. *Charlie's Antique Mall.*

Handle, plastic, "Coca-Cola," bottle shaped for use on newer door coolers, EX, $100.00 – 135.00 C. *Metz Superlatives Auction.*

Big wheel, metal, "Drink Coca-Cola," delivery vehicle, 1970s, EX, $75.00 – 85.00 C.

Buddy L #5546, metal, "Enjoy Coca-Cola the Pause That Refreshes!" complete with original box and all accessories, yellow, 1956, NM, $725.00 B. *Metz Superlatives Auction.*

Buddy L #5646, metal, "Drink Coca-Cola the Pause That Refreshes!" with original box, yellow GMC, 1957, EX, $675.00 B. *Metz Superlatives Auction.*

Buddy L, metal, "Drink Coca-Coca the Pause That Refreshes!" with original miniature cases and bottles, 1960s, EX, $325.00 – 450.00 C.

Buddy L, metal, "Drink Coca-Cola the Pause That Refreshes," Ford, with original box and all accessories, 1960, NM, $550.00 B. *Metz Superlatives Auction.*

Buddy L, metal, "Enjoy Coca-Cola," route truck complete with hand dolly that fits in a side compartment, 1970s, EX, $100.00 – 135.00 C. *Metz Superlatives Auction.*

German #426-20; metal, rubber, and plastic; "Drink Coca-Cola," wind-up with fantastic detailing and a load of cases and bottles, 1949, EX, $2,600.00 B. *Metz Superlatives Auction.*

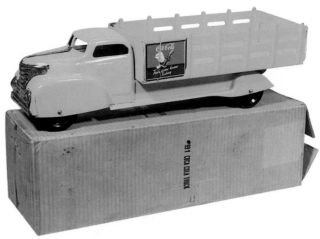

Marx #991, metal, "Coca-Cola...Take Some Home Today" with Sprite Boy, same as the other #991 listed but this one has a different paint scheme, still with original box, 1951, NM, $625.00 B. *Metz Superlatives Auction.*

Marx # 991, metal, "Coca-Cola...Take Some Home Today" with Sprite Boy in advertising on side panel, gray cab and body with yellow bed, in original box, 1953, NM, $900.00 B. *Metz Superlatives Auction.*

Marx, metal, "Drink Coca-Cola Delicious Refreshing," side load, with wheel skirts on both back and front fender wells, 1950s, G, $250.00 – 325.00 C. *Metz Superlatives Auction.*

Marx, metal, "Drink Coca-Cola Delicious Refreshing," snub-nose cab with full load of cases and bottles, 1950s, VG, $450.00 – 500.00 C.

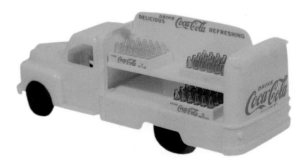

Marx, plastic, "Drink Coca-Cola Delicious Refreshing," Ford style with side load full of cases and bottles, 1950s, EX, $375.00 B. *Metz Superlatives Auction.*

Maxitoys, metal, "Coca-Cola 5¢ at soda fountains," vintage delivery truck made in Holland, only 500 produced, difficult to locate, 1980s, 11" long, NM, $300.00 C.

Marx, plastic, "Drink Coca-Cola Iced," in original box with double cases on sides and wooden wheels, Canadian, 1950s, EX, $1,400.00 C.

Metalcraft, metal, "Coca-Cola...Every Bottle Sterlized," rubber tires, with glass bottles on loading bed, 1930s, G, $775.00 C. *Mitchell Collection.*

Model, plastic, "Vending Machine," ⅕₅ scale, still in plastic sealed box, 1970s, NM, $75.00 – 115.00 C.

Sanyo, metal, "Drink Coca-Cola," made in Japan and distributed by Allen Haddock Company in Atlanta, GA, working head- and taillights, still with original box, 1950 – 1960s, EX, $325.00 B – 395.00 C. *Metz Superlatives Auction.*

Taiyo, metal, "Coca-Cola," metal wind-up, friction motor, in original box, red and white, 1950 – 1960s, 8¾" x 3" x 2", NM, $525.00 B. *Wm Morford Investment Grade Collectibles.*

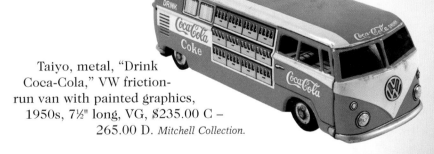

Taiyo, metal, "Drink Coca-Cola," VW friction-run van with painted graphics, 1950s, 7½" long, VG, $235.00 C – 265.00 D. *Mitchell Collection.*

Tractor trailer, metal, "Drink Coca-Cola...," red with spotlight carton on trailer, still in box, but the box is less than EX, $225.00 – 245.00 C.

Bang gun, cardboard, "Compliments of Coca-Cola," with clown, 1950s, EX, $20.00 – 30.00 C. *Metz Superlatives Auction.*

Bang gun, cardboard, "Compliments of Coca-Cola," with Santa in his sleigh, 1950s, M, $20.00 – 30.00 C. *Mitchell Collection.*

Bang gun, cardboard, "It's the Real Thing," model of a government issue .45 caliber automatic pistol, 1960s, EX, $20.00 – 30.00 C.

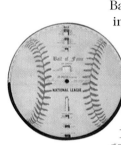

Baseball hall of fame information, cardboard, Coca-Cola premiun, baseball-shaped source of information about the Hall of Fame for both the National and American Leagues, 1901 – 1960, EX, $95.00 B – 150.00 D. *Metz Superlatives Auction.*

Toy, Buddy Lee, composition, "Drink Coca-Cola" patches on doll uniform that stills has the original tag, 1950s, 12" tall, EX, $875.00 B. *Metz Superlatives Auction.*

Buddy Lee, composition. Doll is in homemade uniform made from an original Coke uniform and patches, all worn by Earlene Mitchell's father when he worked for Coke in Paducah, KY. 1950s, 12" tall, EX, $650.00 C. *Mitchell Collection.*

Max Headroom, paper, mask with rubber band to hold it in place, 1980s, EX, $25.00 – 35.00 C. *Metz Superlatives Auction.*

Puzzle, cardboard, "Coke Adds Life to Everything Nice," potpourri puzzle with over 2,000 pieces in original unopened box, EX, $55.00 – 65.00 C. *Mitchell Collection.*

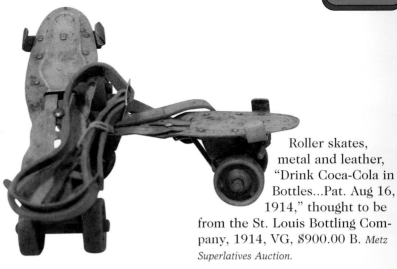

Roller skates, metal and leather, "Drink Coca-Cola in Bottles...Pat. Aug 16, 1914," thought to be from the St. Louis Bottling Company, 1914, VG, $900.00 B. *Metz Superlatives Auction.*

Train, Express Limited, plastic and metal, Coke train with advertising on each car, in original box with all accessories present, 1960s, EX, $450.00 C – 525.00 D.

Shopping basket, metal and cardboard, child's size with products printed on sides, a six-pack of Coca-Cola in plain view and small boxes of products inside basket, 1950s, EX, $450.00 C – 600.00 D. *Mitchell Collection.*

Train, Lionel, plastic and metal, Coca-Cola train with different flavors advertisied on each car, still in original box with all accessories, 1970s, EX, $425.00 C – 500.00 D. *Collectors Auction Services.*

Train, plastic and metal, "Enjoy Coke," tank car, HO gauge, 1980s, EX, $55.00 C – 75.00 D. *Mitchell Collection.*

Yo-yo, wooden, "Drink Coca-Cola in Bottles," red, EX, $110.00 C – 125.00 D. *Mitchell Collection.*

Can, metal, "Bevete Coca-Cola," dynamic wave logo for the foreign market, top money drop, EX, $95.00 – 115.00 C.

Can, metal, "Coca-Cola" diamond can with top money drop, NM, $85.00 – 95.00 C.

Building, plastic, "You'll Feel Right At Home Drinking Coca-Cola," EX, $135.00 – 165.00 C.

Pig, plastic, "Drink Coca-Cola...Sold Everywhere," top coin drop, EX, $25.00 – 40.00 C.

Truck, metal, "Coca-Cola...Advertising Dept." in original box with top coin drop on bed of truck, NM, $35.00 – 65.00 C. *Metz Superlatives Auction.*

Truck, metal, "Drink Coca-Cola...Coca-Cola Bottling Co.," panel design with money drop on top, in original box, NM, $45.00 – 75.00 C. *Metz Superlatives Auction.*

Truck, plastic and metal, "Coca-Cola," delivery van with dynamic wave on side, top money drop, EX, $35.00 – 65.00 C.

"Play refreshed" introduced in 1948.

Vending machine, plastic, "Drink Coca-Cola," dual chute design, coin drop on top, 1948, 2¼" x 3", EX, $150.00 – 175.00 C. *Mitchell Collection.*

Vending machine, plastic, "Drink Coca-Cola...Play Refreshed," 1950s, EX, $145.00 – 195.00 C. *Mitchell Collection.*

Cards, plastic, "Drink Coca-Cola," lady with dog in unopened package, 1943, M, $235.00 – 250.00 C.

Cards, plastic, "Drink Coca-Cola," military nurse in uniform with a bottle of Coke, 1943, M, $145.00 – 185.00 C. *Mitchell Collection.*

Game, cards, plastic, "Drink Coca-Cola," wartimespotter lady, 1943, M, $125.00 – 145.00 C. *Mitchell Collection.*

Game, cards, plastic, "Drink Coca-Cola," stained glass look, in original unopened package, 1974, M, $15.900 – 20.00 C.

Cards, plastic, "Enjoy Coca-Cola," dynamic wave logo, in original unopened package, 1985, M, $20.00 – 25.00 C.

Cards, plastic, "...It's the Real Thing," bottle and food, in original unopened package, 1974, M, $25.00 – 30.00 C.

Cards, plastic, "Have a Coke and a Smile...Coke Adds Life," unopened double deck, 1979, M, $40.00 – 50.00 C.

In 1943, two decks of aircraft spotter cards were issued at a cost of 33¢ each; one deck had a nurse on back, and the other had an operator.

Cards, plastic, "It's the Real Thing," pretty long-haired girl sitting in field, 1974, M, $20.00 – 25.00 C.

Cards, plastic, "Refresh," in unopened original package, 1958, M, $85.00 – 120.00 C.

Cards, plastic, "Santa Claus," poised with a bottle of Coke, full deck in unopened package, 1979, M, $30.00 – 35.00 C. *Collectors Auction Services.*

The diamonds suit had German planes, and clubs bore Italian and Japanese planes. United States planes were on the spades suit, and British planes were on the hearts.

Cards, plastic, "Spring Fling '82...Kansas City," unopened, 1982, M, $55.00 – 75.00 C.

Cards, plastic, Sprite Boy with bottle cap hat and bottle of Coke, in unopened package, 1979, M, $45.00 – 60.00 C.

Checkers, wood, "Coca-Cola" in script on top of each checker, in original cardboard box that is marked "Compliments of the Coca-Cola Bottling Company," 1940 – 1950s, EX, $45.00 – 75.00 C. *Mitchell Collection.*

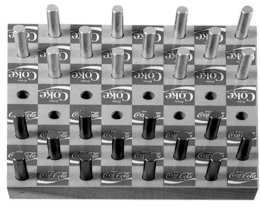

Checkers, wood and metal, "Coca-Cola" with dynamic wave logo on board, modern version with metal pegs for the actual checker pieces, 1970s, EX, $65.00 – 85.00 C. *Mitchell Collection.*

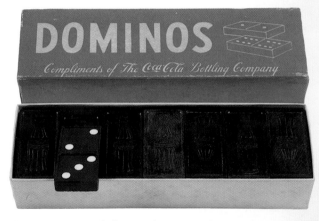

Dominos, wood, "Compliments of the Coca-Cola Bottling Company," in original cardboard box, 1940 – 1950s, EX, $65.00 – 95.00 C. *Mitchell Collection.*

Flip game, cardboard, "Drink Coca-Cola in Sterlized Bottles," framed and under glass, 1910 – 1920, VG, $875.00 – 1,000.00 C. *Mitchell Collection.*

Frisbee, plastic, "Coke Adds Life to Everything Nice," with dynamic wave logo, 1960s, EX, $12.00 – 20.00 C. *Mitchell Collection.*

Puzzle, cardboard, "Drink Coca-Cola 5," victorian lady with a glass of Coke in a glass holder, 500 pieces, VG, $75.00 – 95.00 C.

Puzzle, cardboard, "Coca-Cola," featuring various poster scenes, completed and mounted on wall board, VG, $100.00 – 115.00 C.

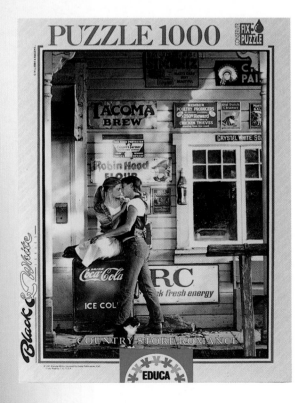

Puzzle, cardboard, "Drink Coca-Cola Ice Cold," 1,000 pieces in original box with scene of young lovers on a Coke cooler in front of an old country store, EX, $25.00 – 45.00 C. *Metz Superlatives Auction.*

Jewelry

Charm bracelet, metal, "Coca-Cola" bottles and glasses on large chain, EX, $130.00 – 145.00 C. *Mitchell Collection.*

Case, metal, Coca-Cola bottle in raised center top position, snap-front closure, EX, $75.00 – 100.00 C. *Mitchell Collection.*

Charm bracelet, metal, NFL-related charms, 1960s, EX, $125.00 – 155.00 C. *Mitchell Collection.*

Cuff links, metal, "Enjoy Coca-Cola" on glass-shaped links, gold finish, 1970s, EX, $65.00 – 85.00 C. *Mitchell Collection.*

Earrings, metal, Coca-Cola bottles, for pierced ears, still on original card, dynamic wave logo, NM, $20.00 – 25.00 C.

Key chain, "Compliments of Coca-Cola Bottling Works, Nashville, Tennessee" in original box with customer appreciation Christmas card inside box, VG, $75.00 – 100.00 C. *Mitchell Collection.*

Key chain, metal, "Drink Bottled Coca-Cola," 1900s, EX, $135.00 – 165.00 C. *Mitchell Collection.*

Money clip, metal, "Compliments Coca-Cola Bottling Works, Nashville, Tennessee," EX, $55.00 – 85.00 C. *Mitchell Collection.*

Tie tac, metal, "Coca-Cola," employee recognition for 30 years of service, with original box, NM, $45.00 – 60.00 C. *Mitchell Collection.*

Apron, cloth, "Be Really Refreshed! Drink Coca-Cola," full front with two pockets, 1959 – 1960s, VG, $35.00 – 55.00 C. *Mitchell Collection.*

Apron, cloth, "Drink Coca-Cola," two front pockets, red trim, 1950s, EX, $55.00 – 75.00 C.

Bandana, cloth, "Kit Carson" and "Drink Coca-Cola." A newer version of the original, this one has a white background while the original has a red background. EX, $25.00 – 35.00 C. *Mitchell Collection.*

Backpack, cloth, "Coca-Cola...Official Soft Drink of the 1984 Olympics," never used, 1984, EX, $20.00 – 30.00 C. *Metz Superlatives Auction.*

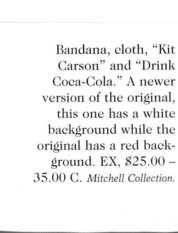

Bandana, cloth, "Kit Carson" and "Drink Coca-Cola," red with Kit in center and western scenes plus Coke logos in each corner, 1950s, 20" x 22", EX, $75.00 – 125.00 C. *Mitchell Collection.*

Belt, leather, "Enjoy Coca-Cola," red lettering on white belt, regular harness-type buckle, 1960s, EX, $20.00 – 30.00 C.

Belt, web, "Enjoy Coca-Cola" on metal buckle with dynamic wave logo, 1960s, NM, $20.00 – 30.00 C.

Belt, web, "Enjoy Coca-Cola" on metal buckle with white and red dynamic wave logo, EX, $20.00 – 30.00 C.

Belt, web, "Enjoy Coke" on metal military-type slide buckle, newer version of this belt, EX, $15.00 – 20.00 C. *Mitchell Collection.*

Coat, cloth, "Enjoy Coca-Cola...Central States Bottling Co.," green waist-length driver's jacket with zip-in quilted lining for light or heavy weather use, EX, $45.00 – 65.00 C.

Coat, cloth, "Enjoy Coca-Cola," dynamic wave logo on front. This driver's uniform was known as the "hunting jacket" due to the large pockets, the length, and the duck material. Riverside manufacturer's tag still in place, unused, brown, EX, $55.00 – 75.00 C. *Metz Superlatives Auction.*

Hat, cloth, "Drink Coca-Cola...Delicious and Refreshing," felt beanie with red, white, and green panels, 1930 – 1940s, 8" dia., VG, $55.00 – 95.00 C. *Mitchell Collection.*

Hat, cloth, "Drink Coca-Cola," driver's hat with round patch at crown and hard bill. These hats are becoming very difficult to locate. EX, $125.00 – 200.00 C.

Hat, cloth, "Drink Coca-Cola," round logo on side of folding soda fountain attendant-type hat, NM, $55.00 B – 125.00 C. *Autopia Advertising Auctions.*

Coveralls, cloth, "Drink Coca-Cola" round patch on front, 38R, VG, $125.00 – 145.00 C.

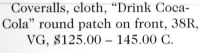

Hat, cloth, "Drink Coca-Cola," round logo patch on folding driver's cap, 1950s, VG, $70.00 – 100.00 C. *Mitchell Collection.*

Hat, cloth, "Drink Coca-Cola" soda jerk cap in unusual yellow and red color, EX, $25.00 – 45.00 C. *Mitchell Collection.*

The term "soda jerk" wasn't coined until the 1940s.

Hat, cloth, "Drink Coca-Cola," soda person folding, red and white, 1940s, EX, $30.00 – 50.00 C. *Mitchell Collection.*

Hat, cloth, "Enjoy Coca-Cola" on crown of cowboy hat, employee award item still in original hat, never worn, NM, $150.00 – 185.00 C.

Kerchief, cloth, "The Cola Clan" with silhouette girl from the 1970s, banquet item, 1970s, EX, $35.00 – 75.00 C. *Mitchell Collection.*

Pants, cloth, "It's the Real Thing," beach pants with drawstring waistband, EX, $20.00 – 30.00 C. *Metz Superlatives Auction.*

Patch, cloth, "Coca-Cola" shoulder uniform patch, VG, $10.00 – 20.00 C. *Mitchell Collection.*

Patch, cloth, "Drink Coca-Cola in Bottles," fishtail patch, 1960s, EX, $8.00 – 20.00 C. *Mitchell Collection.*

Patch, cloth, "Enjoy Coca-Cola," round jacket patch, 1950 – 1960s, EX, $20.00 – 40.00 C. *Mitchell Collection.*

Shirt, cloth, "Coca-Cola" golf shirt with logo over pocket, VG, $25.00 – 35.00 C. *Collectors Auction Services.*

Shirt, cloth, "Drink Coca-Cola," round patch on back of striped driver's shirt, VG, $45.00 – 55.00 C. *Mitchell Collection.*

Shirt, cloth, "Coca-Cola Winning University" T-shirt, G, $10.00 – 15.00 C.

Shirt, cloth, "Things Go Better with Coke," bowler's shirt with lettering on back, 1960s, EX, $30.00 – 45.00 C. *Mitchell Collection.*

Shirt, cloth, "Drink Coca-Cola," round patch on back of driver's shirt with "Things Go Better..." patch on one sleeve and hard-to-find "Fresca" sleeve patch on the other arm, 1960s, VG, $60.00 – 85.00 C. *Mitchell Collection.*

Suspenders, elastic, "Enjoy Coke," with metal snaps, issued to employees, NM, $35.00 – 50.00 C. *Collectors Auction Services.*

Swimsuit, cloth, "Coca-Cola," VG, $20.00 – 25.00 C.

226

Tie, cloth, "Enjoy Coca-Cola," with dynamic wave in red box on brown background, EX, $15.00 – 20.00 C.

Uniform pants and shirt, cloth, "Enjoy Coca-Cola," driver's issue by Riverside, still in original packaging, dynamic wave cloth patch, NM, $65.00 – 95.00 C. *Collectors Auction Services.*

Uniform pants and shirt, cloth, "Enjoy Coca-Cola" driver's issue by Riverside still in original packaging, cloth dynamic wave logo patch, brown with stripes, NM, $85.00 – 125.00 C.

Uniform pants and shirt, cloth, "Enjoy Coca-Cola" with dynamic wave cloth patch, solid green, never worn, EX, $65.00 – 95.00 C.

Uniform pants and shirt, "Enjoy Coca-Cola," driver's set with dynamic wave cloth patch, white shirt with green pants, EX, $55.00 – 75.00 C.

Vest, cloth, "Drink Coca-Cola" round cloth patch on front of driver's uniform vest, large "Drink" patch on back, elastic waist, EX, $70.00 – 100.00 C.

Vest, cloth, "Enjoy Coca-Cola" cloth patch on chest, green, issued to drivers, EX, $35.00 – 55.00 C.

Vest, cloth, "Enjoy Coca-Cola," dynamic wave cloth patch on quilted insulated uniform vest, EX, $35.00 – 45.00 C.

Vest, cloth, "Enjoy Coca-Cola," insulated uniform item with dynamic wave cloth patch over front pocket, this style seems to be the most popular with collectors, red, EX, $35.00 – 55.00 C.

Visor, foam, "Coke Is It!" Kentucky Fair souvenir visor with punch-out head section that can be used for a Coke coupon, 1983, EX, $25.00 – 30.00 C.

Bi-fold, leather, "Drink Coca-Cola, Delicious Refreshing" in gold lettering, 1920s, EX, $95.00 – 125.00 C. *Mitchell Collection.*

Bi-fold, leather, "When Thirsty Try a Bottle," gold engraving, ribbed texture, 1920s, EX, $100.00 – 130.00 C.

Coin purse, "Compliments of the Coca-Cola Bottling Co., Memphis, Tenn.," metal and celluloid top and snap, 1910 – 1920s, VG, $195.00 – 225.00 C. *Mitchell Collection.*

Coin purse, leather, "Whenever You See an Arrow Think of Coca-Cola," with arrow logo, all in gold lettering, metal snap latch, 1909, VG, $185.00 – 215.00 C. *Metz Superlatives Auction.*

Coin purse, leather, "When Thirsty Try a Bottle," 1907, EX, $100.00 – 125.00 C. *Mitchell Collection.*

Ti-fold, plastic, "Enjoy Coca-Cola" in gold lettering, 1960s, EX, $15.00 – 20.00 C. *Mitchell Collection.*

Ad, paper, "...And Now the Gift for Thirst...Drink Coca-Cola," Santa with Coke and kids with gifts, 1952, 7" x 10", VG, $8.00 – 10.00 C. *B. J. Summers.*

Ad, paper, "And the Same to You," Santa in armchair with bottle of Coke, *National Geographic,* 1939, 7" x 10", VG, $8.00 – 12.00 C. *B. J. Summers.*

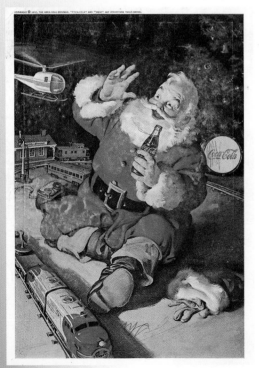

Ad, paper, "Coca-Cola," Santa with Coke bottle in the middle of train setup and with helicopter, 1962, 7" x 10", VG, $8.00 – 10.00 C. *B. J. Summers.*

Ad, paper, "Coca-Cola," Santa with Coke bottle and trying to keep a small dog quiet, 1961, 7" x 10", VG, $8.00 – 10.00 C. *B. J. Summers.*

Ad, paper, "Coca-Cola," Santa with little boy at referigerator with bottle of Coke, 1959, 7" x 10", VG, $8.00 – 10.00 C. *B. J. Summers.*

Ad, paper, "Drink Coca-Cola...Talk about Being Good," Santa with good boys and girls list and a bottle of Coke, 1951, 7" x 10", VG, $8.00 – 10.00 C. *B. J. Summers.*

Ad, paper, "Give and Take Say I," Santa with a Coke and a turkey leg, with black and white inset promoting cold Cokes "from your own refrigerator," 1937, 7" x 10", VG, $8.00 – 10.00 C. *B. J. Summers.*

Ad, paper, "That Extra Something!...You Can Spot It Every Time," with Santa and advertising 5¢ Coke, 1942, 7" x 10", VG, $5.00 – 8.00 C. *B. J. Summers.*

Ad, paper, "The Pause That Refreshes...Coca-Cola," Santa in easy chair and surrounded by elves, 1960, 7" x 10", VG, $8.00 – 10.00 C. *B. J. Summers.*

Bottle hanger, paper, " 'Twas the Night Before Christmas,' " 1950s, M, $25.00 – 45.00 C. *Mitchell Collection.*

Bottle hanger, paper, " 'Twas the Night Before Christmas,' " Santa at refrigerator, 1950s, EX, $45.00 – 55.00 C. *Mitchell Collection.*

Calendar, paper, "A Merry Christmas Calls for Coke," reference edition with Santa in an easy chair with a glass of Coke and surrounded by elves, 1961, M, $45.00 – 55.00 C. *Mitchell Collection.*

Calendar, paper, "Drink Coca-Cola," reference edition with fireplace scene, 1964, M, $35.00 – 45.00 C. *Mitchell Collection.*

Calendar, paper, "A 1954 Calendar for Your Home," reference edition with graphics of Santa with bottle, 1954, EX, $125.00 – 135.00 C. *Mitchell Collection.*

Calendar, paper, "Drink Coca-Cola," Santa on small ladder helping with decorating, reference edition, 1966, M, $35.00 – 45.00 C. *Mitchell Collection.*

Coca-Cola distributed the first Sundblom Santa Claus in 1931, using a model named Lewis Prentiss, whom the company paid $3 an hour.

It is generally believed that after Prentiss died of a heart attack in 1946, Haddom Sundblom used himself as a model for Santa.

Calendar, paper, "Flower Paintings," reference edition, 1956, EX, $35.00 – 45.00 C. *Mitchell Collection.*

Calendar, paper, "Me, Too!" full monthly sheets, former owner had recorded the temperatures on each day, 1954, VG, $150.00 B.
Metz Superlatives Auction.

Calendar, paper, "Flower Prints," with Santa in his workshop with a bottle of Coke, 1957, M, $35.00 – 45.00 C. *Mitchell Collection.*

Calendar, paper, "Presented by your Coca-Cola Bottler," with helicopter flying around Santa who is holding a bottle, reference edition, 1963, M, $50.00 – 75.00 C.
Mitchell Collection.

Calendar, paper, "Season's Greetings," santa holding up a Coke bottle, reference edition, 1970, M, $25.00 – 30.00 C.
Mitchell Collection.

Calendar, paper, "Things Go Better with Coke," small black dog and Santa, 1965, M, $45.00 – 55.00 C. *Mitchell Collection.*

Calendar, paper, "Things Go Better with Coke," with Santa sitting at desk, reference edition, 1967, EX, $30.00 – 40.00 C.
Mitchell Collection.

Carton stuffer, cardboard, "Good Taste for All," Santa with a bottle of Coke, EX, $75.00 – 85.00 C. *Mitchell Collection.*

In America, we, too, like to use words in our own way. No doubt the Dutch "Sant Nikolaas" was changed to the easier said "Santa Claus" by the little boys and girls of long ago who waited so eagerly for his yearly visit.

Many countries have contributed to the history of Santa Claus, to what he should wear, how he should travel, even to his personal appearance. His reindeer must have come from the icy areas of northern Scandinavia where reindeer and sleigh are used for travel. The chimney he descends on Christmas Eve with his sack and his short pipe are Dutch traditions. The fur-trimmed clothes could have been added by anxious folk of cold lands who were fearful lest Santa's comfort be disturbed in his long night's journey.

But his twinkling eyes, cherry nose and plump body are purely American. It was a scholarly New Yorker, Dr. Clement Moore, who saw the "jolly old elf" most clearly and recorded for the whole world, the classic picture of him in the poem which begins, "'Twas the night before Christmas."

Here Santa Claus comes to life, merry, affectionate, a friend of little children; one who finds a great joy in giving. Through him the spirit of mankind is lifted, soaring up the snow-blown path of the sleigh and eight tiny reindeer to a happy world where anything is possible.

Copyright 1950, The Coca-Cola Company

Card, paper, Christmas information about the possible origin of Santa Claus, VG, $85.00 – 100.00 C. *Mitchell Collection.*

Display, cardboard, "Coca-Cola," die-cut easel back that folds out to 3-D effect with little boy in pj's surprising Santa, 1950s, VG, $235.00 – 275.00 C. *Mitchell Collection.*

Carton stuffer, cardboard, "Serve Coca-Cola...Stock up for the Holidays," Santa holding sign and a Coke bottle, 1950s, EX, $150.00 – 195.00 C. *Mitchell Collection.*

Display, cardboard, "Coca-Cola" die-cut Santa on a stool holding a small wooden rabbit, EX, $125.00 – 150.00 C. *Mitchell Collection.*

Display, cardboard, "Coca-Cola" die-cut easel back with Santa holding a bottle of Coke, very similar to a 1946 display, big difference here is holly wreath behind his head, 1960s, EX, $100.00 – 135.00 C. *Mitchell Collection.*

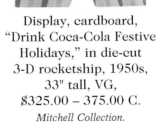

Display, cardboard, "Drink Coca-Cola Festive Holidays," in die-cut 3-D rocketship, 1950s, 33" tall, VG, $325.00 – 375.00 C. *Mitchell Collection.*

Display, cardboard, "Drink Coca-Cola...Bring Home the Coke," Santa in his workshop with a bottle of Coke and a hammer, 1956, 14" x 28", EX, $235.00 – 255.00 C. *Mitchell Collection.*

Display, cardboard, "Get Your Santa Collector's Cup," with Santa on a stool and a device that will hold a giveaway Coke glass, EX, $20.00 – 30.00 C. *Mitchell Collection.*

Display, cardboard, "Greetings for Coca-Cola," die-cut standup with a Coke, 1948, 5' tall, F, $240.00 – 275.00 C.
Mitchell Collection.

Display, cardboard, "Greetings from Coca-Cola," die-cut Santa with elbow on newel post enjoying a bottle of Coke, 1946, 6" x 12", EX, $225.00 – 245.00 C.
Mitchell Collection.

Display, cardboard, "Host for the Holidays...Take Enough Coke Home," die-cut easel back with Santa and a six-pack of Coke, 1952, 13" x 24", EX, $500.00 B.
Metz Superlatives Auction.

Display, cardboard, "It's the Real Thing...," with Santa and elves, die-cut easel back, 1970s, G, $45.00 – 60.00 C. *Mitchell Collection.*

Display, cardboard, "Serve Coca-Cola...Sign of Good Taste," die-cut easel back with Santa holding six bottles of Coke, 1950s, VG, $200.00 – 275.00 C.
Mitchell Collection.

Display, cardboard, "The Gift for Thirst," die-cut easel back with Santa in front of gifts, 1953, 9" x 18", EX, $230.00 – 250.00 C.
Mitchell Collection.

Display, cardboard, "Things Go Better with Coke," die-cut easel back; boy, black dog, and Santa; very similar in context to the 1965 reference calendar, 1960s, 36" tall, EX, $50.00 – 75.00 C. *Mitchell Collection.*

Santas

Figurine, porcelain, animated Santa holding the book with the lists of good and bad children, EX, $120.00 – 145.00 C. *Mitchell Collection.*

Display, cardboard, "Things Go Better with Coke," die-cut easel back of Santa with a bottle of Coke and various scenes of people over his head, 1960s, 36" tall, EX, $65.00 – 85.00 C. *Mitchell Collection.*

Figurine, porcelain, Royal Orleans, limited edition with Santa standing beside a sack of toys and a glass of Coke, 1980s, EX, $165.00 – 185.00 C. *Mitchell Collection.*

Figurine, porcelain, Royal Orleans, Santa trying to silence a small dog, 1980s, EX, $150.00 – 175.00 C. *Mitchell Collection.*

Figurine, porcelain, Royal Orleans, Santa beside fireplace, 1980s, EX, $135.00 – 150.00 C. *Mitchell Collection.*

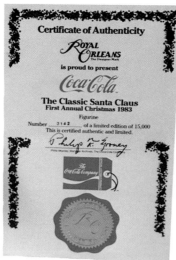

Figurine, porcelain, Royal Orleans, Santa with a globe and bottle of Coke, complete set contains six figures, 1980s, EX, $200.00 – 225.00 C. *Mitchell Collection.*

Figurine, porcelain, Santa with a string of lights in a tangle in front of a footstool, EX, $145.00 – 185.00 C. *Mitchell Collection.*

Poster, cardboard, "Coca-Cola...Christmas Greetings," Santa with bottle of Coke and note left for him by child, 1932, NM, $4,200.00 B. *Metz Superlatives Auction.*

Figurine, porcelain, Royal Orleans, Santa and boy with dog, 1980s, EX, $140.00 – 155.00 C. *Mitchell Collection.*

Playing cards, vinyl, Santa with Coke bottle, 1979, M, $30.00 – 40.00 C.

Poster, cardboard, "Drink Coca-Cola...Delicious and Refreshing," Santa holding a bottle of Coke, 1940s, 43" x 32", EX, $1,000.00 B. *Metz Superlatives Auction.*

Poster, cardboard, "Take Home Coca-Cola Santa Packs," price area at right of Santa, NOS, NM, $30.00 – 45.00 C.

Serving tray, metal, "Drink Coca-Cola," Santa at fireplace, many variations of this exist, EX, $15.00 – 25.00 C.

Sign, cardboard, "A Merry Christmas Calls for a Coke," Santa in chair with elves, graphics are the same used on the 1961 reference calendar, 1960s, 16" x 24", VG, $70.00 – 100.00 C. *Mitchell Collection.*

Sign, cardboard, "Add Zest to the Season," string hanger with Santa and a bottle of Coke, Canadian, 1949, 10½" x 18½", EX, $900.00 B. *Metz Superlatives Auction.*

Sign, cardboard, "Coke Adds Life to Holiday Fun," with pricing area blank, 1960s, EX, $35.00 – 55.00 C. *Mitchell Collection.*

Sign, cardboard, "Coke Adds Life to Holiday Fun," Santa holding a bottle of Coke, 1960s, EX, $100.00 – 115.00 C. *Collectors Auction Services.*

Sign, cardboard, "Extra Bright Refreshment...Stock Up for the Holidays," Santa beside a Christmas tree with a carton of Coke, 1955, 16" x 27", VG, $65.00 – 95.00 C. *Mitchell Collection.*

Sign, cardboard, "Feel the Real Magic of the Holidays," Santa and a small boy and dog, courtesy panel for pricing at bottom empty, 30½" x 47", EX, $40.00 – 55.00 C.

Sign, cardboard, "Holiday Refreshment Starts Here Enjoy Coca-Cola," Santa with present and unused courtesy price area, $60.00 – 80.00 C. *Mitchell Collection.*

Sign, cardboard, "Is There Plenty of Coke & Sprite at Your House?" Santa in chair and Coca-Cola lamp in background, 1970s, EX, $30.00 – 45.00 C. *Mitchell Collection.*

Sign, cardboard, "Real Holidays Call for the Real Thing...Coke," Santa with Coke bottle and wreath, 1970s, 36" tall, EX, $40.00 – 75.00 C. *Mitchell Collection.*

Sign, cardboard, "Santa's Helpers," Santa with six bottles, 1950s, VG, $115.00 – 135.00 C. *Mitchell Collection.*

Sign, cardboard, "Sign of Good Taste...Anytime," Santa drinking from a bottle of Coke, EX, $95.00 – 145.00 C. *Metz Superlatives Auction.*

Sign, cardboard, "The Pause That Refreshes," Santa in armchair with elves, 24¼" x 11½", EX, $75.00 – 85.00 C.

Sign, paper, "Coke Adds Life to... Holiday Fun," Santa beside fireplace, EX, $30.00 – 45.00 C. *Mitchell Collection.*

Sign, cardboard, "The Gift for Thirst...Stock Up for the Holidays," Santa with a bottle of Coke, EX, $75.00 – 100.00 C. *Mitchell Collection.*

Sign, cardboard, "Things Go Better with Coke," string hanger with couple kissing under mistletoe, 13½" x 16", EX, $65.00 – 85.00 C. *Mitchell Collection.*

Sign, cardboard, wreath with Santa inside the circle, 1958, EX, $50.00 – 65.00 C. *Mitchell Collection.*

Sign, paper, "Gift of Refreshment,"
pole-mounted promotional advertising for a giveaway with purchase of a glass of Coke Classic,
22" x 30", NM, $15.00 – 20.00 C.
Collectors Auction Services.

Sign, paper, "Santa's Helpers," truck-sized advertisement
with Santa holding six bottles of Coke, 1960s, 66" x 32",
G, $125.00 B – 195.00 C. *Metz Superlatives Auction.*

Sign, paper, "The
Pause That
Refreshes...,"
Santa in his
workshop, EX,
$25.00 – 35.00 C.
Mitchell Collection.

❧ Sprite Boy ❧

The Sprite Boy was conceived by the D'Arcy advertising agency in St. Louis in 1941. He was first used in advertising Coca-Cola in January 1942 and continued selling Coca-Cola until phased out in 1957 – 1958.

Ad, paper, "Come in...Thirst Knows No Season...Refreshment...Real Refreshment...Awaits" with Sprite Boy at soda fountain and wearing the soad fountain hat instead of the bottle cap, 1949, VG, $30.00 – 40.00 C.

Ad, paper, "Come in — Have a Coke," framed, under glass, EX, $175.00 – 200.00 C.

Mitchell Collection.

Ad, paper, "Host of the Highway," vending machine and Sprite Boy on *National Geographic*, 1950, 6⅞" x 10", G, $8.00 – 15.00 C.

Ad, paper, "Travel Refreshed," back cover of *National Geographic*, Santa and Sprite Boy with bottle of Coke, 1949, 6⅞" x 10", G, $10.00 – 15.00 C.

Ad, paper, "Where There's Coca-Cola There's Hospitality," with Santa looking in refrigerator, 1948, EX, $40.00 C.

Bag holder, metal, "For Home Refreshment...Coca-Cola," 36" x 17", VG, $695.00 D.

Birthday card, paper, "A Treat in Store...for Your Birthday," employee item from the company, EX, $20.00 – 25.00 C.

Blotter, cardboard, "Good," bottle of Coke in snowbank, 7¼" x 3½", EX, $30.00 – 40.00 C.

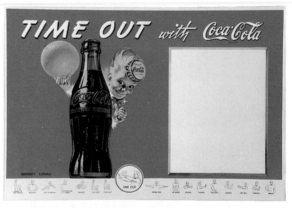

Book cover, paper, "Time Out with Coca-Cola," for school books, 1940 – 1950s, EX, $12.00 – 18.00 C. *Mitchell Collection.*

Button sign, metal, "Coca-Cola," lightweight, designed to be a string hanger, 1940s, 12¼" dia., EX, $775.00 C.

Button sign, metal, "Have a Coke," with decal of Sprite Boy and bottle, 1950s, 16" dia., NM, $775.00 B. *Metz Superlatives Auction.*

Button sign, metal, "Yes! Coke is still 5¢," 1950s, 16" dia., EX, $775.00 B. *Metz Superlatives Auction.*

Calendar, paper, wall sized, with front cover of Sprite Boy in bottle cap hat, framed under glass, EX, $1,200.00 C – 1,500.00 B.

Calendar, cardboard, pocket sized for easy use, Sprite Boy around a bottle of Coke, 1945, EX, $55.00 – 75.00 C. *Mitchell Collection.*

"Have a Coke"

Coaster, paper, "Have a Coke," 1950s, M, $12.00 – 15.00 C. *Mitchell Collection.*

Decal, vinyl, "We Have," showing a glass of Coke and Sprite Boy in soda fountain hat, late 1940s – early 1950s, 21" x 9", EX, $300.00 B. *Metz Superlatives Auction.*

Decal, vinyl, "Take Home a Carton," unused, framed under glass, Sprite Boy with bottle cap hat, 1940s, 8" x 10", EX, $250.00 B. *Metz Superlatives Auction.*

Domino set, plastic, "Double Six Dominos" with complete set in original vinyl case featuring Sprite Boy and a bottle of Coke, 1970s, EX, $40.00 – 55.00 C. *Mitchell Collection.*

Fan, cardboard, "A Way to Win... Wherever You Go," on paddle stick from the Mt. Vernon, IL, bottler, 1950s, EX, $115.00 – 125.00 C. *Mitchell Collection.*

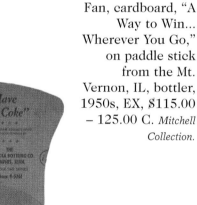

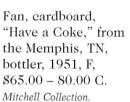

Fan, cardboard, "Have a Coke," from the Memphis, TN, bottler, 1951, F, $65.00 – 80.00 C. *Mitchell Collection.*

Fan, cardboard, "Bottles, Bottles, Who's Got the Empty Bottles?" on wooden paddle stick from the Paducah, KY, bottler, 1950s, EX, $140.00 – 155.00 C. *Mitchell Collection.*

Fan, cardboard, "Have a Coke" on wooden stick, 1950s, EX, $85.00 – 100.00 C. *Mitchell Collection.*

Game, metal and glass, small ball game with Sprite Boy and Coke bottle, VG, $130.00 – 185.00 C.

Hat, paper, "Coca-Cola," soda jerk fold-out hat, 1950s, VG, $30.00 – 50.00 C. *Mitchell Collection.*

Napkin holder, metal, "Have a Coke" on side panel, 1950s, VG, $725.00 B. *Metz Superlatives Auction.*

Playing cards, plastic, Coca-Cola bottle and Sprite Boy, 1979, M, $45.00 – 60.00 C.

Sign, cardboard, Coca-Cola six-pack with bottle cap Sprite Boy, 34" x 43", G, $350.00 – 400.00 C.

Sign, cardboard, Coca-Cola six-pack with Sprite Boy in bottle cap hat, 1946, 41½" x 27½", EX, $525.00 B. *Metz Superlatives Auction.*

Sign, cardboard, "Have a Coke," easel back with advertising for King Size Coke, 1957, 18" sq., EX, $170.00 B – 200.00 C. *Metz Superlatives Auction.*

Sign, cardboard, "Coca-Cola...Take Some Home," Sprite Boy case insert, 1944, 10" x 13", NM, $220.00 B – 295.00 C. *Metz Superlatives Auction.*

Sign, cardboard, die-cut concession stand, part of larger sign with bottle cap Sprite Boy, 37½" x 29", EX, $250.00 – 275.00 C. *Metz Superlatives Auction.*

Sign, cardboard, "Now! Family Size Too!" in original wood frame, 1955, 36" x 20", EX, $550.00 B. *Metz Superlatives Auction.*

Sign, cardboard, "Now! King Size
Too!" with bottle cap Sprite Boy
and two different sizes of six-
packs, 1955, 16" x 27", G,
$145.00 – 165.00 C. *Mitchell Collection.*

Sign, cardboard,
"Pause...Refresh," easel back
with Santa drinking from a
bottle, 1940s, 26" x 52", EX,
$525.00 B – 550.00 C. *Metz
Superlatives Auction.*

Sign, cardboard,
"Quality in Cups,"
promoting the sale of
genuine Coke cups,
1940s, 15" x 12", F,
$375.00 B. *Metz
Superlatives Auction.*

Sign, Masonite and metal, "Sundaes...Malts," beautiful Kay Displays wings
with center 12" button and Sprite Boy and bottle at each end, 1950s,
78" x 12", EX, $1,050.00 B. *Metz Superlatives Auction.*

Sign, Masonite, "Beverage Department," featuring a "Drink..." button
in center of wings that have Sprite Boy on each end, Kay Displays,
1940s, 78" x 12", EX, $850.00 B – 1,000.00 C. *Metz Superlatives Auction.*

Sign, Masonite,
"Drink Coca-Cola,"
arrow through
chest-type cooler,
1940s, EX,
$850.00 – 100.00 C.
Mitchell Collection.

Sign, metal, "Drink Coca-Cola," horizontal, with Sprite
Boy and bottle in yellow spotlight, 57" x 18", VG,
$595.00 D.

Sign, metal, "Have a
Coke...Take Some
Home," designed for
bottle rack use, 1940 –
1950s, 16" x 23", EX,
$300.00 B. *Metz Superla-
tives Auction.*

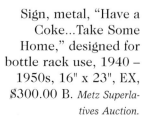

Sign, paper, "Come In...We Have Coca-Cola...5¢," line of marching glasses and Sprite Boy, 1944, 25" x 8", VG, $350.00 B. *Metz Superlatives Auction.*

Sign, paper, "Take Some Home Today...6 Bottles 25¢," window sign, NOS, 1950s, 25" x 10", NM, $300.00 B. *Autopia Advertising Auctions.*

Sign, porcelain, "Buvez Coca-Cola...Glace," French, 1954, 17½" x 54", EX, $235.00 C.

Sign, poster, "Now! Family Size *too!*" displaying two bottles, 1955, 16" x 27", NM, $225.00 B. *Metz Superlatives Auction.*

Sign, porcelain, "Buvez Coca-Cola," spotlight Sprite Boy and Coke Bottle, 1940s, 58" x 18", EX, $750.00 B. *Metz Superlatives Auction.*

Sign, wood, "Welcome Friend...Have a Coke," die cut with Sprite Boy and a bottle of Coke, 1940, 32" x 14", EX, $595.00 – 695.00 C. *Mitchell Collection.*

Sign, wood, "Drink Coca-Cola in Bottles," wing sign with Sprite Boy and bottle on each end and 12" button in center, 1940s, 36" x 12", NM, $1,300.00 B. *Metz Superlatives Auction.*

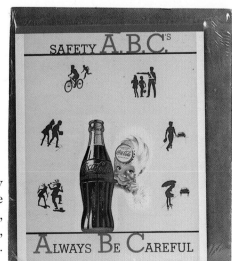

Tablet, paper, "Safety A.B.C.'s...Always Be Careful," full pad, never used, EX, $18.00 – 25.00 C.

Countertop, ceramic, "Coca-Cola," early soda fountain syrup dispenser from the Wheeling Pottery Co., 1896, VG, $5,500.00 B. *Metz Superlatives Auction.*

Countertop, metal, "Drink Coca-Cola...Ice Cold." Bolt-on type with single spigot, this style is sometimes referred to as the "outboard motor" due to the resemblance. 1940 – 1950s, VG, $750.00 – 825.00 C. *Patrick's Collectibles.*

Countertop, metal, "Drink Coca-Cola," single spigot with lift top by Dole, 14½" x 11½" x 25", G, $675.00 B. *Metz Superlatives Auction.*

Countertop, metal and plastic, "Drink Coca-Cola" painted on side, salesman's sample with fabric zippered carrying case, three heads, 1960s, EX, $975.00 C.

Countertop, metal and plastic, "Have a Coke," three spigots for Coke and Sprite, VG, $300.00 – 375.00 C.

Countertop, porcelain and glass, "Drink Coca-Cola," frosted glass lid and top section, red pottery base, 1920s, NM, $6,200.00 B. *Metz Superlatives Auction.*

Counter urn, composition, 75th anniversary pencil holder, 7" tall, EX, $220.00 B. *Metz Superlatives Auction.*

Coca-Cola was first served by soda fountain manager Willis Venable at Jacobs Pharmacy.

Countertop, rubber, "Coca-Cola," reproduction of 1896 dispenser, 1950s, EX, $350.00 B. *Metz Superlatives Auction.*

Play toy, plastic, in shape of single-spout dispenser, "Drink Coca-Cola," 1950s, EX, $175.00 – 210.00 C. *Mitchell Collection.*

Stadium, plastic and metal, "Carry Pack...Drink Coca-Cola," plastic outer housing with a two gallon tank and the original cup dispenser on the side, 1940s, EX, $800.00 B. *Metz Superlatives Auction.*

Play toy, plastic, "Things Go Better with Coke," with all original items including glasses, 1970s, VG, $90.00 – 125.00 C. *Metz Superlatives Auction.*

Wall hanging, metal, for paper Coke cups, 26" tall, EX, $425.00 B. *Metz Superlatives Auction.*

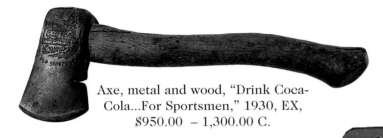

Axe, metal and wood, "Drink Coca-Cola...For Sportsmen," 1930, EX, $950.00 – 1,300.00 C.

Bench, wooden, "Drink Coca-Cola..." The rest is somewhat obscured, but probably says "In Bottles," 1940 – 1950s, F, $850.00 B.

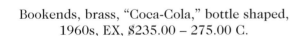

Bookends, brass, "Coca-Cola," bottle shaped, 1960s, EX, $235.00 – 275.00 C.

Bookmark, celluoid, "Refreshing... Drink Coca-Cola...Delicious 5¢," 1900s, 2" x 2¼", F, $575.00 C.

Bood mark, paper, "Drink Coca-Cola 5¢," 2" x 6", EX, $400.00 – 475.00 C.

Bookmark, paper, "Drink Coca-Cola," with Lillian Nordica holding large hand fan and beside a tall table, 1900s, 2¼" x 5¼" NM, $1,500.00 B.

Bottle lamp, composition, "Coca-Cola," brass base, rare and highly desirable, 1920s, 20" tall, NM, $7,200.00 B.

Bowl, china, "Drink Coca-Cola...Ice Cold," scalloped-edge Vernonware, green, 1930s, EX, $450.00 B.

Bookmark, ribbon, "Coca-Cola...Tell City," white cat on front, EX, $95.00 D – 115.00 C.

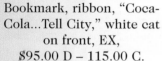

Card table, metal and composition, advertising in each corner for Coke and advertising sheet on underside that boasts the table is so strong it will hold the weight of a grown man, 1930s, VG, $275.00 – 325.00 C.

Camera, plastic, "Coke Adds Life to Happy Times," Polaroid camera, EX, $75.00 – 125.00 C.

Cigarette case, glass, "50th Anniversary Coca-Cola...1886 – 1936," frosted glass, EX, $700.00 – 800.00 C.

Coupons, paper, "Take Time Out for the Pause That Refreshes," uncut sheet, EX, $20.00 – 35.00 C.

Cup, waxed cardboard, "Drink Coca-Cola," cone shaped, metal rings at top and bottom, EX, $15.00 – 20.00 C.

Cup, waxed cardboard, "Enjoy Coca-Cola," cone shaped with metal top and bottom rings, EX, $10.00 – 15.00 C.

Desk set, plastic, "Drink Coca-Cola," pen and music box, cooler shaped, 1950s, EX, $275.00 – 295.00 C.

Display counter box, cardboard, "Coca-Cola Chewing Gum," originally held twenty 5¢ packages of chewing gum, 1920s, VG, $1,500.00 – 2,000.00 C.

Door lock, metal, "Drink Coca-Cola in Bottles Delicious and Refreshing," 1930s, EX, $75.00 – 100.00 C.

Educational wheel, cardboard, "United States At-a-Glance," EX, $90.00 – 110.00 C.

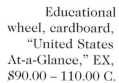

Flower hanger, wall hung, metal, glass and wire, "Drink Coca-Cola," 1950s, EX, $450.00 B.

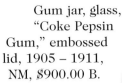

Gum jar, glass, "Coke Pepsin Gum," embossed lid, 1905 – 1911, NM, $900.00 B.

Key tag, composition, "Coca-Cola Bottling Co.," postage guaranteed, VG, $40.00 – 50.00 C.

Light globe, glass, "Coca-Cola 5¢," rectangular with glass bead fringe around bottom, "Pittsburg Mosaic Glass Co., Inc., Pittsburg, Pa.," 1910, 11" x 22" x 7¼", EX, $12,000.00 – 14,000.00 C.

Light globe, glass, "Coca-Cola," round leaded glass globe, 1920s, EX, $10,000.00 – 14,000.00 C.

Light globe, glass, "Coca-Cola," originally had a beaded bottom fringe. Top of band reads "Property of the Coca-Cola Co. to be returned on demand." I wonder how many made it back to the bottler? 1920s, 18" dia., EX, $5,000.00 – 7,500.00 C.

Light globe, glass, "Drink Coca-Cola," 1930 – 1940s, EX, $400.00 – 500.00 C.

Light globe, glass, "Coca-Cola," schoolhouse design with original hardware, 1930s, EX, $1,300.00 – 1,575.00 C.

Light globe, glass, "Drink Coca-Cola," 1930s, EX, $700.00 – 1,100.00 C.

Milage meter, metal, "Drink Coca-Cola...in Bottles...Travel Refreshed," 1950s, EX, $1,550.00 B.

Napkin holder, metal, "Drink Coca-Cola," foreign, resembles a box-type cooler, 1940s, F, $525.00 B.

Needle case, paper, Coca-Cola calendar girl with both a glass and bottle of Coke, 1920s, EX, $65.00 – 95.00 C.

Night light, plastic, "Courtesy of Your Coca-Cola Bottler," EX, $5.00 C.

 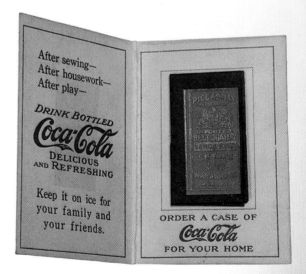

Needle case, paper, "Drink Bottled Coca-Cola Delicious and Refreshing" with fox fur girl on front with a glass of Coke, 1920s, EX, $65.00 – 95.00 C.

Note pad, celluloid, "Drink Coca-Cola in Bottles," 1920s, EX, $900.00 B.

Pencil sharpener, metal, in shape of hobbleskirt bottle, 1930s, VG, $15.00 – 25.00 C.

Pin set, metal and wood, "100 Centennial Celebration Pin Series," in framed presentation box, 1986, EX, $275.00 – 375.00 C.

Popcorn box, cardboard, "Good with...Drink Coca-Cola," 1950s, EX, $30.00 – 35.00 C.

Record holder, plastic, "Hi-Fi," premium for 45 rpm records on revolving base, 10" x 10¾", NM, $100.00 B.

Radio broadcast, vinyl, *Superman* original show presented by Coke, with dynamic wave logo in upper right-hand corner, EX, $25.00 – 45.00 C.

Radio, wooden, "Drink Coca-Cola," small transistor radio built to resemble the larger version of this radio, 1940s, 7" x 4" x 5", EX, $400.00 – 450.00 C.

Record set, vinyl and cardboard, "Got a Long Thirst?...Get a Long King!" record and 45 rpm autographed by Ricky Nelson. This is difficult to find and of course crosses collecting lines, so it's very much in demand. 1960s, 18" x 14½", G, $575.00 B.

Record, vinyl, "*Trini Lopes Sings His Greatest Hits*" on dust cover, for Fresca, 1967, EX, $30.00 – 40.00 C.

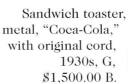

Sandwich toaster, metal, "Coca-Cola," with original cord, 1930s, G, $1,500.00 B.

Shaving kit, canvas, "Enjoy Coca-Cola," with zipper top, EX, $20.00 – 30.00 C.

Statue, composition, "Tell Me Your Profit Story, Please," man holding bottles of Coke, used as a selling training tool, 1930 – 1940s, EX, $175.00 – 195.00 C.

Straws, cardboard box, "Be Really Refreshed... Drink Coca-Cola," with fishtail logo, 1960s, EX, $250.00 B.

Straws, cardboard box, "Delicious and Refreshing," Coke bottle on all sides, 1930s, VG, $400.00 B.

Straws, cardboard box, "Drink Coca-Cola," with straw in bottle, 1940s, EX, $325.00 B.

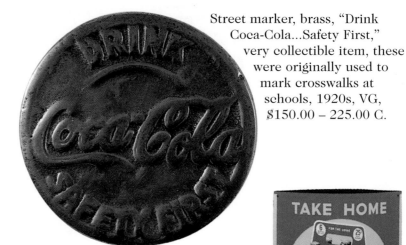

Street marker, brass, "Drink Coca-Cola...Safety First," very collectible item, these were originally used to mark crosswalks at schools, 1920s, VG, $150.00 – 225.00 C.

Straws, cardboard box, "Have a Coke," Coke cup on each-side, 1960s, EX, $225.00 C.

Straws, cardboard box, "The Pause That Refreshes," bottle with straw on each side, 1930s, EX, $575.00 B.

String holder, metal, "Take Home Coca-Cola in Cartons," yellow spotlight with carton, 1930s, 14" x 16", EX, $1,000.00 B.

Thimble, metal, "Coca-Cola" on blue background, 1920s, EX, $95.00 – 115.00 C.

Thimble, metal, "Coca-Cola" on red background, 1920s, EX, $95.00 – 110.00 C.

Tape, vinyl, "Coke Adds Life To..." reel-to-reel tape with 16 advertising spots for radio play, in original cardboard sleeve, 1970s, EX, $25.00 – 35.00 C.

Tote bag, canvas, "Coca-Cola," white on red, NM, $35.00 C.

Tote bag, canvas, "Introducing Diet Coke," with handles, 13½" x 13½", NM, $45.00 – 50.00 C.

Umbrella, canvas, "Drink Coca-Cola in Bottles" with bottle image, 1932, VG, $550.00 B.

Umbrella, canvas, "Drink Coca-Cola...the Pause That Refreshes," designed for beach use, 1930s, G, $110.00 B.

Umbrella, fabric, "Drink Coca-Cola...Be Really Refreshed," F, $500.00 – 600.00 C.

View Master, plastic, original reels of Coke displays, ads, merchandising, and assorted sales helps, 1940 – 1950s, EX, $130.00 B.

Wall pocket, fiberboard, "Drink Coca-Cola," 9" x 13", EX, $650.00 – 800.00 C.

COLLECTOR BOOKS
informing today's collector

www.collectorbooks.com

For over two decades we have been keeping collectors informed on trends and values in all fields of antiques and collectibles.

DOLLS, FIGURES & TEDDY BEARS

6315	**American Character Dolls**, Izen	$24.95
6317	**Arranbee Dolls**, The Dolls that Sell on Sight, DeMillar/Brevik	$24.95
2079	**Barbie Doll** Fashion, Volume I, Eames	$24.95
4846	**Barbie Doll** Fashion, Volume II, Eames	$24.95
6319	**Barbie Doll** Fashion, Volume III, Eames	$29.95
6022	The **Barbie Doll** Years, 5th Ed., Olds	$19.95
5352	Collector's Ency. of **Barbie** Doll Exclusives & More, 2nd Ed., Augustyniak	$24.95
5904	Collector's Guide to **Celebrity Dolls**, Spurgeon	$24.95
5599	Collector's Guide to **Dolls of the 1960s and 1970s**, Sabulis	$24.95
6030	Collector's Guide to **Horsman Dolls**, Jensen	$29.95
6224	**Doll Values**, Antique to Modern, 7th Ed., Moyer	$12.95
6033	**Modern Collectible Dolls**, Volume VI, Moyer	$24.95
5689	**Nippon Dolls** & Playthings, Van Patten/Lau	$29.95
5365	**Peanuts Collectibles**, Podley/Bang	$24.95
6336	Official **Precious Moments** Collector's Guide to Company **Dolls**, Bomm	$19.95
6026	**Small Dolls** of the 40s & 50s, Stover	$29.95
5253	Story of **Barbie**, 2nd Ed., Westenhouser	$24.95
5277	**Talking Toys** of the 20th Century, Lewis	$15.95
2084	**Teddy Bears**, Annalee's & Steiff Animals, 3rd Series, Mandel	$19.95
4880	World of **Raggedy Ann** Collectibles, Avery	$24.95

TOYS & MARBLES

2333	Antique & Collectible **Marbles**, 3rd Ed., Grist	$9.95
5900	Collector's Guide to **Battery Toys**, 2nd Edition, Hultzman	$24.95
4566	Collector's Guide to **Tootsietoys**, 2nd Ed., Richter	$19.95
5169	Collector's Guide to **TV Toys** & Memorabilia, 2nd Ed., Davis/Morgan	$24.95
5593	Grist's Big Book of **Marbles**, 2nd Ed.	$24.95
3970	Grist's Machine-Made & Contemporary **Marbles**, 2nd Ed.	$9.95
6128	**Hot Wheels**, The Ultimate Redline Guide, 1968 – 1977, Clark/Wicker	$24.95
5830	**McDonald's** Collectibles, 2nd Edition, Henriques/DuVall	$24.95
1540	**Modern Toys**, 1930–1980, Baker	$19.95
6237	**Rubber Toy Vehicles**, Leopard	$19.95
6340	**Schroeder's Collectible Toys**, Antique to Modern Price Guide, 9th Ed.	$17.95
5908	**Toy Car** Collector's Guide, Johnson	$19.95

FURNITURE

3716	American **Oak** Furniture, Book II, McNerney	$12.95
1118	Antique **Oak** Furniture, Hill	$7.95
3720	Collector's Encyclopedia of **American** Furniture, Vol. III, Swedberg	$24.95
5359	Early **American** Furniture, Obbard	$12.95
3906	**Heywood-Wakefield** Modern Furniture, Rouland	$18.95
6338	**Roycroft** Furniture & Collectibles, Koon	$24.95
6343	**Stickley Brothers** Furniture, Koon	$24.95
1885	**Victorian** Furniture, Our American Heritage, McNerney	$9.95
3829	**Victorian** Furniture, Our American Heritage, Book II, McNerney	$9.95

JEWELRY, HATPINS, WATCHES & PURSES

4704	Antique & Collectible **Buttons**, Wisniewski	$19.95
6323	**Christmas Pins**, Past & Present, 2nd Edition, Gallina	$19.95
4850	Collectible **Costume Jewelry**, Simonds	$24.95
5675	Collectible **Silver Jewelry**, Rezazadeh	$24.95
3722	Collector's Ency. of **Compacts**, Carryalls & Face Powder Boxes, Mueller	$24.95
4940	**Costume Jewelry**, A Practical Handbook & Value Guide, Rezazadeh	$24.95
5812	Fifty Years of Collectible **Fashion Jewelry**, 1925 – 1975, Baker	$24.95
6330	**Handkerchiefs**: A Collector's Guide, Guarnaccia/Guggenheim	$24.95
1424	**Hatpins** & Hatpin Holders, Baker	$9.95

5695	**Ladies' Vintage Accessories**, Bruton	$24.95
1181	100 Years of Collectible **Jewelry**, 1850 – 1950, Baker	$9.95
6337	**Purse Masterpieces**, Schwartz	$29.95
4729	**Sewing Tools** & Trinkets, Thompson	$24.95
6038	**Sewing Tools** & Trinkets, Volume 2, Thompson	$24.95
6039	Signed Beauties of **Costume Jewelry**, Brown	$24.95
6341	Signed Beauties of **Costume Jewelry**, Volume II, Brown	$24.95
5620	Unsigned Beauties of **Costume Jewelry**, Brown	$24.95
4878	Vintage & Contemporary **Purse Accessories**, Gerson	$24.95
5696	Vintage & Vogue Ladies' **Compacts**, 2nd Edition, Gerson	$29.95
5923	**Vintage Jewelry** for Investment & Casual Wear, Edeen	$24.95

ARTIFACTS, GUNS, KNIVES, TOOLS, PRIMITIVES

6021	**Arrowheads** of the Central Great Plains, Fox	$19.95
1868	Antique **Tools**, Our American Heritage, McNerney	$9.95
6469	Big Book of **Pocket Knives**, 2nd Edition, Stewart/Ritchie	$19.95
4943	Field Gde. to Flint **Arrowheads** & Knives of the N. American Indian, Tully	$9.95
3885	**Indian Artifacts** of the Midwest, Book II, Hothem	$16.95
4870	**Indian Artifacts** of the Midwest, Book III, Hothem	$18.95
5685	**Indian Artifacts** of the Midwest, Book IV, Hothem	$19.95
6132	**Modern Guns**, Identification & Values, 14th Ed., Quertermous	$14.95
2164	**Primitives**, Our American Heritage, McNerney	$9.95
1759	**Primitives**, Our American Heritage, 2nd Series, McNerney	$14.95
6031	Standard **Knife** Collector's Guide, 4th Ed., Ritchie & Stewart	$14.95
5999	**Wilderness Survivor's Guide**, Hamper	$12.95

PAPER COLLECTIBLES & BOOKS

5902	**Boys' & Girls' Book** Series, Jones	$19.95
5153	Collector's Guide to **Children's Books**, 1850 to 1950, Volume II, Jones	$19.95
1441	Collector's Guide to **Post Cards**, Wood	$9.95
5926	**Duck Stamps**, Chappell	$9.95
2081	Guide to Collecting **Cookbooks**, Allen	$14.95
2080	Price Guide to **Cookbooks** & Recipe Leaflets, Dickinson	$9.95
3973	**Sheet Music** Reference & Price Guide, 2nd Ed., Pafik & Guiheen	$19.95
6041	Vintage **Postcards for the Holidays**, Reed	$24.95

GLASSWARE

5602	Anchor Hocking's **Fire-King** & More, 2nd Ed.	$24.95
6321	**Carnival Glass**, The Best of the Best, Edwards/Carwile	$29.95
5823	Collectible **Glass Shoes**, 2nd Edition, Wheatley	$24.95
6325	Coll. **Glassware** from the 40s, 50s & 60s, 7th Ed., Florence	$19.95
1810	Collector's Encyclopedia of **American Art Glass**, Shuman	$29.95
6327	Collector's Encyclopedia of **Depression Glass**, 16th Ed., Florence	$19.95
1961	Collector's Encyclopedia of **Fry Glassware**, Fry Glass Society	$24.95
1664	Collector's Encyclopedia of **Heisey Glass**, 1925 – 1938, Bredehoft	$24.95
3905	Collector's Encyclopedia of **Milk Glass**, Newbound	$24.95
5820	Collector's Guide to **Glass Banks**, Reynolds	$24.95
6454	**Crackle Glass** From Around the World, Weitman	$24.95
6559	**Elegant Glassware** of the Depression Era, 11th Ed., Florence	$24.95
6334	Encyclopedia of **Paden City Glass**, Domitz	$24.95
3981	Evers' Standard **Cut Glass** Value Guide	$12.95
6462	Florence's **Glass Kitchen Shakers**, 1930 – 1950s	$19.95
5042	Florence's **Glassware Pattern Identification** Guide, Vol. I	$18.95
5615	Florence's **Glassware Pattern Identification** Guide, Vol. II	$19.95
6142	Florence's **Glassware Pattern Identification** Guide, Vol. III	$19.95
4719	**Fostoria**, Etched, Carved & Cut Designs, Vol. II, Kerr	$24.95
6226	**Fostoria** Value Guide, Long/Seate	$19.95

5899	**Glass & Ceramic Baskets**, White $19.95
6460	**Glass Animals**, Second Edition, Spencer $24.95
6127	The **Glass Candlestick** Book, Volume 1, Akro Agate to Fenton, Felt/Stoer .$24.95
6228	The **Glass Candlestick** Book, Volume 2, Fostoria to Jefferson, Felt/Stoer .$24.95
6461	The **Glass Candlestick** Book, Volume 3, Kanawha to Wright, Felt/Stoer ...$29.95
6329	**Glass Tumblers**, 1860s to 1920s, Bredehoft $29.95
4644	**Imperial Carnival Glass**, Burns $18.95
5827	**Kitchen Glassware** of the Depression Years, 6th Ed., Florence $24.95
5600	Much More Early American **Pattern Glass**, Metz $17.95
6133	**Mt. Washington Art Glass**, Sisk $49.95
6556	Pocket Guide to **Depression Glass** & More, 14th Ed., Florence $12.95
6448	Standard Encyclopedia of **Carnival Glass**, 9th Ed., Edwards/Carwile $29.95
6449	Standard **Carnival Glass** Price Guide, 14th Ed., Edwards/Carwile $9.95
6035	Standard Encyclopedia of **Opalescent Glass**, 4th Ed., Edwards/Carwile ...$24.95
6241	**Treasures of Very Rare Depression Glass**, Florence $39.95

POTTERY

4929	**American Art Pottery**, Sigafoose $24.95
1312	**Blue & White Stoneware**, McNerney $9.95
4851	Collectible **Cups & Saucers**, Harran $18.95
6326	Collectible **Cups & Saucers**, Book III, Harran $24.95
6344	Collectible **Vernon Kilns**, 2nd Edition, Nelson $29.95
6331	**Collecting Head Vases**, Barron $24.95
1373	Collector's Encyclopedia of **American Dinnerware**, Cunningham $24.95
4931	Collector's Encyclopedia of **Bauer Pottery**, Chipman $24.95
5034	Collector's Encyclopedia of **California Pottery**, 2nd Ed., Chipman $24.95
3723	Collector's Encyclopedia of **Cookie Jars**, Book II, Roerig $24.95
4939	Collector's Encyclopedia of **Cookie Jars**, Book III, Roerig $24.95
5748	Collector's Encyclopedia of **Fiesta**, 9th Ed., Huxford $24.95
3961	Collector's Encyclopedia of **Early Noritake**, Alden $24.95
3812	Collector's Encyclopedia of **Flow Blue China**, 2nd Ed., Gaston $24.95
3431	Collector's Encyclopedia of **Homer Laughlin China**, Jasper $24.95
1276	Collector's Encyclopedia of **Hull Pottery**, Roberts $19.95
5609	Collector's Encyclopedia of **Limoges Porcelain**, 3rd Ed., Gaston $29.95
2334	Collector's Encyclopedia of **Majolica Pottery**, Katz-Marks ...$19.95
1358	Collector's Encyclopedia of **McCoy Pottery**, Huxford $19.95
5677	Collector's Encyclopedia of **Niloak**, 2nd Edition, Gifford $29.95
5564	Collector's Encyclopedia of **Pickard China**, Reed $29.95
5679	Collector's Encyclopedia of **Red Wing Art Pottery**, Dollen ...$24.95
5618	Collector's Encyclopedia of **Rosemeade Pottery**, Dommel $24.95
5841	Collector's Encyclopedia of **Roseville Pottery**, Revised, Huxford/Nickel .. $24.95
5842	Collector's Encyclopedia of **Roseville Pottery**, 2nd Series, Huxford/Nickel. $24.95
5917	Collector's Encyclopedia of **Russel Wright**, 3rd Editon, Kerr $29.95
5921	Collector's Encyclopedia of **Stangl Artware**, Lamps, and Birds, Runge $29.95
3314	Collector's Encyclopedia of **Van Briggle Art Pottery**, Sasicki $24.95
5680	Collector's Guide to **Feather Edge Ware**, McAllister $19.95
6124	Collector's Guide to **Made in Japan Ceramics**, Book IV, White $24.95
1425	**Cookie Jars**, Westfall $9.95
3440	**Cookie Jars**, Book II, Westfall $19.95
6316	Decorative **American Pottery & Whiteware**, Wilby $29.95
5909	**Dresden Porcelain** Studios, Harran $29.95
5918	Florence's Big Book of **Salt & Pepper Shakers** $24.95
6320	Gaston's **Blue Willow**, 3rd Edition $19.95
2379	Lehner's Ency. of **U.S. Marks** on Pottery, Porcelain & China $24.95
4722	**McCoy Pottery**, Collector's Reference & Value Guide, Hanson/Nissen $19.95
5913	**McCoy Pottery**, Volume III, Hanson & Nissen $24.95
6333	**McCoy Pottery Wall Pockets** & Decorations, Nissen $24.95
6135	**North Carolina Art Pottery**, 1900 – 1960, James/Leftwich $24.95
6335	Pictorial Guide to **Pottery & Porcelain Marks**, Lage $29.95
5691	**Post86 Fiesta**, Identification & Value Guide, Racheter $19.95

1670	**Red Wing Collectibles**, DePasquale $9.95
1440	**Red Wing Stoneware**, DePasquale $9.95
6037	**Rookwood Pottery**, Nicholson & Thomas $24.95
6236	**Rookwood Pottery**, 10 Years of Auction Results, 1990 – 2002, Treadway $39.95
1632	**Salt & Pepper Shakers**, Guarnaccia $9.95
5091	**Salt & Pepper Shakers II**, Guarnaccia $18.95
3443	**Salt & Pepper Shakers IV**, Guarnaccia $18.95
3738	**Shawnee Pottery**, Mangus $24.95
4629	Turn of the Century **American Dinnerware**, 1880s–1920s, Jasper $24.95
5924	**Zanesville Stoneware** Company, Rans, Ralston & Russell $24.95

OTHER COLLECTIBLES

5916	Advertising **Paperweights**, Holiner & Kammerman $24.95
5838	Advertising **Thermometers**, Merritt $16.95
5898	Antique & Contemporary **Advertising Memorabilia**, Summers $24.95
5814	Antique **Brass & Copper** Collectibles, Gaston $24.95
1880	Antique **Iron**, McNerney $9.95
3872	Antique **Tins**, Dodge $24.95
4845	Antique **Typewriters & Office Collectibles**, Rehr $19.95
5607	Antiquing and Collecting on the **Internet**, Parry $12.95
1128	**Bottle** Pricing Guide, 3rd Ed., Cleveland $7.95
6345	**Business & Tax Guide** for Antiques & Collectibles, Kelly $14.95
6225	Captain John's **Fishing Tackle** Price Guide, Kolbeck/Lewis ...$19.95
3718	Collectible **Aluminum**, Grist $16.95
6342	Collectible **Soda Pop** Memorabilia, Summers $24.95
5060	Collectible **Souvenir Spoons**, Bednersh $19.95
5676	Collectible **Souvenir Spoons**, Book II, Bednersh $29.95
5666	Collector's Encyclopedia of **Granite Ware**, Book 2, Greguire $29.95
5836	Collector's Guide to **Antique Radios**, 5th Ed., Bunis $19.95
3966	Collector's Guide to **Inkwells**, Identification & Values, Badders $18.95
4947	Collector's Guide to **Inkwells**, Book II, Badders $19.95
5681	Collector's Guide to **Lunchboxes**, White $19.95
4864	Collector's Guide to **Wallace Nutting Pictures**, Ivankovich ...$18.95
5683	**Fishing Lure** Collectibles, Vol. 1, Murphy/Edmisten $29.95
6328	**Flea Market Trader**, 14th Ed., Huxford $12.95
6459	**Garage Sale** & Flea Market Annual, 12th Edition, Huxford ...$19.95
4945	**G-Men and FBI Toys** and Collectibles, Whitworth $18.95
3819	**General Store** Collectibles, Wilson $24.95
5912	The **Heddon** Legacy, A Century of Classic **Lures**, Roberts & Pavey $29.95
2216	**Kitchen Antiques**, 1790–1940, McNerney $14.95
5991	**Lighting Devices** & Accessories of the 17th – 19th Centuries, Hamper $9.95
5686	**Lighting Fixtures** of the Depression Era, Book I, Thomas $24.95
4950	The **Lone Ranger**, Collector's Reference & Value Guide, Felbinger $18.95
6028	Modern **Fishing Lure** Collectibles, Vol. 1, Lewis $24.95
6131	Modern **Fishing Lure** Collectibles, Vol. 2, Lewis $24.95
6322	Pictorial Guide to **Christmas Ornaments** & Collectibles, Johnson $29.95
2026	**Railroad** Collectibles, 4th Ed., Baker $14.95
5619	**Roy Rogers and Dale Evans** Toys & Memorabilia, Coyle $24.95
6570	**Schroeder's Antiques** Price Guide, 23rd Edition $14.95
5007	**Silverplated Flatware**, Revised 4th Edition, Hagan $18.95
6239	**Star Wars** Super Collector's Wish Book, 2nd Ed., Carlton ...$29.95
6139	Summers' Guide to **Coca-Cola**, 4th Ed. $24.95
6324	Summers' Pocket Guide to **Coca-Cola**, 4th Ed. $12.95
3977	Value Guide to **Gas Station Memorabilia**, Summers & Priddy $24.95
4877	Vintage **Bar Ware**, Visakay $24.95
5925	The Vintage Era of **Golf Club Collectibles**, John $29.95
6010	The Vintage Era of **Golf Club Collectibles** Collector's Log, John $9.95
6036	Vintage **Quilts**, Aug, Newman & Roy $24.95
4935	The **W.F. Cody Buffalo Bill** Collector's Guide with Values ...$24.95

This is only a partial listing of the books on antiques that are available from Collector Books. All books are well illustrated and contain current values. Most of these books are available from your local bookseller, antique dealer, or public library. If you are unable to locate certain titles in your area, you may order by mail from **COLLECTOR BOOKS**, P.O. Box 3009, Paducah, KY 42002-3009. Customers with Visa, Master Card, or Discover may phone in orders from 7:00 a.m. to 5:00 p.m. CT, Monday – Friday, toll free **1-800-626-5420**, or online at **www.collectorbooks.com**. Add $3.00 for postage for the first book ordered and 50¢ for each additional book. Include item number, title, and price when ordering. Allow 14 to 21 days for delivery.

1-800-626-5420   Fax: 1-270-898-8890

www.collectorbooks.com

PAST TYME PLEASURES

**Purveyors
of
Fine Antiques & Collectibles
Presents Annual
Spring and Fall Antique Advertising Auctions**

Call, fax, or e-mail today to be added to our mailing list to receive future auction information.
To receive the next color catalog and prices realized, send your check for $15.00 today to:

PAST TYME PLEASURES • PMB #204-2491 San Ramon Valley Blvd., #1 • San Ramon, CA 94583
PHONE: 925-484-6442, 925-484-4488 / FAX: 925-484-2551
CA Bond 158337

e-mail: pasttyme1@comcast.net   website: www.pasttyme1.com

Sales include many items with a fine selection of rare signs, trays, tins, and advertising items
relating to tobacco, sporting collectibles, breweriana, soda, talc, general store, etc.

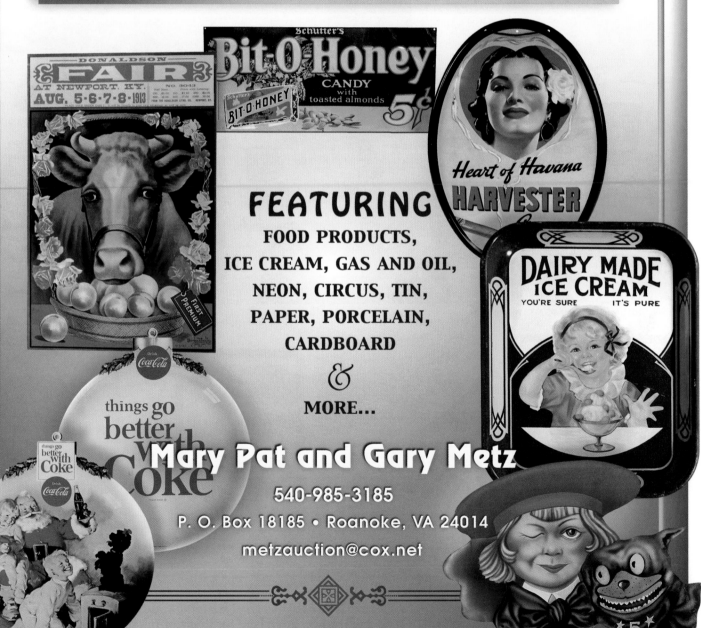

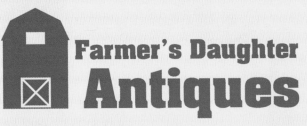
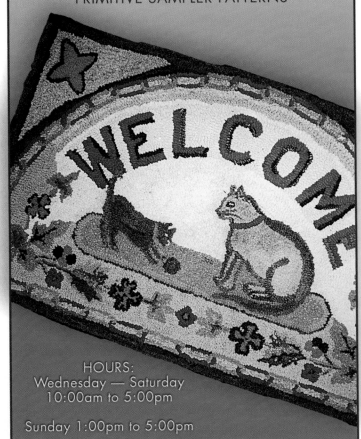

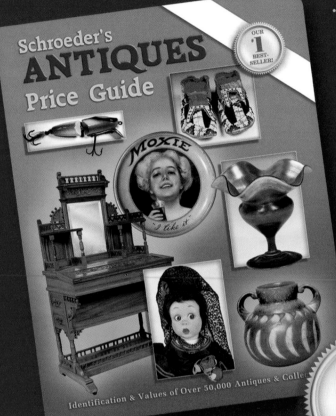